Writing the Four-Blocks® Way

by

Patricia M. Cunningham,

James W. Cunningham, Dorothy P. Hall, and

Sharon Arthur Moore

Carson-Dellosa Publishing Company, Inc.

Greensboro, North Carolina

Credits

Editors
Joey Bland
Tracy Soles Marion

Layout Design
Jon Nawrocik

Inside Illustrations
Wayne Miller
Van Harris

Cover Design
Annette Hollister-Papp

Cover Photos
Photo www.comstock.com
© 2001 Brand X Pictures
© 1999 EyeWire, Inc. All rights reserved
© Photodisc
© Digital Vision® Ltd. All rights reserved

ISBN 1-59441-195-6

Table of Contents

Chapter 1
A Peek into Classrooms Doing Writing the Four-Blocks® Way

- mini-lesson
- children write

In Four-Blocks® classrooms, the Writing Block always begins with a mini-lesson taught by the teacher as she writes for the children, followed by the children writing and the teacher encouraging them or conferencing with them about their writing. The block ends with a brief period of sharing. This chapter will give you an idea of what the Writing Block might look like "early in the year." Exactly what happens in each classroom during the Writing Block may be different depending on the class, grade level, teaching style, and time of the year.

This chapter begins with an imaginary trip to Fourblox Elementary. Tom Baldman is the reading/language arts supervisor for a large school district that includes Fourblox Elementary. Tom has helped all of the schools in his district implement the Four-Blocks® framework. His goal for the school system is good, balanced reading/writing instruction for the entire school district at all grade levels. Tom previously taught kindergarten, first, and fifth grades. He is comfortable in classrooms and knows the teachers and the administrators, having grown up and taught in this school system. Tom also has become quite an expert at writing since he learned about the Four-Blocks® framework. He realizes that some young children really learn to read in the Writing Block! He also has noticed that children who write daily seem to do better on the state-mandated tests. Tom is accompanied on this visit by Margaret Wright, a reading resource teacher at another elementary school in the district. Prior to this position, Margaret was a Four-Blocks teacher at Fourblox Elementary. Her expertise is in writing instruction. She took a workshop titled "Writer's Workshop" several years ago and since then has become a quiet but effective local writing leader. This year, she is teaching a semester-long workshop on writing for teachers in the school district. Tom and Margaret will go into many, but not all, of the classrooms today. The focus of their visit is to watch the Writing Block and see what should be included in the upcoming writing workshops Tom is sponsoring for different grade levels and which Margaret will be teaching.

First, Tom and Margaret stop by the office to greet the principal, Claire Leider. Claire has recently been nominated for a "Principal of the Year" award. The three of them talk a little about the backgrounds and training of the teachers who will be observed. Most of the teachers know about writing instruction from their Four-Blocks training and followed up on this training by reading the *Writing Mini-Lesson* books written by Pat Cunningham, Dottie Hall, Denise Boger, Debra Smith, Cheryl Sigmon, Sylvia Ford, and Amanda Arens. "Here is your schedule for today," says Claire, handing Tom a piece of paper with times, teachers, grade levels, and classrooms. Tom and Margaret will be spending the day at this large elementary school with time for only a quick lunch. The busy schedule puts a smile on both Tom's and Margaret's faces. They know they will be observing some of the best teachers at this school, who are also some of the best Four-Blocks teachers. They both feel they are sure to learn some new ideas that will help them help other teachers and students. Here is what their schedule for today looks like:

Time	Teacher	Grade Level	Room No.
8:30–9:00	Bea Ginning	Kindergarten	Room 4
9:00–9:35	Deb Webb	Grade 2	Room 25
9:35–10:05	Cece Southern	Grade 1	Room 11
10:05–10:40	DeLinda DeLightful	Grade 2	Room 22
10:40–11:20	Amanda Amazing	Grade 3	Room 33
11:20–12:00	Randy Reid	Grade 4	Room 44
12:00–12:30	Lunch	(get lunch in cafeteria/eat in the office area)	
12:30–1:00	Joe Webman	Grade 1	Room 10
1:00–1:30	Kendra Garden	Kindergarten	Room 3
1:30–2:15	Will Teachum	Grade 5	Room 50
2:15–3:00	Susie Science	Grade 3	Room 30

8:30–9:00 Bea Ginning Kindergarten Room 4

As Tom Baldman and Margaret Wright walk down the hall and around the corner, they come to the kindergarten classrooms. Tom shares with Margaret that Bea Ginning had a wonderful first year teaching kindergarten. Tom tells Margaret that last year Bea loves teaching "Building Blocks," the Four-Blocks kindergarten model, and reminds Margaret that Bea knows the Building Blocks model well, having learned it in college and having student-taught with a wonderful Building Blocks teacher. As Tom and Margaret enter Bea's kindergarten class, they slip quietly into the back of the room, almost unnoticed. The children are gathered in a "big group" on a colorful carpet with Bea sitting in a rocking chair and the children sitting in four little rows in front of her. The calendar is to the left of the big group and can be seen by all. Both Tom and Margaret watch Bea finish the calendar and weather. They are about to watch Ms. Ginning as she writes a morning message for children. Early in kindergarten, the emphasis in writing in Building Blocks is putting down on paper what you want to tell. Teachers write daily morning messages and tell the children what will happen in school that day. They also write predictable charts. Later, the teacher will do some interactive charts and interactive writing when the children are ready and most of the class knows what writing is and can use letter/sound correspondence to "write." Early in the year, Building-Blocks teachers show the children different ways in which they can write. The teachers model "driting" and let children drite (draw and write). They encourage every child's attempt, acting as both coach and cheerleader. At this stage of learning to write, young children do not need an editor!

When teachers write a morning message, they provide a model for writing. Children need to know how people think as they write and what they do when they write. As the children watch Bea and listen, they begin to understand what they are to do when they are asked to write later in the year. Young children learn many skills, such as riding a bike or swimming, by first watching someone else. This happens with writing when they watch a teacher write the daily morning message. Morning message is one of the most powerful ways for young children to understand what writing is and how people think as they write. For children further along in their literacy learning, watching the teacher write a morning message can move them quickly toward independence in writing.

Bea Ginning has a large piece of lined, manila paper clinging to the white board with two colorful magnets, one in each of the top corners. (Plain or lined paper could also be used.) She places the paper at a comfortable level for her to write on. With a large, black marker, Bea begins to talk and write.

Dear Class, ("Dear, Capital D-e-a-r, space, Class, Capital C-l-a-s-s, comma")

Today is Tuesday. ("Today, Capital T-o-d-a-y, space, is, i-s, space, Tuesday, Capital T-u-e-s-d-a-y, period.")

We have two visitors today. ("We, Capital W-e, space, have, h-a-v-e, space, two, t-w-o, space, visitors, v-i-s-i-t-o-r-s, space, today, t-o-d-a-y, period.")

Love, ("Capital L-o-v-e, comma")

Ms. Ginning ("Capital M-s, period, Capital G-i-n-n-i-n-g")

Bea writes and talks about what she is writing in her morning message; she lets her students know what she is writing and why she is writing it. Bea is doing all of the work, and the children are just listening and learning what to do and why. When Bea finishes the message, she asks her kindergarten students to count the sentences (2), to count the words in the first sentence (3), and to count the words in the second sentence (5). Then, Bea asks the children which sentence has more words (the second). Next, she asks students to count the letters in the first sentence (14) and to

count the letters in the second sentence (22). Finally, she asks which sentence has more letters (the second). Bea does all of the counting with the children to find the correct answers, then calls on a child to answer her questions. "You're right!" she says. "The second sentence has more words and more letters than the first sentence." In another week or so, she will ask individual children to do the counting and call on those who can do the task easily. Then, she will call on the children who need more help with counting. This gives her a chance to assess individual students, and it gives students who need a little extra practice that opportunity.

Ms. Ginning also talks about the morning message by asking, "What day did I say it is?" (Tuesday) "What letter did I write at the beginning of Tuesday?" (T) "What else did I tell you in my message today?" (We have two visitors.) "Do we have two visitors?" When many of the children turn around to look at the visitors, Bea stops to introduce Mr. Baldman and Mrs. Wright to her class. Bea then lowers the message to the children's level and asks them, "What do you notice about the morning message?" The children talk about Today and Tuesday in the first sentence starting with capital "Ts" and two and today in the second sentence starting with small "ts." One student tells Bea that he notices she always starts on "that side" (pointing to the left) and goes "that way" (pointing to the right)! When Bea asks what words they can find, the students raise their hands for the opportunity to come up and circle **Dear**, **Class**, **we**, **love**, **Today**, **today**, **Tuesday**, and **is**. They have had all of these words in previous morning messages, and these words have become familiar words to some students already.

As Tom leaves the classroom, he shares with Margaret how last year Ms. Ginning had the best kindergarten writers in the school because she waited until after a few weeks of morning messages before asking the children to write by themselves. By then, ALL of the children knew what writing was, regardless of their experiences before entering school. Tom and Margaret left the classroom talking about the importance of writing for children.

9:00–9:35 Deb Webb Grade 2 Room 25

Tom and Margaret are on schedule as they enter Deb Webb's second-grade classroom. The children are all sitting on the carpet with their knees and noses pointed at Mrs. Webb, who is standing in front of a white board. Mrs. Webb is ready to write. Since it is early in the year, her second graders need to work on building the habit of using the Word Wall every time they write. Mrs. Webb has decided to model using the Word Wall as the focus of her writing mini-lesson today. She thinks aloud, "What should I write about today? I could write about walking along the shore of the lake this weekend with my family. I could write about taking Andrew and Ashleigh to the grocery store. Or, I could write about my dog, Quincy. I know; I will write about our latest trip to the grocery store." Deb thinks aloud, talks, and writes:

> Last night, I went ("**Went** is on the Word Wall. Who can tell me what color **went** is? When I want to write **went**, I look at the Word Wall and copy it, because Word Wall words have to be spelled right!") to the grocery store with ("**With** is on the Word Wall.") Andrew and Ashleigh. ("Our family rule is that each child gets to pick one treat.") First, Ashleigh picked cookies. ("**Cook** rhymes with **look**, so I can use the Word Wall word **look** to help me with the beginning of **cookies** and add **ies**.") In the snacks aisle, Ashleigh picked up potato chips, so she put away the

cookies. Then, ("**Then** is on the Word Wall.") she picked up ice cream and put away the potato chips. Finally, Ashleigh wanted ("**Wanted** is on the Word Wall.") to buy gum. She returned the ice cream so that she could get the gum. Andrew waited in the checkout aisle and bought peanut butter cups. Ashleigh left with ("**With** is on the Word Wall.") gum. As usual, she just had to touch some ("**Some** is on the Word Wall.") other things first! ("**First** is on the Word Wall.")

Deb reminds her students, "Since many of you are waving your hands to tell me your own grocery store stories, why not tell me on paper, and write your stories for me to read?" She sends them off to write, saying, "As you are writing today, remember to use the Word Wall to spell Word Wall words and rhyming words." The children return to their seats and begin to write. They know they can finish previously started pieces, and some children do just that; other children begin new pieces about the grocery store or other topics of their choice.

Deb roams around the classroom making sure her second graders are on task writing and using the Word Wall to write words correctly. She helps a student who has spelled a word wrong see

Last night, I went to the grocery store with Andrew and Ashleigh. First, Ashleigh picked cookies. In the snacks aisle, Ashleigh picked up potato chips, so she put away the cookies. Then, she picked up ice cream and put away the potato chips. Finally, Ashleigh wanted to buy gum.

how the Word Wall word could help to spell the word correctly. Mrs. Webb then moves on to another desk nearby and conferences with another child, David, pointing to two Word Wall words that are misspelled and reminding him that Word Wall words have to be spelled correctly even in a first draft. Another student is sitting there thinking but not writing, so Deb goes over to him and asks what he is thinking about. He tells his teacher that he remembers going to the grocery store before a snowstorm. It was crowded, the milk was almost gone, and there was an empty shelf where his favorite kind of bread was usually found. His mother bought wheat bread, not white bread, and he found out he liked wheat bread even better than white! "You have a lot to tell us, don't you?" Deb asks. "How are you going to start the story?" When he tells her his beginning sentence, she tells him to write it down and smiles. Deb then "oohs" and "aahs" over how well a few other students are writing. Margaret notes that Deb has spent the writing time encouraging 10 or more children and having three different conversations with children who were nudged forward in their literacy learning!

9:35–10:05 Cece Southern Grade 1 Room 11

Cece is gathering up the children in front of the room around her overhead projector as Tom and Margaret enter and find two "big chairs" waiting for them in the back of the room. They sit and watch as Cece begins to talk to her students about what she will write about today in her mini-lesson. "Today, I could write about my two daughters; I've told you about them before. I could write about the new car my husband wants to buy and tell you about all of the magazines he is bringing home with pictures and information about new cars in them. Or, I could write and tell you about me when I was in first grade like you. That's what I think I will write about today—me in first grade! I am going to tell you about the first day in first grade when my teacher, Mrs. Tillman, called the roll, and I did not know my first name was Cecelia. You see, my family had always called me Sissy at home, so I thought that was my name. Then, Mrs. Tillman said, 'Cecilia! That's much too big a name for such a pretty little girl! How about we just call you Cece?' And I have been Cece to my friends ever since. I still think of Mrs. Tillman and how she helped me that day." First, Cece Southern draws a simple picture of a woman and a little girl. Then, she talks and writes:

I ("I begin my sentence with a capital letter, and I is always a capital letter when we talk about ourselves.") remember ("That's a big word, I have to stretch it out to spell it: **re-mem-ber**.") first grade. My ("I begin my sentence with a capital letter.") teacher was Mrs. Tillman. ("Names begin with capital letters, so we need one at the beginning of **Mrs.** and one at the beginning of **Tillman**.") When ("I begin my sentence with a capital letter.") she called my name, Cecelia, ("Names begin with capital letters.") I did not answer. Then, she said, "I ("I is always a capital letter.") will call you Cece." ("Names begin with capital letters.") I ("I is always a capital letter.") loved my new teacher and my new name.

I remember first grade. My teacher was Mrs. Tillman. When she called my name, Cecelia, I did not answer. Then, she said, "I will call you Cece." I loved my new teacher and my new name.

Cece tells the children they can go back to their seats and continue the writing they started yesterday. Or, if they want to start writing about new things today, they can return to their seats and write about themselves, or school, or anything else they want to tell about. Mrs. Southern begins by wandering around the room and chatting with a few students about their writing. She then sits at a table on one side of the room and calls children over, one by one, to conference with her. The children know to bring their writing folders over to Mrs. Southern. She looks at any papers in the folder that have been started since the last time she visited with these children. All of the children are prepared to read or tell about what they wrote or the pictures they drew. The children seem to love this special time alone each week with their teacher to talk about their writing.

On his way out of the classroom, Tom remarks to Cece that he remembers when first graders at this school, for the most part, could not write early in first grade; some children did not even write later in first grade! Cece says she, too, remembers and adds, "Since we began doing Four Blocks, the children are both reading and writing better, and teaching is certainly more fun, too!"

10:05–10:40 DeLinda DeLightful Grade 2 Room 22

As Tom and Margaret enter the classroom, DeLinda DeLightful greets them. "This is the block my second graders look forward to each day; we all love to write!" she informs her visitors. The children are also entering the room now, having just returned from physical education on the playground. They sit in their places on a colorful carpet. Mrs. DeLightful goes over to her overhead projector and sits in front of it. DeLinda seems delighted at what she will tell the children today and then write for her mini-lesson. "I am so excited about what I will write about today. I've wanted to tell you my news all morning, but I waited until our writing time, because that is when I usually share something about my family, my friends, or what we are doing at school. Today, I have the best news so far this year. This weekend my son, Zach, got engaged! He is going to get married. I am so-o-o excited! Watch as I write about this for you." DeLinda then talks and writes on an overhead transparency at her projector:

> My son, Zach, is getting married. ("Let me stretch that out and spell it: **mar-rie-d**.")
> I am so excited! ("Let me stretch that out and spell it: **ex-ci-ted**.")

Then, she puts down her felt-tipped pen and says, "Well, that's it. I'm finished." The children have a look of surprise on their faces; they want their teacher to tell them more. Many little hands go up, and the children begin to ask some questions. "Who is he marrying?" one student wants to know. Another child asks, "When is he getting married?" Each child DeLinda calls upon has another question; "Where is he getting married?" "Will we get to go to the wedding?" "Will you be a bridesmaid?"

DeLinda is pleased that they want to know more. "You have lots of questions, just like I do when some of you don't write enough and I want to know more. We have talked before about how a good story tells us who, what, where, when, and sometimes why. Did I do that in my story?" she asks. She then returns to her writing and tells the children the answers to their questions as she writes more.

My son, Zach, is getting married. I am so excited! His wedding will be next October. His girlfriend's name is Kelly. She has blond hair and a beautiful smile. They will get married in Mahomet, Illinois. My daughter, Randa, will be a bridesmaid. I will be the mother of the groom. I am going to buy a new dress. I am so happy!

DeLinda says, "The questions you asked helped me write more sentences about my son's wedding. When you write today, think about some questions that someone might ask you about your writing that could help you write more. I am going to walk around the room as you write today, and I will read what you are writing and ask you a question or two. The answers to these questions will make your writing more interesting."

Mrs. DeLightful sends the children back to their seats, reminding them they can finish pieces they started yesterday—and add more to them—by thinking of some questions and then answering them. Or, they can start writing new things today. When the children are all quietly in their seats and writing, DeLinda begins to walk from desk to desk, silently reading what her second graders have written and asking questions to help them write more. She continues her "quick conferences," making each one a special time for the student she is working with. It is evident that each child is delighted by the teacher's questions and eager to please her by answering each question orally and then adding the answers to his writing!

DeLinda ends her conferences by announcing that it is time now for the "Share Chair." The big, red, comfy upholstered chair in the classroom is the teacher's chair to read in each day and becomes the "Share Chair" when necessary. Beside the chair is the "Share Chair Chart," listing the five school days of the week and the names of the children who will share their writing each day. On their special days, the children get to read something they have written into a karaoke microphone. It is turned up a notch for the quiet children and all the way down for those who can be heard "a mile down the road." After the children read their writing aloud, their classmates are allowed to tell what they liked and then ask questions. The rule is, "Say something nice first, and then you get to ask questions." Mrs. DeLightful reminds students to "ask a thinking question, not a parrot question." A parrot question, she explains, is one that is always asked. After questions are asked, some children remark, "I will add on to my story tomorrow and answer that question." Tom and Margaret notice that these second graders are already mindful of adding "detail" to their writing and trying to answer most questions before the class "sharing time." It is time for Tom and Margaret to leave this delightful teacher and her class to visit the next class on their agenda. Time goes by fast when you are having fun, and that includes watching good teaching!

10:40–11:20 Amanda Amazing Grade 3 Room 33

As Tom and Margaret enter the next classroom on their schedule, they see Mrs. Amanda Amazing sitting behind her overhead projector with her third-grade students gathered in front of her. "Today, I am going to write another piece about my family. We have been talking about how we use quotation marks when we write conversation. So, today I will be sure to use conversation when I write so that I can tell you just how and why I use these quotation marks when writing." She begins by telling her students that Lafe, her youngest child and youngest son, is in first grade this year. He loves elephants, jumping on the trampoline, and taking care of their cats who live in their garage and play in their big backyard during the day.

> Lafe is my youngest child. He is six years old and in first grade this year. ("No talking here, just me telling you about Lafe, so no quotation marks—just a period at the end of each sentence.") If you met Lafe, he may say, ("Now I need beginning quotation marks because I am writing conversation. So, I begin what Lafe says with beginning quotation marks that look like this.") "I love elephants. I have books about elephants, an elephant lamp, elephant towels, and a collection of elephants on a shelf near my bed." ("I place ending quotation marks after what Lafe may say.") If you asked him, ("Now I need beginning quotation marks because I am writing about something you might say.") "Do you like anything besides elephants?" ("I place ending quotation marks after what was said.") Lafe may tell you about his cats. He may say, ("I place beginning quotation marks before what Lafe may say.") "I like cats, too. Some people have only one cat. I have three cats! Their names are Socks, Smokey, and Trucko." ("I place ending quotation marks after what Lafe said.")

Amanda continues, "So you see, each time a person talks you need to place quotation marks around what was said. You also have to remember to start a new paragraph each time a different person speaks. Many people find writing dialogue hard, so they choose not to use it in their writing. As you can see, it is **not** hard if you think as you write. You can do it, just like I did! Tomorrow, I will add more to this writing. As you write today, think about some conversation you can add to your writing. Would some added conversation make it more interesting? If you think it would, you can add it to your writing; just think as you write!" The students are sent off with a reminder to look at their writing, old or new, information or story, to see if dialogue can be added to their pieces. Amanda wanders around her classroom, helping several students find places to add dialogue to stories they have written. She helps other students think of how many times the person talking changes and reminds them to begin a new paragraph each time. Mrs. Amazing remembers to "ooh" and "aah" at the nice job some students have done without offering any help at all. After the students write for 20 minutes, she asks them to stop writing. She lets the students know that if it is their day to share, she wants them to share some writing they have written that contains dialogue or conversation. One girl, Merrill Kaye, begins to read her piece. She reads some conversation between her dad and brother Alex. The first comment from a fellow student is that the conversation does make the writing interesting.

Tom glances at the clock and realizes another 40 minutes have flown by; it is time to head down the hall to the next classroom on their list. He says to Margaret, "That Amanda, she's amazing. While many teachers wonder how to teach grammar and mechanics without worksheets or a language arts text, Amanda teaches her students day in and day out that they are learning grammar and mechanics because they need to use it when writing. Children don't need to learn much about quotation marks if they aren't going to write daily and use them, that's for sure."

11:20–12:00 Randy Reid Grade 4 Room 44

Randy Reid is reading to his fourth-grade class as Tom and Margaret enter this last room on their list before lunch. The teacher is sitting in the front of his classroom with his students gathered around him. They are just finishing a Guided Reading lesson using a "big book" biography of Martin Luther King, Jr. Randy reads aloud the first chapter of another biography of Martin Luther King, Jr., and uses a think-aloud about how the two books are alike and different. Sitting behind an overhead projector, he talks about how the books are alike and begins to write about Martin Luther King, Jr., by creating a matrix. (See page 94 of *Writing Mini-Lessons for the Upper Grades* by Hall, Cunningham, and Arens, Carson-Dellosa, 2003.) Randy has filled in the column for the sources he has read and the columns for the information he found in those sources. So far, Randy has found when and where Martin Luther King, Jr., was born, important contributions he made, actions that helped readers understand him better, when and how he died, and what others thought of King. Randy knows that fourth graders like facts, so he also has collected lots of informational books, including biographies, for Self-Selected Reading.

Today, Randy is talking about writing a biography. He stresses reading as much as possible about the person, taking notes on important facts, using a graphic organizer like a matrix to organize the information, and then writing. He is modeling this organizational strategy for the students today based on what they have read about Martin Luther King, Jr. As Randy reads and talks, he is creating a matrix to organize the information.

Questions / Resources	When was Martin Luther King, Jr., born?	When and how did he die?	What were his most important contributions?	Where there actions to help readers know him better?	What did others think about him?
Biography Adler, A Picture Book of Martin Luther King, Jr.	Atlanta, GA January 15, 1929	MLK was shot in April of 1968	led peaceful protests, fought for equal rights		200,000 people went to Washington with him.
Encyclopedia					
Magazine(s) Weekly Reader	January, 1929	He was assassinated.		Nonviolent	
Internet					
Videos March on Washington		Standing on a balcony of a motel, he was shot		voice made you want to listen	People went to Washington because they thought he was right.

After entering the information from the two books, Randy reminds students that they have been reading biographies during Self-Selected Reading and on their own at home. He asks students to choose a person whose name appears in their fourth-grade social studies book, a study of their state, and begin to organize information and write a biography.

Randy has a list of names on a clipboard, and he uses this list to confer with students. Following the list, Mr. Reid goes to each student's desk for the conference. When all students have had conferences, he will begin again. During the last five minutes of class, Randy lets the students "pair and share." He has paired each student with someone sitting nearby, and they end the Writing Block by telling each other what they are writing about, what they are trying to tell, what is easy, what they are having trouble with, etc. While each student pair is sharing, Randy wanders around the room and "spies on the students," which means he listens to find out what the students are writing about and how it is going. Margaret Wright and Tom Baldman realize that another 40 minutes have gone by, and it is time for them to head to the next thing on their schedule—lunch! They are happy they do not have to drive someplace to eat because there is not enough time. They will eat what the children eat, but they will eat with some other grown-ups in the office area.

12:00–12:30 Lunch

Tom and Margaret join a class and go through the lunch line, choosing from the menu along with the students. Next, they walk down the hall to Claire Leader's office where they sit at a small, quiet table. Both realize that they have only 25 minutes to eat and talk—there are no leisurely lunches in elementary school. They have so much to say about all they have observed this morning and what they want to remember to share with teachers at future writing workshops. "Every time I watch a good Four-Blocks teacher, I learn something new," says Margaret. "I've noticed that, too," remarks Tom as they review the morning: what they saw, what they liked, what they learned, and what they want to tell other teachers. Before they know it, it is time to rush down the hall to finish their visits.

12:30–1:00 Joe Webman Grade 1 Room 10

Joe Webman is a first-grade teacher and the first teacher they visit after lunch. Mrs. Wright and Mr. Baldman enter the classroom as the eager first graders return from their lunch and outside recess. The children gather in front of Mr. Webman, who is sitting on a stool ready to write on a large chart tablet. Mr. Webman reminds the children that writing is telling about something. "I have read you some books about *Clifford, the Big Red Dog* by Norman Bridwell and several of the *Harry the Dirty Dog* titles by Gene Zion. Today, I am going to tell you a story about my dog and then write a short story about him." The class shouts their approval. They like to hear about their teacher, his family, his friends, and his new house, and now they want to know about his dog. Mr. Webman tells about how his dog watches television. He tells about the weatherman on Channel 10 that his dog doesn't like and barks at (the children laugh), about the cartoon dogs his dog watches and likes, about the animals on the science shows and commercials that he likes, and about the cat commercials he doesn't like (the children laugh again). The children listen to Mr. Webman's story and watch spellbound as he writes on the chart tablet. First, he draws a simple picture of his dog watching television.

Then, he begins to write on the overhead projector some of what he has told them, telling the children as he writes how he begins his sentences with capital letters, ends his sentences with periods, and uses the Word Wall for help with a few words.

Aussie is my dog. He likes television. He likes to watch cartoons with dogs in them. He likes commercials with dogs, too. He doesn't like commercials with cats. He doesn't like the weatherman on Channel 10. Aussie barks at him. What a funny dog!

When he is finished writing, Mr. Webman points to the picture of the dog and the TV, saying, "This is my dog Aussie. This is my TV." Then, he reads aloud what he has written. Finally, he dismisses the children to write and tells them they can write about their dogs, their cats, or whatever they want to tell him about. The youngsters return to their assigned tables and chairs and begin to draw and write. Soon, Mr. Webman is walking around the classroom making positive comments about what his students are drawing or writing. Once the children are settled, Joe starts to spend a few minutes individually with five preselected students. He listens as each child reads her writing and then "coaches" her to write a little more. He ends the conference by praising the student's efforts during the Writing Block. In each conference, he "coaches" and "cheers" his young students, making them feel good about whatever they can do and then stretching them to do a little more. Some students are drawing and labeling. Some are driting (drawing, then writing a sentence or two). Most are drawing and writing four to five sentences. A few are filling up whole pages with sentences and then drawing pictures to match. After about 15 minutes, the timer goes off, indicating that the Writing Block is over. The students quickly stop what they are doing and return to the carpet to wait for "five friends" to read what they have written and ask for comments. It's only a few weeks into first grade, and they have the Writing Block format down! Margaret and Tom long to stay and listen to all five students read their writing and hear the "stars" (good comments) and "wishes" (what the children wish they knew about the writing), but it is time for the visitors to go. From what Margaret and Tom observed by walking around the classroom during the Writing Block, these young students are all well on their way to becoming writers, and more importantly, they can all read their own writing!

1:00–1:30 Kendra Garden Kindergarten Room 3

Miss Kendra Garden uses a large piece of plain paper to write on; the paper is on a chart paper stand. This will be the first real writing mini-lesson for her kindergarten class. She knows her students are ready for writing by themselves because they have watched her write during morning messages (writing for children) and predictable charts (writing with children). Today, she will ask them to write by themselves. Kendra has gone through many of her students' names in Getting to Know You activities, so she has talked about most of the letter names and sounds with her class. She thinks that many children are ready to use their phonemic awareness and demonstrate what they have learned by writing the letters that represent the sounds they hear. Kendra no longer writes words for her kindergarten students during their writing time. She knows the importance of developing phonemic awareness in young children, and she wants to give her students the opportunity to stretch out words and listen for sounds. Their real work at writing time is to listen for sounds and then to try to represent those sounds with letters.

This first writing lesson begins with Kendra Garden talking about the different ways people write. She tells her class, "Some people use pictures when they write." She draws a smiling face on the piece of paper to illustrate this.

"When teachers put smiling faces on papers they are saying, 'I like your work!' People sometimes use pictures to help them say what they want to say. You can use pictures when you write if that will help you. If you want to say, 'I love my cat,' you may want to write the word I, then draw a heart and a cat." Kendra does just what she told the children they could do—she writes a capital I and draws a heart and a simple picture of a cat.

"This says, 'I love my cat.'" (She points to the letter I as she says, "I," the picture of the heart as she says, "love," and the picture of the cat as she says, "my cat.")

"Some children make wavy lines and call it writing. They think about what they want to say and then write, 'I like playing ball.' It looks something like this."

"You can write like this if you want." (She points to the scribbling as she says this and reads what she said, 'I like playing ball,' as she points to the lines.)

"Another way children write is to use the letters and sounds they know." Kendra says aloud," I play with my sister," stretching out the words as she says them and writing down the beginning sounds she hears. For **sister,** she writes a beginning and an ending sound.

I p w m sr

She reads this back, as "I play with my sister." The letters help the children remember what words were said.

"Another way children write is to use some words they know. If you can write your name, then do that. If you can write 'cat' or 'dog' or 'mom,' then do that."

Tess CAT Mom

"Tess can read her sentence: 'Tess has a cat and a Mom.' If you know some words, you can use those words to help you write."

"Some people write just like I do every day when I write the morning message—they use words and write sentences. When children do this, they think about what they want to tell the class and then they stretch out the words and write them down as best they can."

Apples are red, green, and yellow.

"If you want to use words and write sentences today, you can do that," Kendra says. She then reads her sentence to the class. She tells the children that if she wrote this sentence on her paper, she would draw red, green, and yellow apples with her crayons. She then takes out red, green, and yellow markers and models just what she wants the children to do.

"So when you write today, remember that there are lots of way you can do it: you can draw pictures, you can make some lines or letters, you can try some words you know, or you can write sentences. Use whatever will help you to tell me about something."

Kendra sends the children back to their tables where plain pieces of newsprint and their crayon boxes are waiting for them. She walks around, asking the children what they will write about and encouraging both drawing and printing. When she comes to a student who has only drawn a picture but who knows letters and sounds, Kendra encourages her to stretch out the word and write the letters that make those sounds. After looking at the writing the class produces, Kendra knows she will have to let the children watch her a little longer before she begins daily writing. She will also allow the children to copy words in the writing center and use pencils, pens, and markers to write what they want on plain paper there. She will continue her morning messages, reading the room for words and modeling how to stretch out words, and write the letters she hears. She will also "coach" some children when they are writing in the writing center. After the winter holidays, Kendra will begin to have her students write daily in their "writing journals" (plain paper bound or stapled into booklets with front and back covers of construction paper).

At the end of writing time, the children form a circle in the big-group area at the front of the classroom, and several children get to share their writing. Proudly, they tell Miss Garden and their classmates what they have written.

Hannah says, "This is me and my mom cooking."

Will says, "This is me and my dad playing ball."

Mary Catherine says, "This is me and my brother and sister."

Cooper says, "I like to play with my dog."

Ryan says, "I play with Madeline at Grandma's house."

Jimmy is next and yells, "Grandpa has a new truck!"

Each child has something to say, even if the teacher and the visitors cannot read their writing. Tom and Margaret are glad that Kendra said, "Tell me what you wrote about." They have seen some kindergarten teachers ask a child to read his writing and the child would reply, "I can't read!" These children feel good about their writing, and with most of the year ahead of them, really will be writing by the end of the year.

1:30–2:15 Will Teachum Grade 5 Room 50

Will loves books and frequently reads aloud quality picture books by favorite authors, such as Eve Bunting and Patricia Polocco, good chapter books, and fascinating facts from informational books. Today, he is writing a book review about a Newbery Award winner book he just finished reading during his read-aloud time. Will wants his students to read "good literature," so he likes to share Newbery winners and Honor Books with his class. Will is a wonderful teacher, and his students both like and respect him. He expects a lot from his fifth graders, but they like him so much, they will do anything and never complain. He talks about how some teachers have students write book reports but points out, "that is a genre only written in school." He prefers writing book reviews, a common genre found in many magazines and newspapers. He tells students, "A book review tells about the book, if the reader/writer liked the book, and also why he did or did not like it. Today, I will write a book review about *Maniac Magee* by Jerry Spinelli, the book I just finished reading to you at Self-Selected Reading time. It was the Newbery Award book in 1990. Then, I will ask you to do a focused writing and write a book review about a book of your choice."

Next, Mr. Teachum begins to think aloud and models how to write a short summary and review of a book.

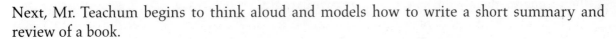

Maniac Magee by Jerry Spinelli (Scholastic, 1990)

Born Jeffrey Lionel Magee, his parents died when he was three. When we meet him, Maniac Magee is living on his own and is a legend. He can outrun, out jump, and play ball better than anyone he meets. Young children love Maniac because he can untie any knot, and it stays untied. Maniac sees no difference between the kids from the black East End of town or those from the white West End of town. Maniac is special!

Maniac Magee is a quick read. It contains forty-five chapters, and fifth graders can read three or four chapters at a sitting. Each chapter tells another enjoyable adventure of the boy named Maniac Magee. When the Newbery Award committee selected this book as a winner, they made a good choice. I enjoy reading this book, and so do my students, year after year!

As Will writes, he explains that his first paragraph is a short summary, telling a little about the book. The second paragraph is what he thinks about the book. After he writes his review, one that fifth graders are capable of writing, he dismisses the students to begin their focused writing. Each student opens his notebook, takes out a piece of lined paper, adds his name and the date on the top line, then lists the name of a book, along with the author and publisher, on the next line. The students know to underline the title of the book; Mr. Teachum has just modeled and explained that in writing his book review. The students then begin to write their two-paragraph book reviews using every other line on their papers. Will wanders around the classroom making sure the students are on task and helping those who need it to get started. Then, he begins to call students up for their weekly conferences. The students looks pleased to go and share their writing with Will and hear his comments. He ends the Writing Block with a quick sharing exercise, "You have one minute to tell which book you are reviewing and to share a little of your review or what you thought of the book. There is not enough time to read everything; you choose what to say. Just remember, we don't like long commercials on television, and we don't have time to hear everything everyone has written. See if you can keep your sharing short but appealing." The students follow his instructions as Tom gives Margaret the signal that it is time to move to their final classroom visit that day.

2:15–3:00 Susie Science Grade 3 Room 30

The last thing on the schedule is Susie Science's writing lesson. Susie's room looks more like a science lab than a classroom. There are plants growing everywhere. There is a rabbit in one cage, two gerbils in another cage, and some fish in an aquarium. (According to Susie's students, one fish is named Gill Phish, and he helps her when Susie is writing.) There are "special spots" in this third-grade classroom to explore with magnets, magnifying glasses, and a microscope. There is a writing center with a computer, an old typewriter, journals, writing/ note paper (a classroom where note writing is OK!!!), and places to explore other science topics. Susie writes at the end of the day with her third graders because, "writing is a nice, quiet, easy activity at the end of the day. My students like to write, and so do I. We also can review something we have learned or discussed and combine that with writing to end our day."

Fourblox Elementary is located in a state that has a "standard course of study" in every subject at every grade level. Susie finds the science objectives for third grade are easy to teach when she integrates them into the Four-Blocks® framework. Currently, her class is studying weather. Susie likes to have the students actively involved in their weather lessons. During Self-Selected Reading, she reads and provides a variety of books that will help her students learn more about weather topics. During Guided Reading, students will read their science text and do "book club groups," with each group choosing a weather book from a selection of four books on different reading levels. During the Working with Words Block, Susie uses the Guess the Covered Word strategy with a weather paragraph to introduce or review weather topics. She also does Making Words using a weather word. She finds that *Making Big Words* (Good Apple, 1994) and *Making More Big Words* (Good Apple, 1997) by Cunningham and Hall contain lots of weather words: temperature, blizzards, precipitation, thunderstorm, snowstorm, etc. Susie has chosen to write a weather report during her writing mini-lesson today.

She thinks aloud and writes:

Warm today with clouds and sunshine. Increasingly cloudy this afternoon with a chance of showers tonight. High temperature today in the mid-60s. Lows tonight in the lower 40s. Colder air to the west will continue to push cooler air into the area for the next few days. Better get those jackets out!

Susie Science loves to teach science, talk about science, write about science, and chat with her children—especially if they are writing about science subjects! After the mini-lesson, she wanders around the room, stopping to see if anyone has chosen to write about science or another interesting subject. She also stops to help children who are having trouble getting started or need help with what they are doing. To Margaret and Tom, it is evident that Susie likes writing almost as much as science.

Leaving Fourblox Elementary, Tom wonders what Margaret will teach in her writing class this year; the teachers they watched are doing a good job and seem to know a lot about writing. Of course, they did not visit every teacher. When he mentions this to Margaret, she tells Tom not to worry. "I have lots of new information and tips to give the teachers who take my workshop. I expect you to come one day for each group to share your wealth of knowledge, too. While we whispered to each other in the different classrooms, made notes, and shared information at lunch, it occurred to me that every teacher can learn more about writing—and should—if he or she wants to be the best writing teacher possible. That is the most wonderful part of our job—we have to keep learning new things ourselves! I love that! But, I like shopping, too, and according to the newspaper, the mall is having the biggest sale of the season. I need some new fall clothes because it's getting colder, and I want to look good when my writing workshop begins next week. So, I'm off to the mall to think about clothes for a while and buy, buy, buy."

Chapter 2
What Is Writing the Four-Blocks® Way?

Four-Blocks is a balanced and comprehensive approach to reading and writing. Children in Four-Blocks® classrooms participate in four different blocks every day, with each block being allotted approximately 30–40 minutes. Each block is structured to be as multilevel as possible. That is, multiple things to be learned are included in each lesson, and the children's attention is directed to the parts of the lesson with the most learning potential for them. Each child needs to feel successful in each block. Every child should learn something each day in each block, but every child does not learn the same thing. In addition to being committed to multilevel instruction, Four-Blocks teachers are committed to transfer and fading to independence. It doesn't really help a child to be good at decoding and spelling words during the Working with Words Block if that child does not actually use this knowledge to decode and spell unfamiliar words during the Writing, Self-Selected Reading, and Guided Reading Blocks. All mechanics and grammar are taught during the Writing Block in mini-lessons where the children watch the teacher write and the teacher coaches the children to use an Editor's Checklist to self-edit their papers. These skills are assessed by observing them in the students' writing. This chapter will provide a brief summary of the Guided Reading, Self-Selected Reading, and Working with Words Blocks. The remainder of the chapter will describe how to do writing the Four-Blocks way. (The most complete source of information about Four-Blocks is in *The Teacher's Guide to the Four Blocks®* by Cunningham, Hall, and Sigmon, Carson-Dellosa, 1999.)

Guided Reading

Guided Reading is the block in which children learn comprehension and oral reading fluency. Guided Reading lessons have a before-reading phase, a during-reading phase, and an after-reading phase. Depending on the text being read, the comprehension strategies being taught, and the reading levels of the children, a great variety of before-, during-, and after-reading variations are used. Before children read, help them build and access prior knowledge, make connections to personal experiences, develop vocabulary essential for comprehension, make predictions, and set purposes for their reading. After reading, guide children to connect new knowledge to what they knew before, follow up predictions, and discuss what they learned and how they are becoming better readers by using reading strategies.

The goals of the Guided Reading Block are:

- to teach comprehension skills and strategies.
- to develop oral reading fluency.
- to develop background knowledge, meaning vocabulary, and oral language.
- to teach children how to read all types of literature.
- to maintain the students' motivation and self-confidence, even if they are struggling readers.

(For more about Guided Reading, see *Guided Reading the Four-Blocks® Way* by Cunningham, Hall, and Cunningham; Carson-Dellosa, 2000.)

Self-Selected Reading

In Four-Blocks classrooms, the Self-Selected Reading Block includes teacher read-alouds. The teacher reads to the children from a wide range of literature. Next, children read on their own level from a variety of materials including the widest possible range of topics, genres, and levels. While the children read, the teacher conferences with approximately one-fifth of the class each day. The block usually ends with one or two children sharing their books with the class in a "Reader's Chair" format. The goals of the Self-Selected Reading Block are:

- to introduce children to all types of literature through the teacher read-aloud.
- to build intrinsic motivation for reading.
- to encourage and develop children's reading interests.
- to provide instructional-level reading.

(Much more elaboration about the Self-Selected Reading Block can be found in the book, *Self-Selected Reading the Four-Blocks® Way* by Cunningham, Hall, and Gambrell; Carson-Dellosa, 2002.)

Working with Words

In the Working with Words Block, children learn the letter-sound relationships which allow them to decode and spell lots of words, and they learn to read and spell high-frequency words automatically. The first 10 minutes of this block are given to reviewing the "Word Wall" words. Students practice new and old high-frequency words daily by looking at them, saying them, chanting the letters, writing the words, and self-correcting the words with the teacher.

The remaining 15–25 minutes of the Working with Words time is given to phonics lessons which help children learn to decode and spell. A variety of different activities are provided on different days. Some of the most popular ones are Rounding Up the Rhymes, Making Words, Reading/Writing Rhymes, Using Words You Know, Guess the Covered Word, and Word Sorting and Hunting. (For grade-level specific descriptions of Working with Words lessons, see *Month-by-Month Phonics for First Grade*, Cunningham and Hall, Carson-Dellosa, 2003, 1997; *Month-by-Month Phonics for Second Grade*, Hall and Cunningham, Carson-Dellosa, 2003, 1998; *Month-by-Month Phonics for Third Grade*, Cunningham and Hall, Carson-Del-

losa, 2003, 1998; and *Month-by-Month Phonics for the Upper Grades*, Cunningham and Hall, Carson-Dellosa, 1998.) The goals of the Working with Words Block are:

- to teach children how to read and spell high-frequency words.
- to teach children how to decode and spell lots of other words using letter-sound relationships.
- to have students automatically and fluently use phonics and knowledge of high-frequency words while reading and writing.

Writing

The Writing Block includes both self-selected writing, in which children choose their topics and how they will write about those topics, and focused writing, in which children learn how to write particular types of writing and on particular topics. Children are taught to use process writing to improve their first drafts, so they don't have to think of everything at one time. Process writing is carried out in "Writers' Workshop" fashion. The Writing Block begins with an 8–10 minute mini-lesson, during which the teacher writes and models one or more things writers do. Next, the children go to their own writing. On some days, they are writing a first draft. On other days, they are working with a chosen piece to eventually revise, edit, and publish it. While the children write, the teacher conferences with individuals or small groups to help them learn how to revise, edit, and publish. The Writing Block ends with "Author's Chair," in which several students each day share work in progress or their published work. The goals of the Writing Block are:

- to have students view writing as a way of telling about things.
- to help all children write fluently.
- to teach students to apply grammar and mechanics to their own writing.
- to teach particular types of writing.
- to allow students to learn to read through writing.
- to maintain the motivation and self-confidence of all students, even if they are struggling writers.

The Five Cycles of Writing Instruction

Writing is perhaps the most complex activity children are asked to engage in. Writing requires the ability to think and organize. The writer must also have a high level of prior knowledge about the topic. The words a student has in her meaning vocabulary store also affect how well and fluently she writes. As students write, they must think about and organize their ideas, write clearly and correctly about their topics, and use precise and powerful words.

Being able to achieve all of these "meaning communication" goals would be complex enough, but as students write, they also must be able to spell words correctly, punctuate and para-graph correctly, and unless they are writing on the computer, use handwriting which can be read easily by others. Because writing is so complex, children must be taught many differ-ent things—some great and some small—but all important. If a teacher focuses on all of the components at once, children are apt to be overwhelmed and frustrated by their inability to write as well as they need to. Writing is a skill everyone can become better at. To become better writers, students need instruction and practice, and they need to focus on just a few things at a time. The cycles of writing allow teachers and the children they teach to focus on particular aspects of writing until students become fluent with them. Here is a brief description of what happens in each cycle.

Cycle 1: Self-Selected Single Draft Writing

Cycle 1 is where instruction begins for all writers. Beginning writers in kindergarten and early first grade will spend a long time in Cycle 1. Older children will begin the school year in Cycle 1 and, depending on their prior experience and willingness to write, might move quickly into Cycle 2. In Cycle 1, all children should learn what writing is, understand how to find topics for writing, enjoy sharing their writing with others, and be willing to write. In Cycle 1, teachers model writing for children through mini-lessons, and the children write and share their writing if they choose to. Students do not revise, edit, or publish writing in Cycle 1.

This is a general description of what happens in Cycle 1. In Chapter 3, you will find more specific suggestions for accomplishing the important goals of getting all children to understand what writing is and to be willing to write and share.

Cycle 2: Process Writing with Editing, Conferencing, and Publishing

In first grade, Cycle 2 begins when the goals of Cycle 1 have been accomplished for all (or almost all) of your students. The children are willing to write and share. They can decide what they want to write about. They know how to write, including what to do about spelling. Of course, this does not mean that the children are all at the same level in their writing. Some children write more, better, and more correctly than others, but they all understand what writing is and actively participate in it. In Cycle 2, children begin to learn about editing, and teachers begin conferencing and publishing.

Mini-Lessons in Cycle 2—In Cycle 2, teachers continue to do mini-lessons that focus on some of the same things as Cycle 1. There may be an occasional mini-lesson on "What to do about spelling" and "Choosing a topic." These mini-lessons usually include the concepts taught in Cycle 1, along with some more sophisticated concepts. By now, the Word Wall is growing, and teachers begin to model how to use Word Wall words to help spell rhyming words. (The Word Wall words that help spell rhyming words are starred or highlighted in some way so that the children know that **play** can be used to spell rhyming words such as **pay**, **clay**, and **spray**. **They** is not highlighted and shouldn't be used to spell any other words, because rather than help you spell, **they** will lead you astray!)

In Cycle 2, teachers continue to think aloud at the beginning of the mini-lesson about topics of interest to the children (some of which may inspire the children, even if the teacher doesn't write about them). Many teachers use their writing mini-lesson time on one day to write their own personal list of topics they know a lot about and to encourage their students to do the same. Teachers also write about things the children are learning in school. "Planning" mini-lessons play a more important role in Cycle 2. Teachers sometimes do a planning mini-lesson in which they make a list, web, or Venn diagram of something they intend to write. In Cycle 2, teachers also do mini-lessons on editing and begin an Editor's Checklist. See Chapter 4 for lots of ideas for editing mini-lessons.

Writing in Cycle 2—The children continue to write every day in Cycle 2. They often write in a notebook or keep their pieces in a writing folder. The time for writing is longer in Cycle 2—15–20 minutes, depending on the age of the children. Drawing is de-emphasized in Cycle 2. When children do draw, they are usually required to write first, then draw. They also may illustrate published pieces.

Sharing in Cycle 2—Cycle 2 is usually when teachers begin a more formal "Author's Chair" sharing time. In an average size class (20–25 students), the children are divided across five days, and each day one-fifth of the class shares one piece, or a portion thereof, that they have written since the last time they shared. There are a variety of ways to share at the different grade levels, and you will learn much more about sharing in Chapter 7.

Editing, Conferencing, and Publishing in Cycle 2—The big, "new" thing that happens in Cycle 2 is that the children select some of their best pieces to publish. In some classrooms, children can each choose one piece to publish when they have three or four good first drafts. In other classrooms, teachers designate a week (or two) for publishing, and each student picks a piece of writing, edits its spelling and mechanics with a friend, conferences with the teacher about it, then publishes it. You will learn much more about editing in Chapter 4, conferencing in Chapter 6, and publishing in Chapter 7.

Cycle 3: Process Writing with Revising, Editing, Conferencing, and Publishing

Cycle 3 is much like Cycle 2, with the addition of revising. Mini-lessons focus on revision, and children begin to learn how to revise their message and organization. Editing, conferencing, and publishing continue in Cycle 3, but children go through a revision step before they edit. Teaching children how to revise their papers is the topic of Chapter 5. In addition to revision, many teachers teach more editing conventions and add them to the Editor's Checklist. Children my share first drafts or published pieces.

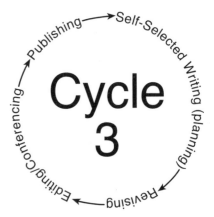

Cycle 4: Focused Writing with Revising, Editing, Conferencing and Publishing

Until Cycle 4, most of the children's writing has been on self-selected topics, topics they think of, know a lot about, and want to write about. In Cycle 4, students continue to do some self-selected writing, but teachers concentrate mostly on focused writing in which all children write on the same topic and/or in the same form or genre. Students learn to write letters, cinquain poetry, reports, stories, and many other forms. Just as in self-selected writing, some—but not all—of the focused pieces that children write go through the writing process of revising, editing, conferencing, and publishing.

Mini-Lessons in Cycle 4—The new focus in Cycle 4 is on how to write specific forms or genres, but students continue to do some self-selected writing. Many teachers alternate the two types of writing, spending one or two weeks on self-selected writing and then three or four weeks on focused writing with a particular genre. During self-selected writing weeks, the mini-lessons continue to focus on strategies needed for all writing, such as adding items to the Editor's Checklist, reviewing, or teaching new revising strategies.

During focused writing weeks, however, the mini-lessons center on the particular genre being taught. Planning, sometimes called prewriting, gets more attention when everyone is writing the same form because the teacher can demonstrate how to use a planning strategy particularly appropriate for that genre. The students can then all use that same planning strategy. Various graphic organizers, such as webs, Venn diagrams, and charts, are taught as planning devices for informational writing. Story maps can be used to plan before writing stories. Some editing conventions are specific to particular forms. Letters have special punctuation and formatting conventions, and these are taught during letter-writing mini-lessons. Revising is also taught as it relates to particular types of writing.
Mini-lessons include how to use a writing scale to evaluate your writing as a particular genre. Genres are the subject of Chapter 8, and you will see examples of genre-based mini-lessons there.

Writing, Revising, Editing, Conferencing, Sharing and Publishing in Cycle 4—These activities continue pretty much the same as they did in Cycle 3. During focused weeks, when everyone is working on the same genre, a class book containing everyone's piece is often the form publishing takes. Focused writing is often integrated with science and social studies topics, and the books published are good summaries of what children have learned during particular units.

Cycle 5: Single Draft Focused Writing

Eventually, children must learn how to write in a particular form and produce good first drafts of that form, including having most words spelled correctly and most basic writing conventions in place. Essay exams and other middle school/high school writing tasks often don't allow time for separate planning, revising, and editing steps. Once children have been taken through the writing process with a particular genre several times and understand clearly the requirements of that genre, they can be asked to write and evaluate first drafts in that genre. In addition, they can be held accountable to spelling most words correctly and applying the most important capitalization, punctuation, and formatting conventions in their first drafts. Cycle 5 writing usually happens late in the elementary school years.

When Do You Do Each Cycle?

When you do each cycle is the big question and one that only you as the teacher can answer. Teachers begin each year with Cycle 1 and usually spend longer in Cycle 1 in the early grades than in upper grades—unless a teacher has a whole class of REALLY reluctant writers.

Cycle 2 begins in first grade, when you observe that most students are writing willingly, know what writing is, and know that what they care most about is WHAT they write! Cycle 2 continues as students are taught procedures for editing and publishing, along with other kinds of mini-lessons.

Revision is the big addition in Cycle 3. (While in Cycle 2, teachers do informal revising instruction with children who are getting ready to publish. They also model in mini-lessons how to change and add to writing to make it better, but they do not focus mini-lessons on revising with the whole class until Cycle 3.) Do NOT wait to start teaching revision until all editing conventions have been taught. In fact, continue to add more editing conventions in Cycle 3.

Cycles 4 and 5 emphasize Focused Writing. Teachers must look at their students and their writing progression to know when to begin each cycle and how much time to spend there. The following chart gives some general guidelines.

	Kindergarten	Grade 1	Grade 2	Grade 3	Upper Grades
EARLY in the Year	Cycle 1	Cycle 1	Cycle 1 Cycle 2	Cycle 1 Cycle 2	Cycle 1 Cycle 2 Cycle 3
MOST of the Year	Cycle 1	Cycle 2	Cycle 2 Cycle 3	Cycle 2 Cycle 3	Cycle 3 Cycle 4
LATE in the Year	Cycle 1	Cycle 2	Cycle 3	Cycle 3	Cycle 4

Organizing Your Classroom for the Writing Block

Teachers who have the most successful writing blocks are usually incredibly well organized. In this section, you will learn some clever devices for organizing your classroom and children during the Writing Block.

Organizing Your Classroom for Cycle 1 Writing

In Cycle 1, children are writing on their own self-selected topics and sharing some of their pieces with each other. Cycle 1 is the easiest cycle from an organizational standpoint. Time is the first variable to organize. The Writing Block usually lasts 30–40 minutes and consists of three parts—mini-lesson, children writing, and sharing. The first 8–10 minutes of each day's Writing Block are devoted to the mini-lesson. Children watch as the teacher writes and thinks aloud about what and how he is writing. Next, the children write "what they want to tell" that day. The time devoted to writing in Cycle 1 is usually 10–15 minutes and often includes drawing to go with the writing. The Writing Block ends with an "informal" sharing each day. Children who want to share their writing volunteer to read or "tell about" what they have drawn or written.

Time in Cycle 1 Writing		
First 8–10 Minutes	**Middle 10–15 Minutes**	**Final 10–12 Minutes**
Teacher teaches mini-lesson.	Teacher roams around and encourages.	Teacher leads informal sharing.
Children watch and listen.	Children write (and draw).	Children read or tell about what they have written (and drawn).

The other organizational consideration is classroom space. Again, in Cycle 1, this is quite simple. Plan your mini-lesson so that all children can easily watch you write and hear what you are thinking as you are writing. Many teachers gather the students around the overhead, chart, or board for the mini-lesson.

Once the mini-lesson is over, children go to their own writing, usually at their desks or tables. As the children write, the teacher circulates, "oohs" and "aahs" about their topics, and makes positive, supportive comments.

Sometimes the sharing is done with the children still at their desks or tables. More commonly, the teacher gathers the children together in a circle and lets volunteers share. Some teachers have the children stand for the sharing since they have been sitting for several minutes.

Organizing Your Classroom for Cycles 2 and 3 Writing

Cycle 2 is when "Writer's Workshop" truly begins, and organization becomes more complex and more critical. The time for mini-lesson and sharing usually remains about the same, but the middle part of the block finds children at different stages of the writing process. Teachers often create a classroom graphic so that they and the children know where everyone is supposed to be and what they are supposed to be doing.

Here are some examples of different graphics.

Status of the Class, Cycle 3

	2/10	2/11	2/12	2/13	2/14	2/17
Merrill	W	W	R	E	C	P
Alex	P	W	W	W	R	R
Lafe	W	W	W	R	E	C
Jeff	W	R	E	C	P	P
Amanda	E	C	P	P	W	W
Cooper	C	P	W	W	R	E

W—Writing P—Planning R—Revising E—Editing C—Conferencing P—Publishing

Status of the Class, Cycle 2

	10/21	10/22	10/23	10/24	10/25	10/28
Suzanne	W	W	E	C	P	W
Ryan	E	P	W	W	W	W
Michelle	W	W	W	E	C	P
Chad	W	W	W	W	W	E
Cooper	W	W	E	C	P	W
Georgia	E	C	P	P	W	W

W—Writing (planning) E—Editing C—Conferencing P—Publishing

The sharing often becomes a more formal Author's Chair in which approximately one-fifth of the students share each day, picking pieces they have written since their last day to share. Some teachers divide the children into sharing groups according to the days of the week. Others just designate groups with numbers—1, 2, 3, 4, and 5. Most teachers spread out their advanced and struggling writers across the days so that each day has a good mix of writers sharing.

Sharing Chart

Monday: Michelle, Ryan, Suzanne, Cooper, Henry
Tuesday: Jerry, Elizabeth, Craig, Dyanne, Matthew H.
Wednesday: Michael, Janice, Charles, Britta, Hoyt
Thursday: Matthew G., Missy, Kristen, Karen, Zach
Friday: Jamie, Judy, Kelly, Thad, Quinton

Sharing Chart

Group 1	Group 2	Group 3	Group 4	Group 5
J. R.	Ashley	Katie	Jeff	Suzanne
Stephanie	Michael	Merrill	Karen L.	Olivia
Georgia	Hannah	Lafe	Kaitlyn	Steve
Deems	Will	Alex	Chris	Cooper
Aidan	Mary	Amanda	Joey	Karen G.

When children are writing in Cycle 2, they usually do not draw every day. Some teachers set a certain amount of time when everyone needs to be writing (10 minutes, perhaps) and then allow children to continue to write or draw for the final 5 minutes. Other teachers tell children that, on their day to share, they can draw pictures to go with the pieces they have chosen to share.

In Cycles 2 and 3, the teacher's time in the middle segment is spent conferencing with children, often those children who are getting ready to publish.

Time in Cycle 2 and Cycle 3 Writing

First 8–10 Minutes	Middle 10–15 Minutes	Final 10–12 Minutes
Teacher teaches mini-lesson.	Teacher holds individual or small group conferences with children.	Teacher leads Author's Chair sharing.
Children watch and listen.	Children write and choose pieces to publish; they then revise (if it's Cycle 3), edit, and publish these pieces with help from peers, the teacher, and volunteers.	Designated children share one piece each, written since their last sharing day. (This may be a published piece, a first draft, or a work in progress.)

Editor's Checklist
1. Name and date
2. Sentences make sense
3. Beginning capital letters
4. Ending punctuation (. ? !)

Circle misspelled words

Classroom space can be organized to support Cycle 2 or Cycle 3 writing. The mini-lesson usually continues in the same space. A "special" chair is often designated as the Author's Chair and is the place around which the class huddles at the end of the writing block. Many teachers designate a place for peer editing (and revising in Cycle 3). This editing/revising center often houses the Editor's Checklist, the revising chart, a handheld electronic spelling checker, colorful pens, scissors, and tape for adding on.

Most teachers also choose a spot for conferencing with children. Some teachers designate this as the "editor-in-chief" center.

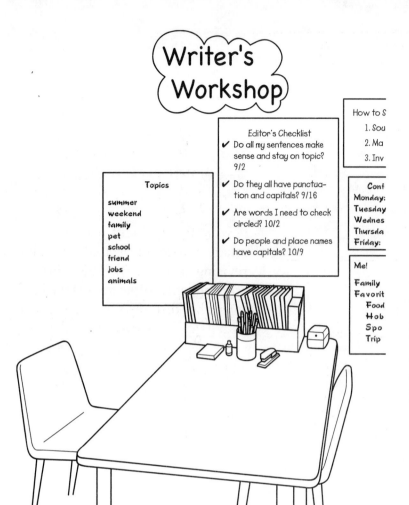

Writer's Workshop

Editor's Checklist
✔ Do all my sentences make sense and stay on topic? 9/2
✔ Do they all have punctuation and capitals? 9/16
✔ Are words I need to check circled? 10/2
✔ Do people and place names have capitals? 10/9

Topics

summer
weekend
family
pet
school
friend
jobs
animals

How to S
1. Sou
2. Ma
3. Inv

Conf
Monday:
Tuesday
Wednes
Thursda
Friday:

Me!
Family
Favorit
Food
Hob
Spo
Trip

Finally, most teachers have a publishing center. This center often contains computers with publishing software and clip art, blank skeleton books, markers and crayons for illustrating, and other enticing supplies that make publishing special.

Organizing Your Classroom for Cycle 4 Writing

Cycle 4 differs from Cycles 1, 2, and 3 in that the children are all participating in focused writing. They are all writing on the same topic and/or in the same genre, rather than writing about their own self-selected writing topics in the ways they want to write about them. Often this writing is connected to science or social studies topics or to what the children are reading in Guided Reading. In Cycle 4, children are not usually producing several different drafts and then picking one to publish, and they are usually all working at the same stage of the writing process each day.

Here is an example of how time might be utilized during a week of focused writing lessons on letter writing.

	Mini-Lesson	Children Write	Sharing
Day One	Teacher models making a list of important things to include in letter.	Children write individual lists; teacher circulates and encourages.	Children share lists in small groups and add to lists based on feedback.
Day Two	Teacher models writing first half of letter.	Children begin their letters; teacher circulates and encourages.	Children share letter beginnings in same small groups and revise based on feedback.
Day Three	Teacher models finishing letter.	Children finish letters; teacher circulates and encourages.	Children share letters in same small groups and revise based on feedback.
Day Four	Teacher models revising letter with help from class.	Children work with peers of similar writing ability to revise; teacher checks revisions.	Children share revised letters in small groups.
Day Five	Teacher and children edit teacher's letter; teacher chooses stationery on which she will copy letter later.	Children work with peers of similar writing ability to edit; teacher checks editing and gives permission to copy.	Children copy revised, edited letters and share these in small groups.

Connecting Writing to the Other Blocks and the Rest of the Curriculum

Each block has its scheduled time in every classroom, but Four-Blocks teachers make many links among the four different blocks and to other areas of the curriculum. There are many possible links to the books read by the children during Guided Reading or to the children during the teacher read-aloud part of Self-Selected Reading. Teachers can point out to children the punctuation and other editing conventions used in books by their favorite authors. Revising is not the favorite part of writing for most children, but they need to understand that all writers revise to make their writing even better. See Chapter 5 for ways to connect revising to books and authors children are familiar with. Teachers can use the books children have read during Guided or Self-Selected Reading to help children understand the particular characteristics of various genres. Suggestions for this are contained in Chapter 9.

The Working with Words Block is essential to a successful Writing Block. High-frequency words and words with common spelling patterns are put on the Word Wall and practiced each day. Children are reminded at the beginning of each writing time to spell words as best they can "unless it is on the Word Wall." Teachers model glancing up at the Word Wall for the spelling of words during their mini-lessons and talk about how helpful the Word Wall is, especially for tricky words. Most teachers highlight or star words with helpful rhyming patterns and model how these words help them spell other words.

The other activities done during the Working with Words Block help children learn the patterns needed for spelling words. As the year goes on, children's sound spelling becomes much more sophisticated as they apply the patterns they learned in Working with Words to their own writing.

Finally, teachers make connections to the subject areas of science and social studies. They often pick topics being studied and write about them during their mini-lessons.

"Today, I am going to write about what I think are the most interesting facts we have learned about the planets."

"We have been studying communities. My grandma has lived in a little community her whole life and was there when the town was actually formed. I am going to write a letter to her and ask her some questions about that."

In addition to modeling writing connected to science and social studies during mini-lessons while the children are doing self-selected writing, teachers connect much of their focused writing to science and social studies. Writing is a way of learning about a topic as you rehearse, organize, and reflect upon new information. Using science and social studies topics during focused writing ensures that everyone has a fairly high level of prior knowledge from which to write. Writing connected to science and social studies results in better writing and more science and social studies learning—a winning combination!

Making the Writing Block Multilevel

In Four-Blocks classrooms, we are always concerned with making the blocks as multilevel as possible. Writing is the most multilevel block because children can only write on their level. When teachers allow children to choose their own topics, accept whatever level of first-draft writing each child can accomplish, and allow him to work on his piece as many days as needed, all children can succeed in writing. One of the major tenets of self-selected writing is that children should choose their own topics. When children decide what they will write about, they write about something of particular interest to them, and consequently, something that they know about. Now this may seem like belaboring the obvious, but it is a crucial component in making writing multilevel. When everyone writes about the same topic, the different levels of children's knowledge and writing ability become painfully obvious. Writing is multilevel when children choose their topics and write about what they know.

The importance of having children choose what they write about to make writing multilevel cannot be overemphasized. One morning late in the first-grade year, one of the authors of this book (Pat) was in a classroom during "Author's Chair." Here is Pat's story of the *My Bike* book and the *Rocks* book.

Two of the authors had just published books and were sharing these with the class. (The other three authors shared first drafts or "works in progress" that day.) The first boy to share his book was one of the most struggling readers/writers in the class. He had written about his bike, and his book was quite simple. Each page had a sentence or two and a picture.

Here is my bike. It is red.

I like to ride my bike.

I ride it to the store.

My brother wants a bike too, but he is too little.

The child proudly (and slowly) read each sentence and showed each illustration. After he finished, he called on children to tell what they liked. Lots of hands were raised, and the general idea was that most of them had bikes, too, and they liked their bikes as well. Many of their bikes were also red! A clear bonding took place between this struggling writer and other members of the class!

The next author was one of the most advanced readers/writers in this first grade class. He proceeded to read his book about rocks. The book was quite long with quite a bit of writing on each page, and it was clear that he had carefully researched this topic.

There are three different kinds of rocks. Some rocks are igneous. Some rocks are metamorphic rocks. Some rocks are sedimentary rocks.

Igneous rocks were formed from melted rock. They are sometimes called fire rocks. Some igneous rocks form underground. Some igneous rocks form above ground.

The book went on for eight pages, and each page had a plethora of information about rocks.

The children listened politely and made some "nice" comments about the rocks book, then the "Author's Chair" time ended.

As the children were having their snack time, Pat circulated and commented on how wonderful both books were. She then asked several children which book they liked best. At first, the children politely told her, "I liked them both!"

When pressed, however, the consensus of opinion in this first-grade class was that they liked the bike book better! No surprise here. Bikes (and all other vehicles) are of enormous interest to most young children.

To any adult, it was obvious which book was better—the rocks book was about three grade levels more sophisticated than the bike book! Had both children written about the same topic, the differences in their writing abilities would have been painfully obvious to all—including the first graders. When children write on different topics, however, the differences in level are usually not noticed by the children, who are focusing on the topic. Letting children write on topics they know and care about "levels the playing field" as far as the other children are concerned. It is possible for a struggling writer to be judged by his peers to have the "better" book if the topic chosen is of more interest to the children. Letting children write on topics they know and care about is essential if all levels of writers are to feel successful!

During focused writing, children are all writing on the same topic or in the same genre or form. When writing on the same topic, make sure that every child has a fairly high level of prior knowledge about that topic by integrating focused writing with topics being studied in science or social studies. When writing in a particular form or genre, teach all children how to write that particular form or genre. Often, teachers use examples from literature which the children have read during Guided Reading or that they have read to the students during the teacher read-aloud part of Self-Selected Reading. By making these reading-writing connections, teachers assure that all children are familiar with the genre they are learning to write.

Teachers also have opportunities to make their teaching multilevel during mini-lessons and conferences. In mini-lessons, the teacher writes and the children get to watch him thinking. In these short daily lessons, teachers show all aspects of the writing process. They model topic selection, planning, writing, revising, and editing, and they write on a variety of topics in a variety of different forms. Some days, they write short pieces. Other days, they begin pieces that take several days to complete. When doing a longer piece, they model adding on by showing how you reread what you wrote previously in order to pick up your train of thought and continue writing. The mini-lessons contribute to making writing multilevel when the teacher includes all different facets of the writing process, writes on a variety of topics in a variety of forms, and intentionally writes some shorter, easier pieces and some more involved, longer pieces.

Another opportunity for meeting the various needs and levels of children comes in the conference with the teacher. In some classrooms, as they develop in their writing, children do some peer revising/editing and then come to the teacher ("editor-in-chief") for some final revision/editing before publishing. As teachers help children publish their chosen pieces, they have the opportunity to truly "individualize" their teaching. Looking at a child's writing usually reveals what the child needs to move forward and what the child is ready to understand. The conference provides the "teachable moment" in which both advanced and struggling writers can be nudged forward in their literacy development.

Success is essential to motivation. Some children do not write as well as other children, but they need to feel that they are succeeding in moving along in their writing or they will stop writing. To make sure that Author's Chair is a successful experience for all levels of writers, teachers often spend a minute or two with a struggling writer before that child shares in the Author's Chair. If the child wants to share from a first-draft piece but is unable to read it (and if the teacher can't read it either), then the teacher will coach the child to "tell" his piece rather than try to read it. If a struggling reader is about to read from a published piece for which the teacher has provided a lot of help, the teacher will read it with the child a time or two to assure that he can read it fluently when he is in the Author's Chair.

Finally, writing is multilevel because, for some children, writing is their best avenue to becoming readers. When children who are struggling with reading write about their own experiences and then read it back (even if no one else can read it!), they are using their own language and experiences to become readers. Often, the children who struggle with even the simplest material during Guided Reading can read everything in their writing notebook or folder. When young children are writing, some of them are really working on becoming better writers; others are engaging in the same activity, but for them, writing is how they figure out reading.

Building-Blocks Variations

The kindergarten program is called "Building Blocks." It shares many features with Four-Blocks, but it is consistent with how kindergarten teachers think and how five-year-olds learn. In kindergarten, teachers do writing for the children in which the children watch them write and hear them talk about what they are writing. This writing for children is often done in the form of a morning message. Teachers write with children and take dictation from them. This writing includes shared writing, interactive writing, and predictable charts. Writing by children is also included. Most of the writing done by kindergartners is Cycle 1 writing, in which the children draw, write, and share. (For lots more information about kindergarten, see *Month-by-Month Phonics, Reading and Writing for Kindergarten* by Hall and Cunningham, Carson-Dellosa, 2003, 1997, and *The Teacher's Guide to Building Blocks*™ by Hall and Williams, Carson-Dellosa, 2000. Books specific to writing in Kindergarten include *Writing Mini-Lessons for Kindergarten* by Hall and Williams, Carson-Dellosa, 2003, and *Predictable Charts* by Hall and Williams, Carson-Dellosa, 2002.)

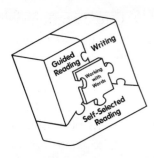

Big-Blocks Variations

Four-Blocks was developed for use in primary classrooms—grades one, two, and three. Seeing the success of the Four-Blocks® framework in primary grades, upper-grade teachers have wanted to use the framework, too. The upper-grades framework is called "Big Blocks," because it is for big kids and the blocks often require bigger amounts of time. It would be nice to think that all upper-grade classrooms could begin writing in Cycle 3 or 4, but in reality, there is often much resistance to writing by children in upper grades. By beginning in Cycle 1, teachers can change children's negative attitudes toward writing and develop their willingness to write and share. Once this is accomplished, teachers move through the cycles as quickly as possible, making sure that the children are learning the things that are the focus of each cycle before moving to the next one. (For more information about upper grades, see *The Teacher's Guide to Big Blocks*™ by Arens, Loman, Cunningham, and Hall, Carson-Dellosa, 2005. Mini-lessons specifically intended for upper-grade children can be found in *Writing Mini-Lessons for Upper Grades* by Hall, Cunningham, and Arens, Carson-Dellosa, 2003.)

Chapter 3
How Do You Get Students to Write and Keep Writing?

How to Start the Year in the Writing Block

How to get a writing program started is the question most often asked about writing. When teachers visit a Four-Blocks® classroom and see the Writing Block running smoothly, they can imagine themselves and their classrooms looking like that. What they can't imagine is how to get started. As they are "debriefed" about what they observed, some common comments are heard:

"Some of my children just refuse to write. How do you get everyone to be willing to write?"

"If I let them choose what to write about, many of mine wouldn't write."

"My class won't write if I don't spell for them!"

"When I let them choose, they just write the same thing over and over."

"A lot of my children don't even know all of the letter names and sounds yet. How can they write?"

"I try to be supportive, but most of my struggling writers refuse to share their writing."

In this chapter, you will find a variety of ideas to get your writing program off "on the right foot."

Getting the Writing Block Off to a Successful Start

Regardless of their age or grade in school, children who are unwilling to write unless the teacher tells them what to write about or spells words for them are beginning writers. They lack the self-confidence, intrinsic motivation, and independence of even the average student in the spring of a kindergarten with a successful writing program. If beginning writers are in kindergarten or first grade, they have yet to learn to write. Most teachers recognize that kindergartners and first graders are beginning writers. What must also be recognized is that many older children are also beginning writers.

Older children reveal that they are like younger, beginning writers by being unwilling to write unless a teacher gives them topics or spells words for them, but they can also reveal this condition in other ways. Some older children will write independently but insist that you tell them how many sentences they must write. Then, they rush to complete that many sentences as quickly as they can, never writing more than the required number. If your required number of sentences is fairly large, these children usually write fewer and then insist they can't think of anything else to say. Some older children will write independently but refuse to share what they have written, even in a paired setting. A very few older children will just write or copy some unconnected words on their papers. By their lack of independence, word quantity, willingness to share, or understanding of what writing is, all of these older children are showing that they are still beginning writers in need of writing experiences that start by assuming nothing. Even excellent writing instruction of a more advanced nature is usually unable to succeed with beginning writers because they lack the prerequisite attitudes and skills to benefit from it. It is like trying to teach reading to beginning readers using a third- or fourth-grade level book and curriculum—even high-quality instruction is doomed to fail.

Several weeks of good writing instruction that assumes nothing can also be helpful for children who are no longer beginning writers. When a class of children begins working with a new teacher, they are often wary of how he will respond to their writing. They know that the teacher is always free to dislike what they write or to nitpick it for its lack of conformity to familiar or even unfamiliar rules. Even as adults, we may know that our mastery of, say, colons and semicolons is less than perfect. That self-awareness can make us reluctant to write for someone whose "pickiness" we are unsure of. Children are even more aware of their vulnerability concerning mechanics and conventions. Several weeks of writing that assumes nothing at the beginning of a new school year can restore the self-confidence, intrinsic motivation, and independence of children who are beyond beginning writing so that they can again write at the levels they achieved last year. This first cycle of writing, which gets all writers off to a successful start and lets children know that what teachers value most in writing is their ideas, is called self-selected, single-draft writing.

Self-Selected Writing and Sharing (Cycle 1)

Self-selected writing is when students come up with their own topics for writing and decide how they will write about those topics. At the beginning of each year, Four-Blocks teachers start with self-selected writing because that is the best way to overcome a child's lack of background knowledge or intrinsic motivation to write.

Every child has a personal life that she lives outside of school—mornings, evenings, weekends, school holidays, and vacations from school. By teaching children that they can write about what they already know about, teachers help them overcome the lack of knowledge they may have about any topics that might be suggested or assigned to them. By teaching children that they can write about what they already care about, teachers help them overcome the lack of interest they may have in writing about topics offered to them. When children refuse to write without the teacher giving them topics, they are showing that they consider writing to be something one does in school that has no relationship to their lives or the things that really matter to them personally. We use self-selected writing so that students will learn to write about topics they know something about and to gradually change their attitude that writing is a school-based, rather than a personal, activity.

At the beginning of each year, don't go through the writing process, only do a single draft. Some teachers of older children do not immediately see the need for this, since many of their children write well and willingly. Every class, however, has some children who "hate writing" and write only the bare minimum. Starting the year with single-draft writing is the only way to overcome some children's lack of self-confidence or intrinsic motivation to write. Children who have not learned to value writing or who avoid writing out of fear of failure or imperfection are likely to fail if expected to revise, edit, or recopy pieces of writing before their intrinsic motivation, self-confidence, or independence in writing significantly improve. Single-draft writing with no standards gets ALL children off to a successful start.

Mini-Lessons That Get Students Writing

Mini-lessons early in the year look quite simple, but they are critical to meeting the goal of having all children develop a willingness to write and share on the topics they know and care about. Mini-lessons provide instruction on deciding what to write about and help to communicate that students should write about what they would like to tell about. The teacher thinks aloud about what she could write:

"Let's see. What do I want to tell you about today? I could write about the new bike my son got for his birthday and how he is learning to ride it. I could write about what happened in our room yesterday when the power went off. I could write about the dog I had when I was your age. That's it! That's what I want to tell you about today. I will write about Icky."

As the children watch, the teacher writes on a chart (or the overhead) a piece about Icky, the pet dog she had when she was their age. The writing is not very long—a label or two or a sentence or two if the children are kindergartners or first graders, and four or five sentences for older children. As the teacher writes, she "thinks aloud" about all aspects of her writing.

"I will write Icky's name here with his picture. This word says 'Icky.'" (when adding labels rather than sentences to pictures)

"I will put a finger space between each word to make it easy to read." (when writing a short sentence for younger children)

"That is a good first sentence. I will put my period here and begin my second sentence with a capital letter."

"I think I should describe what Icky looked like."

"Icky was a funny dog. He was always getting into things. I will tell just one funny thing he did."

When she finishes writing, she reads the piece to the children, letting them join in the reading if they choose. If this is kindergarten or early first grade, she will draw a picture of Icky before writing. With older children, she sometimes draws a picture to go with her writing after she writes. With very young children, a teacher often just writes some label words to go with the picture. After the first few lessons, she might include a short sentence or two. With children who have not yet become writers, teachers do a lot more talking than writing.

In this brief mini-lesson, the children learn what writing is—it is putting down on paper something you want to tell. As the teacher thinks aloud before writing and mentions a few topics of interest that she doesn't choose to write about, such as her son's new bike or the power outage in the classroom yesterday, she is planting some ideas for what the children may want to write about. She does not, however, tell the children what to write about. One of the first things children must understand about writing if they are to become willing writers is that you write about something you want to tell about. If the teacher tells the children to write about their pets, or pets they wish they had, then she is doing for them the essential task that all writers must learn how to do for themselves—deciding on the topic for their writing.

Icky

1. Kindergarten or early in the year in first grade—the teacher talks, draws, and then labels.

When I was young, I had a dog named Icky.

He was short and had short brown hair.

2. Early in the year in first or second grade—the teacher talks, draws, and then writes a sentence or two.

When I was young, I had a short, brown, cocker spaniel named Icky. He loved to run around in our backyard. We were glad that our yard had a fence and he could not run away. He barked at everyone who came near our house, but he did not bite. He was a great family dog.

3. Early in the year in third grade and above—the teacher talks, writes several sentences, and then illustrates if there is time or it is helpful.

CAUTION: DEAD END!

Sometimes, teaching is like driving. You are going along in a logical way and suddenly find yourself lost—sometimes on a dead-end street. "Why didn't they warn me?" you think. "Where was the DEAD END sign?" Throughout this book, we will try to warn you of dead-end roads that many well-intentioned teachers have taken. These roads are often attractive and seem to go in the right direction, but they won't get you where you want to go.

Telling children what to write about, giving them a topic, letting them choose from three topics you give them, etc., are DEAD ENDs. Begin the year by letting the children know you can't tell them what to write about because writing is putting down on paper what the writer wants to tell. How could a teacher possibly know what a student wants to tell??? If your children tell you that their first-grade teacher always told them what to write about, respond (with a straight face) that "second-grade teachers aren't allowed to do that!" In Four-Blocks writing, a teacher thinks aloud about a few topics that she doesn't write about to plant ideas, she writes her mini-lesson about a common topic students might write about (which she neither encourages nor discourages), she "oohs" and "aahs" about what interesting topics other children in the class write about, and she helps children brainstorm lists of what they know about. Except during focused writing lessons, the teacher doesn't give students a topic because she wants them to be able to write at home in the evenings, over the weekend, during vacations from school, and during downtime in school. If she gives them topics, students will be dependent on her and will be unable to write unless she is there to give them topics. Giving students topics to write about is a DEAD END!

Do other mini-lessons early in the year that help children decide what to write about. Many teachers have the children help to create a list of all of the things they know about.

"How many of you went to kindergarten last year? Shall we add **kindergarten** to the list of things you might write about?"

"Raise your hand if you have brothers or sisters. Most of you do. Let's add **brothers and sisters**."

"I like to eat pizza and ice cream. What do you like to eat?" Children will volunteer favorite foods, and the teacher can add them to the growing list.

As the children share at the end of the writing time, other "universal" topics might emerge, and you can add them to the list "Things We All Know About."

Here is a list of topics one group of children helped their teacher create. This class never complained that they didn't know what to write about!

Things We All Know About		
School	My Friends	Grocery Shopping
Fall	Birthdays	Me and Grandma
Spring	Racing	Me and Grandpa
Winter	Weather	Rain
Summer	Holidays	Cats
Ball Games	Magnets	Our Class Trip to . . .
My Dog	A New Baby	A New Bike
Miss Olson, Our Student Teacher		
A Picnic	A New Student	The Substitute
Scary Stories	The Lake	Playing Soccer
Cheerleading	Fun on Saturday	Making Popcorn

In early mini-lessons, teachers model good spelling, punctuation, conventions, etc., and they talk about it as they do it, but teachers don't require that the students do it when they write. Later, some mini-lessons on editing will focus children's attention on the mechanics of writing. Early in the year, however, model and talk about it as you write but don't expect the children to focus on it. Writing is complex, and there are many things to be learned. If students feel that they must learn everything at once, they may end up learning little or nothing!

In other mini-lessons, begin to model what to do about spelling. Stretch out some words, putting down the sounds you hear. Some teachers are uncomfortable pretending they can't spell a word. The solution is to tell this to children as you begin to stretch out a word and "sound spell" it:

"I can spell **restaurant** now, but this is probably how I would have spelled it when I was your age."

When you model sound spelling and imply that this is how you would have done it at their age (and probably would have if anyone had let you!), children are willing to write words they have not yet learned to spell.

In addition to modeling sound spelling, also model how you use the resources in the room to help you spell.

"I can spell **because** because it is on the Word Wall. I'll just glance up there to make sure I'm correct."

"**November** is on our calendar, so I can look over there to spell it."

"**Purple** is on our color chart. There are so many places in our room to look for words we need to spell as we are writing!"

Mini-lessons early in the year focus students' attention on what writing is, how to decide what to write about, and how to write, including what to do about spelling. As you do the mini-lessons, think aloud about whatever is appropriate to the age and writing sophistication of the children you are teaching. (Specific mini-lessons for different grades can be found in *Writing Mini-Lessons for Kindergarten* by Hall and Williams, 2003; *Writing Mini-Lessons for First Grade* by Hall, Cunningham, and Boger, 2002; *Writing Mini-Lessons for Second Grade* by Hall, Cunningham, and Smith, 2002; *Writing Mini-Lessons for Third Grade* by Sigmon and Ford, 2002; and *Writing Mini-Lessons for Upper Grades* by Hall, Cunningham, and Arens, 2003. These book are available from Carson-Dellosa Publishing.)

Getting Children to Write Early in the Year

After you write, the children write. In kindergarten and early first grade, teachers and students draw first and then write. We call this beginning stage of writing "driting" because it combines drawing and writing. Early in the year, some young children only draw. As the weeks go by and they learn how to use the room to spell words and how to stretch out words and write the sounds they hear, all children begin to include some words and letters in their driting, particularly when you brag on them as they begin to include words. As the children write, rove around and encourage all of their efforts at drawing and writing.

"Oh, I see someone else has a pet dog."

"A cat is a good pet, too. I have a cat now. You gave me an idea for writing. I will tell you about my cat tomorrow."

"Do you really go fishing with your grandpa? I have never been fishing. I can't wait to hear more about your fishing trips."

Basically, "ooh" and "aah" about their topics in a voice loud enough for other children to hear. Remember what you are trying to accomplish early in the year—to teach children what writing is, to teach them how to write, and to encourage their willingness to write. Oohing and aahing about what they are writing sends them exactly the right message.

What teachers don't do while the children write is as important as what they do. Teachers don't tell students what to write about. They don't correct anything (hard as that is), and they don't spell words for the children. If a child asks you to spell a word, you should reply with something like:

"I can't spell **bike** for you, but I can help you stretch it out."

Then, help the child to say the word slowly and put down whatever letters he hears. Some children may just write **b** or **k** (the last sound they heard). Others will write the consonant letters **bk**. More sophisticated children will write **bik**. Regardless of how many letters they put down, don't tell them to include other letters but respond with something like:

"That was good listening for the sounds in **bike**, and you will remember that you meant to write **bike** if you choose to share what you wrote."

When they are trying to spell a word displayed somewhere in the room, clue them in on where to look:

"I can't spell **blue** for you, but I bet you can if you use the color chart."

"Aren't you lucky! We just put **my** on the Word Wall."

Early in the year, limit the amount of time that children write. With older children, teachers often start with 5–10 minutes and set a timer. The time increases gradually as the children's willingness to write increases.

CAUTION: DEAD END!

Spelling words for kids is a DEAD END. Once you start, they will never let you stop. Point out places in the room where students can find words. Help them stretch out words and praise their effort, telling them you couldn't have stretched that word nearly as well when you were their age! If they tell you that their kindergarten teacher spelled words for them, tell them, "First-grade teachers aren't allowed to do that!" If you have been spelling words for them all year and it is almost February, have the "How Things Change in February" talk, including that "teachers are no longer allowed to spell words for you once February comes" (and any other DEAD ENDS you have taken and now wish you hadn't!).

Keeping Students Writing

Once children are used to writing at a particular time each day and they are writing most days without complaint, it is time to prepare them for Writer's Workshop. Tell the children that they are writing so well that you soon will start collecting some pieces to edit and publish. Teachers often signal this shift by changing what they are writing in or on. With first and second graders, teachers often move to "half and half" paper, which has a picture space at the top of the page and writing lines on the bottom. Now, instead of drawing first, students are asked to write a sentence or two and then draw. Of course, the teacher models this by shifting to a chart or overhead with drawing and writing spaces and writing a few sentences before drawing the picture.

Teachers of older children often give their students notebooks to make the shift, saying something like:

"You are becoming such good writers that soon we will begin picking some of your best pieces to edit and publish. Starting today, I want you to write in these notebooks—skipping every other line so that you have room to add and change things when we edit and have conferences."

Of course, your mini-lessons from then on will look like notebook paper, and you will write on every other line and remind your students why you are doing this. If you have some published books from previous years, bring these out now to show your students what you are working toward. Brag on your "authors" from previous years and tell students that you know next year you will be bragging on them.

There are no hard and fast rules about what children write in or on. Different teachers have different preferences. Many teachers, however, have found that it helps to prepare students for the next cycle by shifting what they write on. It is also critical that children write on every other line so that there is space to edit and revise. (Imagine how hard it would be to revise and edit a paper that you had single spaced to save paper!) Some teachers create writing notebooks for children by stapling 10–20 pieces of paper between construction paper covers. Some first- and second-grade teachers use notebooks for the children to write on and have them write their sentences on one page and draw their picture (after they write) on the facing page. Most kindergarten teachers continue with unlined paper and drawing first, then writing, for most, if not all, of the kindergarten year.

Once students are writing willingly, it helps to include some mini-lessons on planning and expanding beyond one sentence. You also need to continue to provide some lessons on deciding what to write about and thinking aloud about how to write. Here are some examples of mini-lessons to do toward the end of Cycle 1.

Mini-Lessons on Deciding What to Write About

Early in this chapter, two powerful ways to help children decide what to write about were mentioned—thinking aloud about a few topics of interest to the children that you don't write about and creating a class list of "Things We All Know About." Here are a few other mini-lessons to keep students' "what to write about" ideas flowing.

Making a Personal List of What to Write About

Many of us are list makers. Making a list is simple because you only need to write words, not whole sentences. To do this mini-lesson, tell your students that lots of times you think of good things to write about but then forget them when it is actually time to write. Tell students that today, you are going to make a list of things you know about and want to write about. Let the children watch as you think aloud and make your list. Label your list "Mrs. _____'s Writing Topics" and then number each entry.

"For number one, I am going to put **food**. I love to eat, so this is always a good thing to write about."

Mrs. C's Writing Topics

1. food

"Food is a good topic, but there are particular kinds of foods I like, so I might add some of them to my list."

Mrs. C's Writing Topics

1. food
2. pizza
3. apple pie
4. apples
5. turkey

"**Turkey** makes me think of **Thanksgiving**. That is something else I can write about."

Continue to think aloud and add items to your list, often spinning ideas off one another. Here is what your list on the first day might look like:

Mrs. C's Writing Topics

1. food
2. pizza
3. apple pie
4. apples
5. turkey
6. Thanksgiving
7. Halloween
8. pumpkins
9. cats
10. Squeaky ("My cat")
11. Puddles ("The cat I had when I was your age")
12. soccer
13. Wake Forest basketball
14. football
15. hiking

When you have a good number of topics, tell the children that this list has plenty of ideas for right now.

"I will write about some of these things in the next few weeks, and I will add more ideas to my list as I think of them."

Tell the children that for their writing today, they might make a list of some topics they know a lot about and might want to write about. Let the children who make lists share what is on their lists. Get a few ideas from their lists to add to your own list and encourage children to "borrow" each other's ideas.

Over the next several weeks, model pulling out your list and writing about some of the topics. Check topics off as you write about them. You do not need to write about all of them. Sometimes we think we want to write about a topic, but then we get more interested in other things. If there are some items on your list you decide not to write about after all, cross them off. Encourage the children to do the same. The list should be a help to them on days when they need ideas for writing—not a list of chores to be completed!

Adding to the "Things We All Know About" List

If you began a "Things We All Know About" list early in the year, add to it when appropriate. If someone shares a story about a cousin, ask your children to raise their hands if they have cousins. Assuming almost everyone admits to having cousins, add this topic to the class list.

When you finish a unit of study or theme, add that topic and some of the subtopics to the list.

"We have just finished learning about the solar system. What topics can we add to the list now that everyone in our class knows a lot about the solar system?"

If your class takes a field trip or you have a visitor who talks about a topic the children are interested in, add those topics to your list. If your gerbil gives birth to baby gerbils, you will surely want to add **baby gerbils** to the list. Don't overwhelm your students with the number of topics on the class list but do be on the alert to add to it when there is genuine interest on the part of the children.

Involve the Family in Coming Up with Topics

Send a letter home to your children's families asking them to help come up with topics the children know a lot about. Explain that the topics should not be "family secrets" but could include family members, traditions, places visited, other places lived, favorite activities, etc. Limit the number of topics to five so that no one feels she has to complete an exhaustive list. Keep the letter to the families short, and write the first draft of the letter for your mini-lesson so that the children get to watch you composing it. If your children are beginning readers, have them read it with you a few times so that they can impress their families with their reading skills!

Dear Family,

This year, your child will be writing each day in school. I will be talking about the many things he or she could write about and will model how I choose a topic and write about it. We know children write best about the things they know and care about. Please help your child come up with a list of topics (not family secrets!) that he or she knows about: family members, traditions, favorite activities, places you have visited, things he or she likes to do, friends, etc. Thanks for helping!

Your Child's Teacher,

Ms. Cunningham

Child's Name_____

Please list five topics your child knows a lot about and might want to write about:

1.

2.

3.

4.

5.

Photos to Inspire Writing

Over a week's time, take photos of your children doing various activities in lots of different settings. Take pictures of your kids getting off their buses, on the playground, in the gym, and at lunch. Include some photos of children reading with partners, Making Words, and cheering for the Word Wall words. Take pictures of your children working with math manipulatives and doing science experiments. Refuse to divulge to your students the reasons for these photos. (Every classroom needs a certain amount of intrigue!)

When you have a good number of good pictures, including each of your children in at least one picture, attach these to a bulletin board and number them. Do a mini-lesson in which you describe one of the photos and let the children guess which numbered photo you are writing about. Warning—this may set off a surge of descriptive writing in which children write about various photos, share their writing, and ask the listeners to guess which photos they wrote about!

You can also bring in a photo from home—a family member, a friend, a new baby, or an event—and write about that photo.

This is a picture of my cousin Zannie Murphy. She lives far away in California. I get to see her every summer. She is in second grade now. Zannie is a good reader. I like it when Zannie comes to visit.

Thinking Aloud about How You Write Mini-Lessons

Continue to do some mini-lessons in which you think aloud about what you are doing. For younger children, you will be making very basic statements:

"I will use my finger to make sure I put a good space between the words to make it easy to read."

"I am at the end of that sentence, so I put my period here."

With older children, model more sophisticated things:

"My sentence is a question, so I am putting a question mark here."

"'When the cat jumped out, I was really surprised.' This sentence deserves an exclamation point."

"I am writing about the second spoke on my web, so I will start a new paragraph."

For children of any age, continue to model how to use the words in the room, how to use words that rhyme with other words they can spell, and how to stretch out words to spell.

"I can spell **favorite** because it is on the Word Wall."

"**Carnivorous** is on our big animal bulletin board."

"I want to write **string**. I can spell **thing**, and **string** sounds like **thing**, so I can use the rhyming pattern."

"**Curious** is a word I can spell now, but I would have had to sound it out when I was your age. I will put down the letters I hear and then circle it so that I can remember to check on that spelling if I decide to publish."

For children of all ages, think aloud as you decide what to write next.

"Let's see, I wrote that Penny was a collie and that she had two litters of puppies. What else should I tell about Penny?"

If you have a cluster, web, or Venn diagram to plan your writing, be explicit in how it helps you organize.

"I've written about how dogs and cats are alike. I should write a paragraph telling about the special things about dogs that are in the dogs part of the circle."

Thinking aloud lets children in on how to write. Continue throughout the year to occasionally do mini-lessons in which you let the children "listen in" to that little voice in your head that helps you make decisions while writing.

Mini-Lessons on Planning

Planning what you are going to write before you start and planning what you will write next while you are writing are essential skills for all writers. As soon as your students are willing to write on what they know and care about without asking you to spell words for them, they are ready to learn how to plan their writing. There are many different mini-lessons you can teach to help students learn how to plan or plan better. Here are some ideas to get you started.

Two-Minute Talk

Many teachers let children plan what they are going to write by giving them two minutes (one minute each) to turn to neighbors and talk about what they are going to write. Be sure to set a timer and limit each child to one minute because most children would much rather talk than write. Talking about what they will write helps students plan but must be kept to strict time limits so that everyone has time to actually write.

Clusters, Webs, and Venn Diagrams

Graphic organizers are excellent planning devices for writers, but they need to be kept simple so that the writing—not the making of the organizer—remains the main event. The easiest kind of organizer is a simple listing of ideas related to the topic. To do a mini-lesson on clustering, you might choose one of the topics from your personal list and then let the children watch as you brainstorm words related to that topic. Here is what the cluster for the topic "pizza" might look like:

Pizza

round pie

triangle-shaped pieces

tomato sauce

thin crust

pepperoni

mushrooms

melted cheese

hot, delicious

Writing the cluster—and thinking aloud about how you are making it—would be your mini-lesson for one day. On the next day, take your cluster out and review it before writing about pizza. Refer to your cluster as you are writing to make sure you don't forget any important ideas about pizza. Tell your children that they may want to make clusters of ideas before writing about some of their topics.

Webs are like clusters except that they extend to another level. Webs are more complex and have more organization to them. Many teachers use webs to help children organize ideas learned from informational reading. If your children are used to "webbing" ideas from their reading, it will not be hard to teach them to web their ideas before writing.

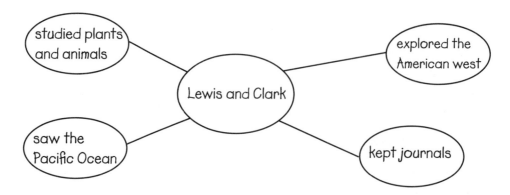

The other planning organizer you might use during Cycle 1 is a Venn diagram or what some like to call a "double bubble." Plan writing in which you compare two things by letting the students watch you create your "double bubble" one day, then write from it the next day.

Clusters, webs, and Venn diagrams are the simplest planning devices, so they can be used towards the end of Cycle 1 to help children begin planning their writing. Don't limit them, however, to Cycle 1 writing. As you continue to move through the cycles of writing and begin editing, revising, and publishing, continue to use these organizing devices and, depending on the age and sophistication of your children, introduce more complex or genre-specific graphic organizers.

Moving Beyond One Sentence and Adding On

Before moving to a Writer's Workshop that includes editing and publishing, it is important to include mini-lessons on writing more than one sentence and on adding on to a piece begun on a previous day. You have already shown the children some ways to move beyond one sentence if you have demonstrated some planning devices, such as clusters, webs, and Venn diagrams. Here are a few other ideas many teachers have used successfully:

Writing One Sentence and Saying, "I'm Done!"

This is something many children do, but they are shocked when you do it in your mini-lesson. Choose a topic. Write one sentence, put your marker down, look at your children, and announce, "I'm done."

My mom came to visit with me for the week.

The children are sure to have questions. Encourage and answer their questions. (Do not write the answers—answer them orally.)

"Where does your mom live?" ("Rhode Island.")

"Your mom is still alive?" ("Yes, she couldn't come to visit if she weren't!")

"How old is your mom?" ("Ninety-two.")

"How did she get here?" ("She flew into Charlotte, and I drove down to pick her up so that she wouldn't have to change planes.")

Let the children continue to ask questions, and answer them orally. Then, with surprise in your voice, say something like, "Goodness. I have lots to tell you about my mom's visit."

Return to your piece and write more, including as much of the information as is relevant. (You don't have to write that she is still alive, although it makes you wonder if they think you are too old to have a living mom!) Do this type of mini-lesson a few more times over the next several weeks until you feel that your children understand how to expand beyond their first sentences by thinking about questions people might ask about them.

On another day, give all of the children index cards and ask them to write only one sentence about a topic they know a lot about. Collect the cards and choose a sentence to write on the overhead or chart. Here is Billy's sentence:

I went to a birthday party.

Encourage the children to ask Billy questions and have Billy answer them. Give Billy back his card and comment that he certainly knows what his friends would like to know about the birthday party.

Choose another card and write the new sentence on the overhead or chart. Here is Chandra's sentence:

Our team won the soccer game.

Encourage the children to ask Chandra questions, and again, hand her card back and comment on how much everyone would like to know. Continue to write a few more children's sentences and let others ask questions until your mini-lesson time is up. If you think more practice is needed, write a few more of your children's sentences for a second day's mini-lesson.

On another day, follow this up by giving your children index cards and asking them to write one sentence. Have the children count off so that you have four or five children in each group. Ask each group to gather somewhere in the room, then have each child read his sentence and let the other children in his group ask questions.

Writing one sentence and saying "I'm done" is an amazingly simple—and also amazingly effective—device for helping all children learn to expand their writing beyond one sentence.

Who? What? When? Where? Why?

Another way to get children to expand their writing is to have other children ask these five W questions. Tell your class that these are questions reporters often try to answer as they write newspaper stories. You may want to read a short newspaper article or an article from a children's magazine, such as *Time for Children* or *Ranger Rick*, and have students determine if the five W questions were answered. Next, write the title of the piece you want to write about and have children ask you Who? What? When? Where? and Why? questions. Give oral answers to their questions, then use some of this information as you write your piece. Many teachers display a chart with these five W questions and also refer to it during reading comprehension lessons.

Use the same procedure described for the one sentence and "I'm done" lessons to get your students involved in asking each other the five W questions.

Adding On

One of the major concepts to get across to children during writing time is that you don't always finish the piece you are working on in one day. Each day as they begin their writing, remind students that they can begin new pieces or add on to the pieces they were working on the day before. When one group of teachers began the editing and publishing cycle, few children added on to their pieces and often had many unfinished pieces in spite of these reminders. Why this happened was a mystery, until one teacher remarked, "Maybe they just don't know how!"

"How could you not know how to add on?" was the response of most of the other teachers. "You just reread what you wrote and continue writing!"

"Aha," chimed in a clever teacher. "That's what my children don't know. They don't know that you have to reread in order to get back your train of thought."

Many among the group were skeptical, but since their reminding and telling efforts had failed, they decided to show the students how to add on and see what happened.

Doing an Adding On mini-lesson is simple. Begin writing your piece as you do every day and plan a fairly lengthy piece. When the time for the mini-lesson is up, stop writing and remark, "I didn't realize I had so much to say about _____ . I will continue this tomorrow."

The children may protest and ask you to continue, but "stick to your guns." Remind them that if you take too much time in the mini-lesson, it will cut into their writing time.

The following day, pull out your piece and reread it to "get back your train of thought." (You may want to have the children read it with you. There is no such thing as too much reading practice.) Once you have reread it, continue writing. Depending on what you are writing about, you may finish on the second day, or you may need to continue on the third day. Regardless of how many days it takes you to complete a piece, be sure to reread everything you have written first, to get back on track with what you have already said and what you still want to say.

After a few Adding On mini-lessons, remind your children that they, too, can add on to their pieces. Ask them what the first thing that must be done before you can add on is, and the children will respond that you have to read what you have already written. You may want to ask the children who want to add on to their pieces to raise their hands; then you can partner them so that they can do the rereading with students who are also adding on.

So, the answer to the question of why so few students continued writing on unfinished pieces appears, indeed, to be, "They did not know how!" Once the teachers started modeling the critical rereading step, their children could and did add on. (We won't tell you how many years it took for the teachers to realize this. Some things are so obvious, you just can't see them. The teachers did learn that whatever their students wouldn't do was apt to be some "obvious" thing they didn't know how to do. This has helped them learn to model other "obvious" things that weren't so obvious to their children.)

Writing Across the Curriculum

While some students may naturally choose to write about what they are learning in science, social studies, health, or reading/literature, it is not likely. While you want students to write about what they know and care about during writing time, it is certainly appropriate to ask them to write about what they have just done or learned in a science, social studies, health, or literature activity in your classroom. Just remember, during self-selected, single-draft writing across the curriculum:

- Children still choose what they will say about what they have just done or learned.
- Children still spell words phonetically.
- Children still only produce a first draft.
- Children still share some of their writing with other students.

Self-selected writing in subject areas increases the quantity and variety of self-selected writing that students do. It also encourages students to self-monitor and evaluate what they are learning in their content subjects and to think more about that new learning. As long as they choose what they will say about their content learning and how they will write about it, rather than attempt to answer specific questions or write to prompts, self-selected, single-draft writing across the curriculum will help your students improve in both learning to write and learning subject matter.

Sharing Early in the Year

Sharing writing is always important, but it is particularly important early in the year. Children get ideas from the writing shared by others, and they like to share about the things that are important in their lives. When the writing time is over, circle the children and let volunteers share what they wrote. (Some teachers have students stand in a circle as they share because they have been sitting while they write and are antsy.) If the students have drawn pictures, let them show the pictures and tell what they have written. Always respond positively to their writing and drawing. Many teachers let each child who shares call on another child to tell something she liked about what was shared. Make sure the comments are positive by requiring the responder to start the sentence with:

"What I liked about that was . . . ."

The child who responded can then share her piece if she chooses to.

The most important rule to keep in mind about sharing early in the year or in Cycle 1 is that children only share if they volunteer to do so. This is not usually a problem with younger children, all of whom often want to share. To keep to your time limits, you may need to write down the names of children who wanted to share today but didn't get to and make sure they get to share first tomorrow. With older children who have not had good experiences with writing, very few children may be willing to share for the first several days. If you only have two children who volunteer to share, let them share and call on one person who tells something he liked. Most teachers find that when no criticism is made of the writing and only positive responses are given by the teacher and other children, more and more older, resistant writers will be willing to share. In fact, you may quickly end up with too many children who want to share and have to start a list of those who get to share first the next day.

Sharing is a key element of writing instruction for those who are unwilling or reluctant to write. As children move up through the grades, it is obvious which ones have not done enough sharing of what they have written because they always write for the teacher. If you point out a gap in the content of what was written, the child may often respond with a puzzled look, "But you already know that!" Such students lack a well-developed sense of audience that permits them to write to real (or hypothetical) audiences who do not already know what they are trying to communicate. Because children really do not think like adults or understand the way adults think, most of them cannot acquire a well-developed sense of audience by writing for adults (their teachers). Only by learning to write for her peers will a student's sense of audience develop properly. Gradually changing children's sense of audience from the teacher to their peers is the main benefit of regular sharing.

Writing Cycle 1

1. Write a first draft.

2. Share some of your first drafts with classmates and teacher.

The Benefits of Starting All Children with Self-Selected, Single-Draft Writing

A writing program with the goal of all children succeeding can assume nothing at the beginning. It cannot assume that the children like to write, want to write, or are even willing to try to write. It cannot assume that the children can even write their own first names or that they can hold pencils properly. It cannot assume that children know sound-letter relationships. It cannot assume that the children know or care about the kinds of topics you would suggest or require them to write about. Yet, because good writing instruction is multilevel, a writing program that assumes nothing at the beginning still has much to contribute to children who do have these attitudes and lack these skills.

When you start your year with self-selected, single-draft writing in which your students learn to plan, write, and share first drafts, you get your writing program off to a successful start for all of your students. Students will never all write on the same level, but they can all develop the willingness to write and the understanding that writing is essentially putting "your story" down on paper. Once students have achieved these goals, it is time to move to what will look more familiar to most of you—a Writer's Workshop in which writers choose pieces to publish, edit with friends and with the "editor-in-chief" teacher, and publish those pieces. To learn how to help your students edit, conference, and publish, read on!

Tips to Get ALL Students Writing

and Keep Them Writing

- Model and think aloud as you write in your daily mini-lesson.
- Model and talk about correct writing but don't expect it from students.
- Model how to come up with topics that are important in your life but don't give students topics to write about.
- Help children "phonic or sound" spell and find words in the room but don't spell words for them.
- "Ooh" and "aah" about students' topics and clever ideas.
- Teach a variety of mini-lessons on "what to write about."
- Teach some mini-lessons on planning, expanding beyond one sentence, and adding on.
- Let volunteers share and allow only positive comments.

Building-Blocks Variations

Building Blocks is the program for kindergarten. It shares many similarities with Four-Blocks, but there are also important differences. Most of the writing kindergartners do should be first-draft writing that they share with others. Drawing and writing on unlined paper would continue for most, if not all, of the year in kindergarten.

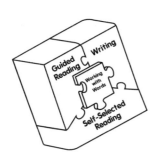

Big-Blocks Variations

Big Blocks is the program for upper grades. Many upper-grade teachers will find it strange to begin their school year with a "no assumptions, no standards" self-selected, single-draft approach, but the writing program for the rest of the year will benefit from it. Attitudes matter in all learning. Almost all upper-grades classrooms have some children who are unwilling and unable to write well. Beginning the year in a success-oriented way that focuses on what students write, not how they write, will allow all of your children to move forward in writing. Try it—we think you will like the results!

Chapter 4
Editing—Fixing It!

Most writers do not like to edit. Editing implies you "messed up" the first time. Why else would you have to go back and "fix it"? Many children think that it is only children who have to edit or fix errors in their writing. The first thing they need to understand is that all writing—even that of the most wonderful writers—needs editing. Of course, you can tell your children that all writers, the very best, edit their own writing and then have professional editors edit it again before it is published. Think how much more powerful this message will be if you can show them an example! Bring a real, "published" writer into your classroom and ask the writer to bring some "before and after" writing.

At this point, you may be thinking that you don't know any writers, but that is not likely to be true. Perhaps you don't know any "famous" writers, but what about people who write pieces for your local newspaper? Newspapers are usually very willing to support school literacy programs, counting on you to produce their next generation of readers. The newspaper publisher might even be willing to send one of their writers and one of their editors to talk to your class, especially if you gather the whole grade level together and make it an event. Wouldn't your children love to meet the person who writes the local sports column and the editor who "fixes it up?" Another possibility is to invite the editor of the high school newspaper. Do you have a local church or community group that publishes a weekly or monthly newsletter? All of those pieces were written—and edited—before they were published. Our guess is that all teachers know people who are "published authors" (or know people who know published authors). If you can arrange for a writer and/or an editor to "Show and Tell" with your children, you can forevermore banish the idea that editing is just what kids have to do because their writing "ain't good enough!"

However you accomplish this important goal, your children's attitudes toward editing will improve immensely if you can convince them that all—even the very best and most famous writers—edit their own writing and then have friends and professional editors do final edits before publishing.

When to Begin

In the previous chapter, you learned how each year should begin with self-selected, single-draft writing in which children learn how to write, share, and plan. When most of the children are writing fluently and willingly, if not well, it is time to teach them how to edit their writing. Depending on the age of the children and their previous experiences (both positive and negative) with writing, the focus on editing might begin a few weeks or a few months into the school year.

The Purpose of Editing

There are three reasons for teaching editing, when children are ready to learn it. The first reason to teach editing is that it is the only proven way to teach children writing rules they actually use when they write. A century of research on teaching writing has shown that grammar instruction outside of editing instruction is of little or no value to most students. Editing is not the opportunity to apply what students already know about writing conventions; it is the only effective way for them to learn those conventions in the first place.

The second reason for teaching editing is related to the first. We need to teach students to edit their own papers so that they will learn the essential skills of proofreading and self-correction. It is these two skills that will enable students to learn the writing rules you and their future teachers teach. Many students can quote writing rules or complete worksheets or language book activities on those rules, but they cannot proofread and correct their own papers for those rules. As far as writing is concerned, they don't know the rules. The first reason to teach editing was that most children learn writing conventions only by learning how to edit for them. However, children cannot learn writing conventions during editing unless they know how to edit! In other words, children should begin learning to edit their own papers soon after the first few writing rules are introduced to them, usually by the middle of first grade. If they are unable to edit their own papers for one or two of the simplest writing rules, they will not be able to use editing to learn the other writing rules you and their future teachers try to teach them.

The third reason to teach editing is to provide students with an incentive to write correctly during their first drafts without penalizing them when they are unable to do so. By having a separate editing step in the writing process, when children are only concerned with finding and fixing their mechanical errors, teachers help them be more successful than they can be when they are also trying to compose sentences and articulate their messages. However, a separate editing step also provides children with an incentive to do things right to start with if they can, since it is easier for a writer to do that while writing than to find and fix the errors later. Teaching editing to children makes it clear that mechanical correctness is important and holds them accountable for an appropriate degree of correctness in their final drafts, without causing the discouragement and change in focus that grading first drafts for correctness inevitably does.

How to Begin

When you begin to teach children to edit, focus first on whatever you think will make the biggest difference in the writing of most of your children. Here is an example from a classroom in which the teacher chose to begin the editing process with a focus on checking to see that all of the sentences made sense.

One Teacher's First Editing Lesson

As I was getting ready to write one morning, I told the children that since they were all real writers now (writing in their writing notebooks every day), they would need to learn how to help each other edit their pieces. We talked about editors and publishing books; how every book that I had read to them, or that they had read, was written by an author who had an editor's help to make the book as exciting and easy to read as possible. I told them a little about how books get published and the many different people who are involved. I then wrote on a sheet of chart paper:

Our Editor's Checklist

1. Do all of the sentences make sense?

I explained to the children that editors always read to make sure that all of the sentences in a story make sense. Sometimes, writers leave out words or forget to finish a sentence, and then the sentences don't make sense. "Each day, after I write my piece, you can be my editors and help me decide if all of my sentences make sense," I told them. I then wrote a piece and purposely left out a word. The children, who were, as always, reading along as I wrote and often anticipating my next word, noticed my mistake immediately. When I finished writing, I said, "Now, let's read my piece together and see if all of my sentences make sense." The children and I read one sentence at a time. When we got to the sentence where I had left a word out, we decided that the sentence didn't make sense because my mind had gotten ahead of my marker, and I had left out some words. I wrote the word in with a different colored marker and thanked the children for their good editing help. I then had a child come and draw a happy face on my paper because although my sentences didn't all make sense when I first wrote them, I checked for that and fixed them.

After I wrote my piece, the children all went off to do their own writing. As they wrote, I circulated around and encouraged them. I didn't tell them what to write, but I did engage them in conversations about what was happening in their worlds and reminded them of possible topics. I didn't spell words for them, but I did help them stretch out words and write down the sounds they heard.

When the 15 minutes of allotted writing time was up, I pointed to the Editor's Checklist we had just begun and said, "Be your own editor now. Read your paper and see if all of your sentences make sense. If you didn't finish a sentence or left a word out, take your red pen and fix it." I watched as the children did their best to see if their sentences made sense, and I noticed a few children writing with their red pens. After just a minute, I said, "Good. Now, use your red pen to draw yourself a little happy face to show that you checked your sentences for making sense."

Every day since then I leave a word out or don't finish a sentence when I write. The children delight in being my editors and helping me make all of my sentences make sense. Every day, when their writing time is up, I point to the checklist, and they read their own sentences for sense. They don't find every problem, but they all know what they are trying to do, and I have noticed almost everyone picking up a red pen and glancing up at the checklist as soon as I ring the bell to signal the end of writing time. I am about to add to our checklist a second thing to read for. I will add: Do all of the sentences have ending punctuation? (. ? !)

CAUTION: DEAD END!

"All of the sentences make sense" is a good writing rule to teach students early in their development as editors because young or struggling writers can understand it without knowing anything about grammar or the jargon of writing. However, be careful not to broaden this rule to mean that a sentence has to be nearly perfect mechanically to "make sense." Some children have had trouble with beginning editing instruction because this rule was taught to them as if to ask, "Are all of my sentences complete sentences?" and/or "Do all of my sentences start with capitals and have ending punctuation?" This broadening of the rule is really a misinterpretation of it. For example, all of the sentences in the following three pieces of writing make sense, but they are not all complete sentences, and they do not all have correct beginning capitals and ending punctuation:

• do you like hip hop I does a lot and so does my older brother and all his friends

• Marnie is beautiful. Gorgeous. Lovely. Sweet. My dream girl.

• Don't be mean. You know, nasty. Like a person with a bad rash.

CAUTION, it is a DEAD END to require children to learn to edit for too many rules or for rules that are too difficult at first.

Many teachers use a "thumbs up/thumbs down" approach when having children edit the teacher's writing and their own. The children read each sentence aloud and give the teacher a thumbs-up if it makes sense or a thumbs-down if it doesn't. When they signal a sentence that doesn't make sense, the teacher fixes it—and offers an explanation:

"I left the word _____ out."

"I lost my train of thought and forgot to finish this sentence."

"I wrote the word _____ , and I meant to write _____ ."

Older children particularly like the thumbs-up/thumbs-down procedure, and teachers often have them draw "one thumb up" on their papers after they have read to see that all of their sentences make sense. If capital letters at the beginning of sentences is what you choose to add as the next writing rule, the children will still read your piece aloud, a sentence at a time, and give you a thumbs-up if the sentence makes sense and a thumbs-up if it starts with a capital. Students read their own sentences in the same way at the end of each writing time. When there are two things to check each sentence for, teachers often refer to this as the "two thumbs-up" checklist. If you next add a check for ending punctuation, you will have moved to the "three thumbs-up" stage.

The biggest concern teachers voice about having children self-edit for items on the checklist is that "children don't find all of their errors." To which we respond, "Neither do real writers!" The four authors of this book (Pat, Jim, Sharon, and Dottie) each edited their own chapters as they wrote before sending them out to each other. Then, each writer sent them to the others, who found things that needed editing that the original writer had overlooked. When the book was finally finished and sent to Carson-Dellosa, our publisher, it was edited again by Joey. Believe it or not, he found more things that needed fixing! When you instruct children: "Be your own editor. Read your piece and give yourself a thumbs-up if your sentence makes sense and another one if it begins with a capital letter," you are not expecting them to find every sentence that doesn't make sense. Some sentences will sound perfectly sensible to them, but you will need to fix these sentences if they choose to publish the piece. As real writers, we all too often get back a book with some sentences marked as "doesn't make sense." "But of course it makes sense," we would like to respond, but we know that if it doesn't make sense to our editor, it won't make sense to our readers. So, we say it differently and hope it makes more sense the second time around.

CAUTION: DEAD END!

Sometimes teachers are tempted to think that the indicator of students' progress in writing is that their final or published drafts are free of mechanical errors. Beware! Such thinking can, and often does, lead down an enticing but wrong road—a road that ultimately goes nowhere. When a goal of writing instruction is to produce an error-free final draft, it can lead you to edit for children, rather than requiring students to edit their own papers while you check their editing and fix a few additional things for them. You or another adult doing all of the editing for students will certainly result in more correct final drafts, but it will also result in much less learning of writing rules by students. It is only when they learn to proofread and correct their own papers for a gradually increasing number of writing rules that students learn those rules. Having someone else edit their papers teaches them nothing except dependence on others. It is a DEAD END.

At this point, your children should quickly reread their sentences and fix anything they see wrong. Your goal is to help them understand what it means to "make sense" or "begin with a capital." Each day during your mini-lesson, as you make a making-sense mistake or forget a capital letter and they read your piece as your editors, your children have the opportunity to watch and participate in the editing process. You ask them to self-edit because you want them to get in the habit of checking for these things in their own writing. For many children, it will be a long time before they become good at this, but once you add something to the checklist, you are going to review it every day and remind them to look at their own writing for this every day. Eventually—if you persevere and don't expect immediate results—most of your children will learn how to write sentences that make sense most of the time, start with capital letters, and have ending punc. (**Punc** is short for punctuation. Once children understand what capital letters and punctuation are, it is just more fun for them to check for "caps" and "puncs" than capital letters and ending punctuation!)

Editing mini-lessons and checklists teach all of the mechanics and conventions of writing. The biggest difficulty with instruction on mechanics and conventions is that unless they are taught in the context of real writing, children never learn to apply them in their writing. How many times have most of us seen classes of children who can capitalize and punctuate sentences correctly on worksheets or tests (or daily oral language lesson!) but can't do it in their writing. The only reason for instruction in mechanics and conventions is for writing. We don't need capitals, punctuation, and indention to speak and be understood. If children do not apply the conventions and mechanics in their own writing, all instructional time and energy in teaching these will be wasted. In a Four-Blocks® classroom, all writing mechanics and conventions are taught in the mini-lessons and added to a checklist. Children are given lots of practice in reading and correcting the teacher's pieces for these writing mechanics and conventions to get them in the habit of reading and correcting their own pieces. Gradually, children learn to edit their writing for whatever the teacher has focused on. Finally, these conventions become automatic and appear in the first-draft writing of most children without the teacher requiring it. All that is necessary is both patience and perseverance. (Some of us think prayer also helps!)

Build Your Editor's Checklist Gradually

Walk into a classroom while children are writing and observe the mechanics and conventions they have control of as they write first drafts. Do most of the children demonstrate that they are automatic at beginning capitalization and ending punctuation by including it as they write for the first time? The items on the Editor's Checklist are not just there so that children will find them as they edit. The goal is that, by focusing on the checklist items as children check the teacher's writing at the end of mini-lessons and by asking children to do a quick self-edit of their own writing each day, students will begin to incorporate these conventions as they write their first drafts. The question of when to add another item to the checklist can be answered by observing the first-draft writing of the children. If most of the children, most of the time, apply the current checklist items as they write their first drafts, it is time to add another item to the checklist. If you add other items before most children can do the current items, many children will not become automatic at any writing mechanics.

The concept of automaticity is important to all learning, but it has a huge effect on how well children write. The brain can do many automatic things—but only ONE nonautomatic thing—at a time. Automatic means just what you would think it means—you do it without thinking. The way you become automatic at something is to do it over and over. The previous chapter stressed the need to begin each school year with self-selected, single draft writing. You want children to become automatic at putting down what they want to tell. You want them to use the Word Wall and other room supports for spelling and to automatically stretch out other words, putting down the sounds they hear. Whatever punctuation and other conventions they use as they write will be things they have become automatic at through previous writing. As teachers watch students write during the first weeks of school, they observe what children have become automatic at, and these observations inform them about what to add to the checklist. Most first graders have little automaticity with conventions, and teachers observe that they need to start with the most basic conventions, spending quite a lot of time on each so that it becomes automatic for most of their children. If children have done a lot of writing in previous grades and learned to apply conventions in their own writing, you can combine things on your checklist and just spend a few weeks on those conventions that most children are already automatic at. Developing your Editor's Checklist is easy if you let your observations of your children's first-draft writing determine what is added, the order in which it is added, and the speed with which items are added.

Questions to ask yourself as you observe children writing early in the year:

- Do most of the sentences make sense?
- Do most sentences begin with capital letters?
- Does each sentence begin with a capital letter?
- Is there ending punctuation at the end of most sentences?
- Is the ending punctuation appropriate to the sentence?
- Do children automatically circle or underline words they stretched out to spell?
- Do most sentences stay on topic?
- Do people and place names have capital letters?

For older children, if the above are mostly automatic:

- Are paragraphs "real paragraphs" and indented correctly?
- Is dialogue appropriately punctuated?
- Are commas used appropriately?
- Does most writing contain appropriate standard English grammar?

Teaching the Editor's Checklist Items

Once you have decided what items to add to the checklist and in what order, teaching the items is easy. This chapter began with a description of how one teacher began her Editor's Checklist and taught children to read her sentences and then their own sentences, thinking about whether or not each made sense. When most children understood what they were editing for and when most of their first-draft sentences made sense, she decided to add: "Do all of the sentences have ending punctuation? . ? !" Here is a description of the mini-lesson on the day this second item was added to the checklist:

"Today as I began my mini-lesson, I pointed to our Editor's Checklist and asked children to read #1 with me. After we had all read it, I told them that, since they were becoming so good at spotting sentences that didn't make sense, we were ready to add something else to our checklist. As the children watched, I added #2: 'Do all of the sentences have ending punc? . ? !' I reminded the children that **punc** was short for punctuation and we used it when editing.

"The children and I read this item together, and I reminded them that we had been noticing and talking about punctuation in the books we read. I also reminded them that most sentences just have periods, but asking sentences have question marks and exciting sentences have exclamation points. I asked the children to once again have 'eagle eyes' and be my editors but told them that today, they needed to watch both for sentences making sense and to see that I remembered to put ending punc. I then wrote a short piece:

> This summer my son is getting married. The wedding will be in California on July 31 I am so excited. I can hardly wait!

"I never read what I am writing aloud as I write it, but the children all try to read as I write. A few noticed immediately that I didn't put a period at the end of my second sentence. I just keep writing, however, and ignored their whispers and knowing looks.

"When I finished writing, I said, 'Now, help be my editors. We will read each sentence, and you will give me a thumbs-up if it makes sense and another thumbs-up if it has ending punc.'

"Together, the children and I read the first sentence aloud, and I got two thumbs-up. We read the second sentence, and the children gave me a thumbs-up for making sense, but a thumbs-down for ending punc. I quickly inserted the period, and we continued to read aloud the final two sentences for sense and ending punc.

"The mini-lesson ended and the children wrote for the allotted time. When the time was up, I pointed to the checklist and said to the children:

'Now, be your own editor. Read each sentence and give yourself a thumbs-up or thumbs-down for making sense and ending punctuation. Give yourself two smiley faces for checking for two things.'

"The children read each sentence, and some added words or punctuation. I watched but didn't help or correct.

"I don't expect all of the children to have learned this rule after just one mini-lesson. I have confidence, however, that after checking my writing every day for these two things, most of the children will learn to put ending punc at the end of most of their sentences as they write first drafts."

Our Editor's Checklist

1. Do all the sentences make sense?
2. Do all the sentences have ending punctuation? . ? !

Once you have two items on your checklist, alternate on different days making a #1 error and a #2 error. Don't make a lot of errors, or your writing will become so hard to read that the children won't be able to catch them. Your children should be intently watching you write, and they should spot the error immediately most of the time. They usually can't wait until it is time to give you a thumbs-down and help fix your error. Also, don't make things too complicated. At this early stage, don't put the wrong punctuation mark. Just leave one out and let the children realize that you left it out and decide what you should put. Do occasionally leave out a question mark or an exclamation point, so that children will learn that question marks and exciting sentences need exclamation points.

How long should you wait before adding a third item to the checklist? Only you can answer that question. When most of your children are putting some ending punctuation at the end of most of their sentences most of the time, you are ready to add #3. However, don't wait for perfection. Some children will think their sentence ends before it actually does and put the punc mark there. Sometimes, they will put a . when a ? is needed. What you are looking for is the understanding that sentences need ending punc and that your children are becoming automatic at putting them where they belong most of the time.

When you add #3, be sure that you continue on some days to make a #1 or #2 error. (Don't make too many errors and make your piece unreadable.) As the children write, ask them to read their sentences for all three things. That does not mean, however, that they read their sentences three times.

Imagine that the third item you add is:

3. Do all the sentences begin with capitals?

As the children read your piece one sentence at a time, you should ask:

"Make sense?" (Thumbs are all up.)

"Ending punctuation?" (Thumbs are down—add the appropriate punctuation.)

"Next word has a capital?" (Thumbs are up.)

Reading what you write each day for these three basic sentence conventions should not take more than a minute or so, as should reading their own daily writing for sense, ending punc, and beginning caps.

There are many lessons for teaching editing in the *Writing Mini-Lessons* series (Carson-Dellosa) for each grade level. Here is an example for a lesson that adds the last item to the Editor's Checklist:

The teacher says:
"You are becoming such good editors that I think it is time to add one more item to our checklist. Most of you do this already. When we write, we try to write all about the topic we have chosen. Sometimes, writers include things they are interested in but that have nothing to do with the topic. This is another thing editors always look for when they are editing a piece. They look to see that everything the writer writes is about the topic." The teacher adds #7 to the checklist and says, "Number seven on our checklist is staying on topic."

Editor's Checklist

1. Name and date
2. Sentences make sense
3. Beginning capital letters
4. Ending punctuation (. ? !)
5. Circle misspelled words
6. Capital letters for names and places
7. Stays on topic

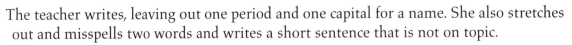

"Today, after I finish writing, you will edit my writing for all seven items on the list."

The teacher writes, leaving out one period and one capital for a name. She also stretches out and misspells two words and writes a short sentence that is not on topic.

Mrs. Cunningham   February 7

Abraham Lincoln

Abraham Lincoln lived long ago. He grew up in a log cabin. He liked to read and lern. (Stretches out and misspells **learn**.) He was a loyer (Stretches out and misspells **lawyer**, then forgets the period.) He was our sixteenth president. Do you remember all of the presidents? (This is the sentence that is not on topic.) Abraham lincoln (Lowercase letter for his last name.) freed the slaves. We remember him each year on Presidents' Day.

The teacher and the class edit the piece, adding the period and capital letter, circling **lern** and **loyer**, and crossing out the sentence about all of the presidents. (From *Writing Mini-Lessons for First Grade* by Hall, Cunningham, and Boger, Carson-Dellosa, 2002.)

Here is a series of lessons to teach children how to punctuate dialogue:

The teachers says:
"I've noticed that lots of you are beginning to have your characters talk to each other. These conversations, or dialogue, require lots of work. There are many things to know about the punctuation marks used to show that people are talking. We also have to work at making sure the dialogue sounds real. Today, we are going to focus on all of the punctuation marks needed to show that a conversation is happening.

"I think one easy way to learn about the marks is to look at an example of dialogue in a book. I chose one section from the book I've been reading to you (choose an excerpt that includes a good chunk of dialogue representing different kinds of punctuation). I decided to put it on the overhead so that we can all look at it together.

"I want us to highlight all of the punctuation we see that is associated with the conversation. Let's use blue for quotation marks, green for commas, pink for periods, and yellow for question marks. Help me make sure we don't miss anything."

The teacher works with his class to highlight or mark all of the punctuation. He is sure not to choose a section that is too large and makes sure that his transparency can be seen by the students.

"Now that we've highlighted the punctuation, let's see if we can work together to make a list of why each mark is used."

Quotation marks:	go at the beginning and end of what is said
Comma:	goes inside the quotation marks before a dialogue tag
	goes after a dialogue tag if the tag comes before the words being said
Question mark:	goes inside the quotation marks if the speaker is asking a question, even if the dialogue tag comes after the quote
Period:	goes inside the quotation marks if the quote is the end of the sentence
	comes after the dialogue tag if the tag is the end of the sentence

"This list will help us as we write dialogue. We will spend the next several days learning about how to use the punctuation correctly. As you're reading today, if you come across some conversation, see if you notice the things from our list."

Adding to the Writer's Checklist

10. I have punctuated quotations correctly.

Reviewing the List

Review the list above. Remind students of the different places you found all of the different punctuation. Glance back over the highlighted text as you talk about it. Now, model writing a conversation or a section of dialogue for the students. Try to incorporate several types of dialogue tags, creating the need for periods, commas, and question marks.

"I am going to write about a conversation I had with my husband on the phone. It was dialogue between two people, and I want to show you how I use the things we learned about punctuating dialogue to write this conversation."

"Hello, Amanda?" asked Jeff.

"Yes, it's me," I said.

"Where are you?" he asked.

"I'm on my cell phone, heading home from the airport."

Jeff asked, "Are you coming into town any time today?"

"Around noon," I answered. "Why?"

"Well, I left that contract on the books behind the couch. I was reading it last night, and I put it down there. But, I need it today," he explained.

"So, do you want me to bring it to the office?" I asked.

"That would be great," Jeff said.

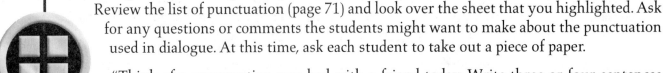

Revisiting and Reviewing Dialogue

Review the list of punctuation (page 71) and look over the sheet that you highlighted. Ask for any questions or comments the students might want to make about the punctuation used in dialogue. At this time, ask each student to take out a piece of paper.

"Think of a conversation you had with a friend today. Write three or four sentences from that conversation, including the appropriate punctuation. Think carefully; this is your chance to show me what you've learned the last couple of days."

Collect these writing samples to find out what instruction needs to be reviewed or continued. After they finish the writing samples, ask students to spend five minutes rereading pieces of writing in their writing folders that had dialogue in them. Have students change any punctuation they think needs changing. (From *Writing Mini-Lessons for Upper Grades* by Hall, Cunningham, and Arens, Carson-Dellosa, 2003.)

Editing is taught before revising because most children are ready to learn to edit before they are ready to learn to revise. Once you teach revising, however, always model revising first and then editing. Here is a lesson which includes both revising and editing:

The teacher reads and thinks aloud about revising the piece she has chosen to publish:

Mrs. Hall
March 8, 2003

My Cat Tommy

Once, I had a cat named Tommy. He was a big, gray Persian cat He was fat and furry. A hurricane was coming up the coast, and weather was rainy and windy. Tommy was lost. I could not find Tommy in the house. I could not see him when I looked out the window. We were afraid he might get hurt. My husband was on his way home from work. He saw Tommy stuck in the storm drain and reskood him. He dug him out of the debree, picked up the wet cat, and brought tommy home to us.

"Let's read my story together, and you help me think about revising it." The class likes the beginning of the story but thinks the sentence "Tommy was lost" needs to be moved after the sentences about not being able to find him. The teacher agrees and does this. The class thinks **soaked** would be a better word than **wet**, and the teacher agrees and changes this. The class wants a better ending and helps the teacher come up with: "We were so happy to have our cat again!"

The teacher chooses a child to be her partner and help edit her writing.
The child takes a red marker and edits the teacher's writing using the checklist.

"Number one: It has the name and date. I put the first check at the top."

"Number two: All the sentences make sense. A second check."

"Number three: Do all the sentences begin with a capital letter? Yes; another check."

"Number four: One of the sentences we added needs a period at the end." The editor adds this and then puts a check at the top.

"Number five: Are the misspelled words circled? Yes, the misspelled words **reskood** and **debree** are circled." The editor puts another check on top, and since this will be published, the teacher writes the correct spelling of **rescued** and **debris** above these words.

"Number six: The name **Tommy** in the last sentence needs a capital letter." The editor fixes this and then puts a check at the top.

"Number seven: The sentences all stay on topic, and a final check goes at the top." (From *Writing Mini-Lessons for Second Grade* by Hall, Cunningham, and Smith, Carson-Dellosa, 2002.)

Self-Editing

When children self-edit they look at their pieces and go over the items on the Editor's Checklist—but don't expect perfection. Just like adults, many students do not find their own mistakes.

Daniel

My Trip to the Orchard

One
~~Wone~~ day my family and I went to an apple orchard. We wint to pick fresh apples. First, I got a big basket. Next, I picked some ripe apples off the trees. I put them in the basket. After about an hour, I was
too
~~to~~ hungry to keep going. Thats when I bit into a juicy, red apple. The sweet, ripe apple tasted better than anything in the world!

Notice that the child did not find the wrong word in the second sentence. The idea is not that students edit perfectly but that they get in the habit of checking their writing and they begin to know what to check for.

Teaching Children to Peer Edit

Once children have had lots of experience editing the teacher's piece each day, they can learn how to edit with partners. Most teachers introduce this by choosing children to be their partners and role-playing how the partners will help with the editing. Here is an example of how you might introduce the concept of peer editing.

"Today, I choose partner editing as the focus of my mini-lesson." Tell the class that they will soon start choosing some of their best pieces to publish, and that once they have chosen, the first step in the publishing process will be to choose friends to help them edit it.

"Boys and girls, we are going to pretend today that I am one of the children in the class, and I am getting ready to publish a piece. I will choose one of you to be my editor."

Write a short piece on the overhead as the children watch. Instead of letting the whole class read the sentences aloud and do "thumbs-up or -down" as you have been doing, choose one child to be your editor. As the children watch, read the sentences with your editor one at a time and edit for the things currently on the checklist. As you and your editor read each sentence, decide if it makes sense, has ending punc, and has a beginning cap. Next, look at the words and decide if any of them need to be underlined because you think they are not spelled correctly. Here is what the edited piece looks like.

I saw a red bird in my yard this *morning* (mrning.)

I think it *was* (saw) a cardinal.

I *it* looked so pretty against the *blue* (bloo) sky.

For the next several days, follow the procedure of choosing a child to be your editor and doing partner editing in front of the children. When you think the children understand how to help each other edit for the items on the checklist, partner them, assigning partners of similar writing ability to work together. Have the children choose pieces to publish and help each other edit as you circulate. Make sure each pair of children understands that they are to read each sentence for the things on the checklist and jointly decide what needs fixing. Depending on how successfully they do this, you may want to have several more peer editing practice sessions before turning them loose to peer edit without your supervision.

Editor's Checklist

1. Name and date
2. Sentences make sense
3. Beginning capital letters
4. Ending punctuation (. ? !)
5. Capital letters for names and places
6. Stays on topic
7. Wise word choices
8. Commas
9. Quotation marks (when needed)

Editor's Checklist

- Do all my sentences make sense and stay on topic? 9/2
- Do they all have punctuation and capitals? 9/2
- Are words I need to check circled? 9/16
- Do people and place names have capitals? 10/2
- Is there a beginning, middle, and end? 10/9
- Do words in a series have commas? 11/9
- Mrs. Smith says, "Check your quotes!" 1/14

Introducing the Writing Process (Writing Cycle 2)

The writing process has students apply different writing skills at different steps, or phases, in producing their final drafts. Therefore, it enables them to achieve an adequate writing product with far less automaticity of skills than writing a first draft that is also an adequate final draft. However, process writing is more difficult for children than single-draft writing because it requires more motivation and the additional skills of remembering and rereading what was previously written.

The writing process is the cycle of steps a writer goes through again and again as he completes one final draft and then begin working toward producing another. Introduce the writing process to children after they have learned to edit their own papers for two or three basic writing rules. There are several different writing processes. The one typically used to introduce students to process writing is this one:

Writing Cycle 2

1. Write or choose a first draft.

2. Use the Editor's Checklist to edit your first draft alone or with a partner.

3. Confer with your teacher to have your corrections approved and to fix things not yet on the Checklist.

4. Publish your piece! (See Chapter 7.)

Editing—A Time to Fix Up Your Writing and Make It More Readable

The most important part of any piece of writing is its meaning. But, we write to communicate our ideas to others, and that communication will be hindered if the writing is hard to read. Mechanics and conventions exist to make writing easier to read. We don't need to put punc at the ends of sentences and caps at the beginnings in speech because the pause between spoken sentences signals the listener. We don't need to spell words correctly when we speak because spelling isn't needed in order to understand the meaning. When we write, we need to use correct mechanics, conventions, and spelling to make our writing easy to read. As children learn to edit for specific mechanics, those mechanics will gradually become automatic in their first-draft writing. As more and more mechanical and spelling skills become automatic, children can focus all of their attention on writing meaningful, entertaining, and informative pieces. Learning to edit is like learning good manners. People just like your writing better when you make it pleasant and easy for them!

Tips on Editing

- Convince your children that even the best writers edit their own writing and have editors do final edits. Show and Tell with a published author if possible.

- Don't begin editing instruction until children are writing willingly and fluently—if not well!

- Observe your children writing to decide which mechanics and conventions they are automatic at and which you need to focus on.

- Begin your checklist with one item. Let children edit your piece for this one item every day. Make no more than two mistakes in your writing.

- When the writing time for the children is up, ask them to be their own editors. Praise their efforts at self-editing but don't expect them to find everything. Be patient and persistent.

- Add a second item to the checklist when most of your children do the first item correctly most of the time.

- Continue to add items to the checklist gradually, using the same procedures to teach each item.

- Teach children to peer edit by role-playing, and then provide supervised practice as children peer edit with writers of similar ability.

- Continue to have children write, share, and plan.

- Introduce Writing Cycle 2 to students. Have them peer edit their chosen pieces for the checklist items and have this editing approved before publishing.

- Later, after they learn to revise, always have them revise BEFORE editing.

Building-Blocks Variations

Building Blocks is the program for kindergarten. It shares many similarities with Four-Blocks, but there are also important differences. Most of the writing kindergartners do should be first-draft writing that they share with others. Editing is not something most kindergarten classes would profit from.

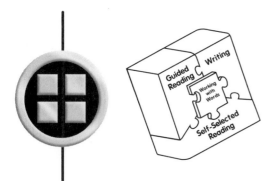

Big-Blocks Variations

Big Blocks is the program for upper grades. Editing is especially important for children in upper grades, and all of the suggestions in this chapter are appropriate for both Four-Blocks and Big-Blocks classrooms. Teachers of upper grades need to be sure not to assume that children can apply the basic mechanics in their writing. The only way to determine what to focus editing lessons on and what belongs on the Editor's Checklist is to observe children as they do first-draft writing early in the year.

If you see that most children write sentences that make sense and stay on the topic; capitalize first words, I, people names, and place names; and use appropriate punctuation, you can begin your checklist with these—devoting perhaps a week of review to each. If most children have sentences that make sense and stay on topic, you can combine these on your checklist. If their first-draft writing indicates that most children are automatic at these things most of the time, your beginning checklist might look like this:

Editor's Checklist:

1. Sentences make sense and stay on topic.

2. First word, I, people names, and place names have capitals.

3. Sentences end with appropriate punctuation.

If, on the other hand, any of these are not automatic with your children, you need to break those out into separate items, follow the procedures in this chapter to systematically teach them in your mini-lessons, and remind children to edit their own writing at the end of each writing period.

Once these writing basics are in place, here are some other items often taught and included on upper-grade checklists:

Uses commas appropriately.

Uses apostrophes appropriately.

Punctuates quotations appropriately.

Uses complete sentences—not choppy or run-on sentences.

Uses appropriate, standard written English.

Chapter 5
Revising—Making It EVEN better!

Do you like to revise your writing? Do you like helping your students revise their writing? While a few of you might be able to enthusiastically answer, "Yes!" to one or both of these questions, for many of us (the authors of this book included!), revising is the hardest part of writing. Yet, all published writers revise, and all high-quality writing has been revised. Students must learn to regard revising not as a chore, but as an essential part of writing that makes their good writing even better! Many teachers must also undergo an "attitude adjustment" about revising and begin to approach it enthusiastically. Remember, attitudes matter and are highly contagious. This chapter will convince you that revising is necessary, doable, and produces very satisfying results. You can then approach revising with your students with an attitude that will help many of them "catch" your enthusiasm for revising.

What Is Revising?

The most important understanding for you and your students to come to is that revising is not editing. Editing, you will recall from the previous chapter, is "fixing" your writing to make it more readable. Most editing would not have to be done if no one but the writer was going to read the piece. Imagine a world in which the only way written information was conveyed to people was through listening. An author would write her story, book, or newspaper article, and then that author would record it on audiotape. People would receive the information by listening, not reading, and there would be almost no need to edit! The listeners would not be bothered by wrong or missing punctuation, misspelled words, or the lack of paragraph indentation because this information is not needed to understand and enjoy while listening. Editing makes writing easy to process and understand for readers.

In this imaginary, no-reading, listening-only world, revising would still be necessary. When a writer revises, he makes the writing better—more clear, more interesting, more dramatic, more informative, more persuasive, more SOMETHING! Even if you were listening to a taped reading of what the author wrote, you would probably notice if revisions were needed. As you listen, you might find yourself thinking:

"I don't understand what the point is."

"I am having trouble following this."

"I wish she would give an example of that."

"This information is not very well organized."

"The ending was a real letdown."

The need for revision is just as obvious when listening as when reading because revision is all about the meaning and how clearly that meaning is conveyed.

How Do Writers Revise?

There are many things writers do as they revise, but the most essential thing—and the starting point for any revision—is captured by the word **revise** itself. The word **revise** is made up of the prefix **re**, meaning "again," and the Latin root **vis**, meaning "to see or look." When a writer revises, he looks again at the writing, asking the essential question:

"How can I make this piece of writing EVEN better?"

The word EVEN in this question is important because it implies that the writing is good as is but can be even better! Using the phrase "even better" is part of the attitude adjustment you and your students may need to make about revising, since many children think that having to revise means they didn't do a good job to begin with. All successful writers revise, and all published writing has been revised. Writers always begin revising by rereading their writing and thinking about how to make it EVEN better.

Sometimes writers revise on their own, by themselves. Everyone does some revising as he writes, such as when he thinks of a better word or realizes his beginning will not grab the attention of the reader, so he stops to rework the first few sentences or paragraph. Most writers reread their writing once it is finished and make some changes to make the piece better. Before publishing a piece, however, most writers need someone else to read the piece while asking the "How could it be even better?" question. Conferring with another person who has read what you have written often helps you see how to improve your piece of writing in ways you didn't think of as you reread it.

Once they decide what is needed to make the meaning or clarity of their drafts even better, writers make revisions by either adding, replacing, removing, or reordering. Sometimes they add, replace, or remove one or more words or phrases, or they reorder some words or phrases. Sometimes they add, replace, or remove one or more sentences or paragraphs, or they reorder some sentences or paragraphs. Occasionally, a writer will add, replace, or remove an entire section or reorder the sections that are already there.

CAUTION: DEAD END!

Even with older children, don't start revision too early in the year. You shouldn't ask students to revise until most of them have developed some self-confidence, intrinsic motivation, and independence in first-draft writing and then in editing. Once children are confident in their writing and have some fluency with the mechanics and editing of writing, they are willing to revise to make their GOOD writing EVEN better.

Teaching the Four General Revising Strategies (Cycle 3)

Every writing teacher has met resistance when asking students to revise their papers. The possible need for an "attitude adjustment" toward revision for you and your students has already been mentioned. It is also important to make sure students know what revising is and how to do it. The general admonitions to "make it better, clearer, and more interesting" are a source of frustration to all writers.

Teach children how to revise by using the general revising strategies of adding, replacing, removing, and reordering. Model this during Cycles 2 and 3 in your mini-lessons. This helps students to understand what revision is, how it is different from editing, and where to begin when trying to make the meaning of a selected piece of writing even better. Model revision when publishing in Cycles 2 and 3; focus your instruction on it in Cycle 4.

In the previous chapter, you learned how to help children edit with partners. Children also need to learn how to revise with partners. Partner editing is easier than partner revising, however, because there is an editing checklist and partners know just what they are looking for. They may not always find it, but they know what they are looking for. Because revision changes meaning rather than correcting errors of mechanics or conventions, it is much harder for students to know what they are looking for. You can help them, however, by teaching them the four general revising strategies. Just as with editing, model and demonstrate these strategies during mini-lessons and then support children doing the strategies with partners. And, just as with editing, teach revising strategies gradually. When students have been taught only one strategy, they should only be expected to use that one strategy. As you conference with children who are getting ready to publish, remind them of the revising strategies you've taught so far and give them help implementing some of these with their pieces.

Many children think revising and editing are the same thing. Unless students are given the opportunity to learn to edit their own papers before they are expected to also revise them, many of them will just edit during revision time. Many teachers have found that it works well to have students learn to edit their first drafts using an Editor's Checklist before they are taught how to revise. This means that they repeat Writing Cycle 2 several times before beginning to learn how to revise. Once students understand what editing is, have learned how to do it with a very basic Editor's Checklist, and have practiced cycling through the writing process with an editing step but not a revision step, then they will understand and can be persuaded when you tell them, "Now we are going to learn how to help the reader understand the meaning of what we are writing even better! After you have revised your first draft, you will edit it like we have been doing for several months." Students won't feel the need to edit during revision because they will know what editing is and that they will still have a chance to do it after they revise.

CAUTION: DEAD END!

There is no sense in editing a piece first if you are going to add, remove, reorder, or replace certain parts; you will need to edit it again after revising. Don't focus on editing during revision. Do have a separate editing step of the writing process following the revision step.

Teach your class the revision strategies you believe they are ready to learn but also make room for individualization. When the children conference with you about their first drafts, you may suggest and help an individual child make her piece even better by using a strategy not yet taught to the whole class. Once revising begins, it becomes the first thing partners do—before they edit. Helping children revise also becomes your first focus during writing conferences.

Teaching the Adding Revising Strategy

Adding is the easiest revising strategy for most children to learn, so it should be taught first. Children are often impressed with themselves when they write long pieces—and adding makes them even longer and more impressive! By starting with the adding revising strategy, you can capitalize on your students' affinity for length and start them off with a positive attitude toward revising.

If you have been writing on every other line on your transparency or chart and having your children write on every other line on their first drafts, adding just a word, phrase or sentence will be easy to do and see right on the original piece. Adding longer sections will require cutting and taping—something else children love to do, which also helps improve their attitude toward revising.

Revising by Adding Words or Phrases

Here is a mini-lesson in which children learn that adding words or phrases can make the meanings of their pieces clearer and more vivid. To do this mini-lesson, choose a piece you wrote recently. Tell the children that you want to revise this piece before you publish it, and one way to revise is to add a few words or phrases to make the meaning clearer. Using a brightly colored marker, show children how to put a caret (^) and then insert a word or phrase in the empty line above at different places to make what you have written better.

The Presidential Election

This year is an election year! On November 2, we don't have school, because it is voting day. Many people will come to Clemmons Elementary to fill out their ballots.
^ and other voting places
The presidential candidate for the Democratic Party is ^Kerry. The current presi-
John
dent, George W. Bush, is the candidate for the Republicans.
^
Party

Once you have revised the piece, have the children read it with you and help you explain how the added words and phrases make it better or clearer.

"We know that in the election people are voting at more places than just our school."

"Now we have the full names of both men running for president this year."

"We said that Kerry is running for the Democratic Party and should have said that Bush is running for the Republican Party, not just Republicans."

Over the next several days, demonstrate adding words or phrases to revise with a few more of your pieces or with a piece volunteered by a child. Whenever you use a child's piece, be sure it is a relatively good piece of writing and that you have the child's enthusiastic permission to use it. Make a transparency of the child's writing and use the same procedure. Monitor the child's reaction as you revise his paper, and finish quickly if you note any discomfort.

When you have done enough mini-lessons to be sure that most of your children understand revising by adding words or phrases, partner them so that children of relatively equal ability are working together. Ask each partner to choose a piece of his writing. Have partners suggest words or phrases to each other that will make their writing clearer or more vivid. Give students brightly colored pens to use and christen these as "our revising pens." Collect the pens when they are finished revising their papers and reserve the pens only for revising. The children will enjoy using these bright, special pens, and this, too, will have a positive effect on their attitude toward revising.

As the children revise, circulate and help the partners who seem to be having trouble adding words and phrases. As you move around the room monitoring and helping the partners, be on the lookout for particularly good additions. Instead of having an Author's Chair today in which specific children share, gather children together and share some of the best revisions you noticed.

My Grandpa is president of a club. They give used glasses to kids who can't see. He knows alot of people. He helps them. He takes the poor kids to see the Tarheels play football. He takes me places to do projeks. I love my Grandpa.

Revising by Adding Dialogue

Another way of making writing clearer and more vivid is to add dialogue. Again take one of your pieces and use it as the first example. (You might want to plan ahead and write a piece with no dialogue that would be improved by a few exact words so that you have a good example to use.) Tell the children that you want to revise this piece. Explain that after you wrote it, you realized that adding some dialogue—the words people or characters actually said—would make the writing "come alive." Use the same procedure that you used with adding words and phrases, except that you also should provide a brief explanation of how quotations are punctuated. Make sure that your emphasis, however, is on how adding dialogue can improve the meaning, not on how quotations are punctuated. How to punctuate quotations correctly is taught and practiced during the editing step of the writing process, not during the revision step.

Before:

Something wonderful happened to me the other day. I met the governor

of our state. He made a speech at our state teachers' meeting. After he

finished, some of us were able to talk to him personally for a little while. I

was the teacher from our district who was chosen to meet with him. I was

impressed with how interested he is in education in our state.

After:

Something wonderful happened to me the other day. I met the governor

He began by saying, "Both my parents were teachers."
of our state. He made a speech at our state teachers' meeting. ^After he

finished, some of us were able to talk with him personally for a little while.
When I introduced myself, he said, "I have been to
Winston-Salem many times. My wife's family lives there."
I was the teacher from our district who was chosen to meet with him. ^I

was very impressed with how interested he is in education in our state.

Do a few more mini-lessons in which you use your writing or the writing volunteered by one of your students to demonstrate how adding dialogue makes the writing come alive. Partner your children and have them help each other find places where adding dialogue will make their writing even better. "Spy" on the partners, helping those who seem to need it, and pick a few good examples of revisions to share with the whole class afterwards.

Before:

Mama was very mad at me because I let the dog out. We had to

hunt all over for him. We found him hiding under a bush in somebody's back

yard. Mama carried him home in her arms. I'm not grounded anymore.

After:

> She said, "Young lady your grounded til you grow up!"

Mama was very mad at me because I let the dog get out. We had to
> I kept calling, "Here Jakey. I got a treat for you."

hunt all over for him. We found him hiding under a bush in somebody's back

yard. Mama carried him home in her arms. I'm not grounded any more.

Before:

My best friend is Jerry. We have fun together. Every day after

school he comes to my house or I go to his. My dad has a tent

he's gonna let us use. It is kamoflog color.

After:

> I called him last night and said, "Hey, Jerry. Let's camp
> out in my yard Friday night." He said "Cool!"

My best friend is Jerry. We have fun together. Every day after

school he comes to my house or I go over to his. My dad has a

tent he's gonna let us use. It is kamoflog color.

> He said, "You and Jerry can
> use my big flash light to."

Revising by Adding a Missing Part

So far, you have taught children how to add words or phrases to make writing clearer or more vivid and how to add dialogue to make writing come alive. There is another important way writers often improve their writing by adding something to it. Sometimes, once the first draft is finished, the writer realizes (often with the help of another pair of eyes) that an important part is missing. Adding the missing part necessitates adding more than a sentence here or there. To add a missing part, teach children how to cut and tape. Here is an example of a cut-and-tape mini-lesson:

Begin this mini-lesson, like the other adding mini-lessons, with a previously-written first draft. For your first mini-lesson of this kind, make sure your first draft obviously lacks important information somewhere in the middle. For example, if your first draft is a narrative telling about a trip you took to a nearby zoo park, it could relate how you traveled to the zoo park and how you returned home, yet tell almost nothing about what you actually saw and did at the zoo park. When you ask the students to read your first draft on the overhead and make suggestions about how you could make it better, you want it to be highly likely that several of them will agree that you need to tell them more than you have. You also want them to agree that it needs to be added somewhere in the middle, rather than at the beginning or the ending of your first draft.

Once everyone has agreed that there is important information missing, have students help you decide exactly where to add the new part. Then, as they watch you, use a pair of scissors to cut your first draft into a beginning and an ending right at the place where the addition will go. Then, put a clean piece of acetate on the overhead and compose the addition while they watch you. Be sure to position the beginning of your first draft so that your addition will continue nicely from it. As soon as you have written the first sentence or two of your addition, you can lay the beginning of the first draft aside. Finish your addition, letting students help you decide when you have told them enough that is new. After completing the addition, use cellophane tape to tape the beginning of your first draft to the top of your addition and the ending of your first draft to the bottom of your addition. Your revised first draft will now probably be as long as two pieces of acetate taped together, so you will need to gradually move it up as the class reads your revised first draft. After they have read it, ask them if they think it is more complete and better now than it was before you revised. Hopefully, most of them will agree that it is.

After you have done one of these cut-and-tape mini-lessons, you will find that several of the students will want to do what you have done. Ask each student to look at her first draft and try to find one with a chunk of missing information at the beginning, in the middle, or at the end. If students need to add parts before their first drafts begin or after they end, they won't need to cut their first drafts, but they will need to tape their additions to them. On several subsequent days, do mini-lessons with pieces your students volunteer or with other pieces you write, in which you cut and tape or just tape to add a missing part. You will soon find that your students love to cut and tape and will be eager to find places in pieces they are going to publish that need more information so that they can work on them with scissors and/or tape.

At first, the beginnings, middles, or endings they add may not be wonderful, but your students can still meet the two goals of instruction in revising by adding a missing part. The first goal is that they start developing the sense that every piece of writing needs a distinct beginning, middle, and ending. Of course, all children have been told that they need these three parts when they write, but they will only begin to understand what this means and to take it seriously if they learn how to notice when one of these parts is missing from their own first drafts, and then work to add it.

The second goal is that they and you begin to talk about what a good beginning and a good ending each do. At first, you should keep this conversation at a very basic, common-sense level. When students learn to revise by replacing their beginnings or endings later on, this will be a better time to teach them a more sophisticated sense of how to begin and end a draft. In other words, it is enough at first to make sure they have distinct beginnings, middles, and endings, rather than be concerned with how good their beginnings and endings are!

At this point, you may want to begin a Revising Chart to post in your room to remind children of the revising strategies writers use. Here is an example of what it might look like at this stage.

Tips on Revising

- Look again at your writing. Pick a friend to look with you.
- Use special revising pens, scissors and tape, or just tape.
- Add: Words that make the writing more vivid or clearer

    Dialogue that makes the writing come alive

    A missing part

Adding details, dialogue, or a missing part are all examples of the general revision strategy of adding. It is usually the easiest way for children to revise, so it is taught first. Children are motivated to find places to add by the lure of special colored pens and scissors and tape. Once children know how to revise by adding, teach them the most important general revision strategy—replacing.

Teaching the Replacing Revising Strategy

Replacing is another revising strategy all writers use. While the adding strategy makes writing better by making it more elaborate and complete, the replacing strategy makes writing better by improving the quality of what is already there. As with adding, you can replace words or phrases, sentences, or whole chunks of text. When replacing a small amount of text, use the special revising pen to cross out the text you want to improve and write the new text clearly above it. When replacing large chunks in order to improve them, use the cut and tape procedure.

Revising by Replacing Words or Phrases

Writers are always seeking "just the right word"—the word that will communicate exactly what they mean. Looking again at their writing and asking themselves the "How can I make it EVEN better?" question often leads writers to replace common or overused words with more descriptive, more vivid words. Here is a mini-lesson designed to teach children how to revise by replacing words:

Write something for your students and use as many "boring, tired, and common" words as you can. Don't tell the children your intent ahead of time. Just write it as you normally write during a mini-lesson.

> Last summer, I went to Yellowstone National Park with my family. We had fun on our trip. We flew on a big plane to Salt Lake City and then to Bozeman, Montana. I was tired after the trip. The mountains we saw were big and had tall trees. We ate good pizza at a restaurant in Gardiner, Montana, on our way to Yellowstone. We saw some animals eating red berries as we drove along the road.

When you finish, have the class read it with you and ask them if they can think of any ways to make your writing even better. Since you have already taught several mini-lessons on revising by adding, they may suggest some words or phrases for you to add. It is all right to quickly add a few of the words suggested, but if no one also suggests replacing some of your "overused" words, you will need to suggest it yourself, in order to move your mini-lesson from the adding to the replacing strategy:

"I notice that I have some common words here that don't create very vivid pictures. **Good**, for example, doesn't even begin to describe how wonderful the pizza was. I think I will cross out **good** and replace it with **delicious**."

Continue replacing some of your boring, overused, or inexact words, eliciting suggestions from your students about which words need replacing and what you could replace them with. Be sure to convey your enthusiasm for "just the right word" when they have helped you find one. Young or struggling writers have to change from seeing words as occasions for making an error to opportunities for expressing themselves in a clear and enjoyable way.

> Last summer, I went to Yellowstone National Park with my family. We had fun on our
>   huge, silver airplane
> trip. We flew on a ~~big plane~~ to Salt Lake City and then to Bozeman, Montana. I was
> exhausted   lofty   giant, green pine
> ~~tired~~ after the trip. The mountains we saw were ~~big~~ and had ~~tall~~ trees. We ate ~~good~~
> a delicious pepperoni
> pizza at a restaurant in Gardiner, Montana, on our way to Yellowstone. We saw ~~some~~
> four small, furry black bears
> ~~animals~~ eating red berries as we drove along the road.
>   bright

You may also want to choose a paragraph from one of your students' favorite authors who uses lots of descriptive words and rewrite it by changing the descriptive words to boring, overused, or inexact words. Here is a paragraph rewritten in this way from *Lilly's Purple Plastic Purse* by Kevin Henkes (Greenwillow, 1996).

> Lilly's stomach **hurt**.
>
> She felt **sad**.
>
> Her **glasses** were gone.
>
> Her **quarters** were gone.
>
> Her **purse** was gone.
>
> Lilly **wanted** her purse all morning.

If you have older students, use a book more suited to them, like E. B. White's *Charlotte's Web* (HarperTrophy, 1974).

> The barn was **big and old**. It **smelled**. It had stalls on one floor and a sheepfold and pigpen below. The barn was filled with **lots of things**. Birds **came** here and children played **here**. Mr. Zuckerman owned it.

After writing this paragraph, explain to students that this may have been the way E. B. White first wrote the paragraph. He (the author) then might have looked back at it and decided he had used a lot of boring words. Let students find the boring words and think of replacements. Write these replacements above the boring words, and then compare the revised paragraph with the one from the actual book. Make sure students understand that you don't know for sure that the author had written a less vivid draft and then revised it by replacing words. Children often think that a wonderful writer just happens to be able to write well. They need to be reminded that all writers revise, and the best writers do the most revision. Finish the lesson by reading the actual paragraph from the book and comparing the boring version, the children's revisions, and the author's actual final words.

Just as with revising by adding, you probably will need to do several mini-lessons on replacing words or phrases, before asking your students to use this strategy on one of their pieces. Again, when they try to apply the strategy to their own writing, have them work with partners, as you move around helping individuals having trouble and looking for good examples of revision to share with everyone afterwards.

Revising by Replacing "Telling" with "Showing"

"Show, don't tell" is a basic guideline for good writing. Unfortunately, many children (and adults!) are not sure what this guideline means. To teach your students what it means, you have to practice what you preach and show them how to "show, don't tell," instead of taking the far easier road of telling them to "show, don't tell!"

To teach children to replace telling words with words and sentences that show, you can use many of the procedures already described in this chapter. Write pieces in which you purposely tell rather than show, and then revise these pieces in mini-lessons with the children's help. Use paragraphs from the children's favorite authors as examples and rewrite these in mini-lessons by replacing the showing words with telling words and sentences. After identifying the places where the children wish the writer had shown them rather than told them, read the original and compare the "telling" version with the "showing" version. After several mini-lessons, partner children and ask them to help each other find examples in their writing where they could make the writing come alive by replacing some of their telling words with showing words and sentences.

When my grandpa died, I ~~was sad.~~ *moped around for a week. Nothing was any fun. Nothing tasted good* One day, my mom asked me to take my grandpa's dog for a walk. He ~~was happy to see me.~~ *jumped and barked and wagged his tail when he saw me with his leash* We went for a long walk and ended up at the river. I threw sticks into the river, and he swam in after them. When I took him back home, Grandma ~~was happy.~~ *smiled, thanked me, and said, "Grandpa would be proud of you."* I took Champ for a walk every day, ~~and I felt~~ *After walking Champ,* *I was hungry and ate seconds of everything. Then I played my favorite computer game.* ~~better.~~ Walking Champ was fun and something I could do for Grandpa!

Revising by Replacing the Beginning

For most children, the first revision they do that replaces a chunk of text is when they make the beginning of a piece noticeably better. Why does the beginning of a first draft so often need replacing? Because a writer rarely knows what kind of beginning would be best until he has written the middle and the ending. Yes, planning your first draft before writing it makes it better, but good writing also involves discovery. No matter how well a writer plans a first draft, he never knows exactly what he will say or how he will solve the problems that inevitably arise until he actually does the writing. Often a writer doesn't discover his voice for a particular topic or story until halfway through the piece!

While some children lack a beginning to their first draft and have to revise by adding one, children who make sure they have distinct beginnings often still end up with poor beginnings or too much of a beginning! A poor beginning often gives away the middle and ending, so there is really no need to read the rest, or it doesn't relate very well to the middle and ending. A beginning is "too much" when it goes on and on previewing what is coming or building background beyond what is necessary for the readers.

The trick in helping children who are first learning how to replace their beginnings with better ones is to teach them what an excellent beginning is. It does little good to tell most students that they should have a better beginning; they need to know what a better beginning for a piece might be.

An excellent beginning tells readers what they need to know to understand the middle and ending. The single most important thing that a good beginning does is to build background knowledge for the readers so that they will understand the middle and ending. If the piece of writing is any kind of narrative, the beginning must tell when and where the narrative begins (the setting). The beginning must also describe or explain what the readers need to know about the time and place in order to understand the narrative. The only exception to the need for such description or explanation is if the setting is your classroom. It doesn't matter whether the narrative is nonfiction, fiction, or fantasy; the setting must be identified and the background built for it in the beginning.

The topic must also be identified in the beginning so that readers will know what it is. Then, background knowledge about the topic must be built so that readers can understand what the writer will say about the topic in the middle and ending of the piece.

An excellent beginning makes readers want to keep reading. There are two main ways that good writers grab readers' attention and keep them reading. One way is to begin with an interesting question that will be answered in the middle or ending of the piece. While a writer can begin his first draft with a question, he usually finds that he writes a better question for the beginning after he has finished the first draft. This is why teaching students to start their first drafts with questions is often not very effective. Whether or not a student has started her first draft with a question, she can usually improve the beginning of her first draft by starting with a good or better question that makes the reader want to keep reading and that the rest of the piece will answer satisfactorily.

Students also have to learn that if they start with a question, they usually must resist the temptation to answer or even begin to answer the question in the following sentence. Rather, now that they have the readers' attention, they need to build some background so that the rest of the piece will be clear and make sense to the readers.

Another way that good writers make readers want to keep reading is to start in the middle of things. "Jack woke up when he heard the explosion. 'Where am I? What's my name?' he wondered aloud" is a beginning that will make most readers want to keep reading. Unfortunately, teachers often tell students who begin in this way that they don't have a beginning! Like starting with a question, after a writer begins a piece in the middle of things, then he must step back and build the background knowledge necessary for readers to understand what will follow. "Jack didn't remember being in the greatest battle of World War II or how long he had lain facedown in this field" could be a second sentence that keeps the reader's attention but begins to tell the reader the setting and situation of the story.

Again, students can try to start the first draft of a narrative they are writing in the middle of things, but they will usually have a better beginning of this kind when they write it during revision. As previously mentioned, the best beginnings are based on the writer knowing what will be said in the middle and ending, and that only fully occurs during revision.

Revising by Replacing the Ending

Any writer can tell you that good endings are hard to write! Children often solve the problem by stopping when they can't think of anything else to say and writing "The End." Consequently, you already should have helped your students to revise by adding an ending that was missing from a first draft. It is easier to get most students to end a piece than it is to get them to end it well. That is why teaching your students to revise by replacing their endings will help almost all of them to write better and more interesting endings than they do now. Again, of course, you must not rely on telling children that they need better endings, but you must strive to teach them what makes an excellent ending.

An excellent ending answers the readers' questions or shows why they can't be answered. One of the best kinds of mini-lessons to help students replace their endings with better ones is to have them read a piece with the ending covered up, then decide as a group on the two or three most important questions they want the ending to answer. Once they have posed these questions for you to write down, have them read the ending to decide whether their questions are answered. If they asked a good question that is not answered, have them decide whether the ending made it clear why that question couldn't be answered. The discussion should end with suggestions for how the ending could be changed so that it does answer all of their most important questions or show why one or more of them can't be answered.

After several mini-lessons of this kind, students should be able to work with partners to read several of their first drafts and decide what questions readers would probably want the endings to answer. Then, they should each revise an ending that doesn't answer these questions by replacing it with one that does or with one that shows why these questions can't be answered.

An excellent ending should feel right to readers. While it may seem simple, one of the most valuable experiences for helping students write better endings is for them to engage in discussions about whether they like the ending to a particular piece of writing and why or why not. These discussions should begin only after several mini-lessons on making sure the ending answers the most important questions that remain in the reader's mind. Endings can answer these questions without the answers being "satisfying" to the reader. There are no rules for what makes an ending "feel right" to readers, and readers will never completely agree with each other, but good writers have a sense of what readers will enjoy. Certainly, your children want their classmates to like what they write. Discussions of whether they liked an ending, why or why not, and what would have made it one they liked more helps students develop this sense of what their audience wants and doesn't want.

An excellent ending can surprise the reader . . . but not too much. The third insight that you want to give students about what makes an excellent ending is that it often surprises the reader. The reason it is the last of the three is that it is an insight definitely prone to abuse. Armed with this idea, many children will leap to replace their ending with one that surprises but also raises more questions than it answers and does not satisfy. An ending can surprise the reader and is probably better if it does, but the surprise should not be so great that it leaves the reader saying, "What? Where did that come from? I don't get it." It is probably best to give examples of good surprise endings and bad surprise endings and talk with the children about what makes a good one.

CAUTION: DEAD END!

One of the temptations you and your students can fall prey to is using precious writing energy to achieve premature neatness. Unfortunately, writing always requires effort and labor. That is the main reason why students need to experience an extended period of single-draft writing in which they are not expected to expend extra effort and labor to revise, edit, or copy/type their writing, until they develop enough self-confidence, intrinsic motivation, and independence to do so willingly. So, you must always be careful to keep the effort and labor required for students to write to that which is really necessary, at least if you want all of your students to learn to write well and like doing it. The chief way to accomplish this goal during process writing is to eliminate all recopying. Students should only copy or type once; there is usually no reason for them to recopy or retype. Enforce it as a rule, "Copy or type only once during the writing process." Have students make small revisions in the space above each line of their writing, and have them make larger revisions by cutting and taping. Then, have students edit their revised drafts without allowing them to copy them over first. Once students know that they will only be allowed to copy their first drafts over after they have been revised and edited, they will be more willing to revise them. Allowing students to recopy pieces before they are revised, edited, and approved is a DEAD END that will leave students too tired to do the real work that revision and editing require.

Integrating Grammar and Mechanics Instruction with Revision Instruction

Revision can provide good opportunities for you to show students how grammar and mechanics can actually improve the meaning of what they write, but doing so too early can confuse students and hinder their learning how to revise. Once students have learned how to revise by adding and replacing and are comfortable doing so in the various ways discussed so far in this chapter, it is appropriate to do some mini-lessons in revision by adding and replacing that also teach grammar and mechanics.

Teaching Grammar through Revision by Adding

Grammar is usually taught in a perfunctory way without regard for how words can be used to improve the quality and clarity of writing. Many of the words added to writing are adverbs that make the meaning of adjectives, adverbs, and verbs clearer and more vivid. Notice the adverbs added in the following sentences and how they enhance the meaning:

> It was a ^{very} hot Saturday. We ate breakfast and did our morning chores ^{slowly}.
> ^{Suddenly,} Dad said, "I think this is a perfect day for our first beach trek of the season." We all ^{enthusiastically} agreed. Even Jeff, our golden retriever, barked and ^{eagerly} jumped up and down. We ^{quickly}
>
> gathered our beach things and piled into the van. An hour later, we were running in
> and out of the ocean. "This was a ^{perfectly} wonderful day," Mom said, as we packed up our
>
> things to head home.

Adverbs often answer the "How?" question. Help your students understand this by writing a paragraph, such as the beach one, without the adverbs, and then let students watch you add the adverbs. Once you have revised by adding these adverbs, explain that adverbs often help clarify **how** something was or **how** something happened, and ask your students "How?" questions:

"How hot was it?"

"How did they eat breakfast and do the morning chores?"

"How did Dad suggest a beach tip?"

"How did everyone agree?"

"How did Jeff jump?"

"How did everyone gather the beach things?"

"How wonderful was the day?"

Children are often taught that adverbs "modify" adjectives, verbs, and other adverbs—a definition they can easily repeat or write without any understanding at all. Writing mini-lessons such as this one actually demonstrate how adverbs work and can enhance the meaning of writing and reinforce the idea that using good adverbs helps writers become EVEN better writers.

This is just one example of how grammar instruction can be integrated with a revision mini-lesson on adding words or phrases. When grammar is taught as something you do during writing rather than some rule you repeat back, children understand and learn it better, and it actually has a positive influence on how they write.

Teaching Mechanics through Revision by Adding

Learning how to punctuate quotations is an editing skill, but if you teach it along with adding dialogue, children will learn how to use it in their own writing. The problem with all grammar and mechanics instruction is one of transfer. The only reason for knowing how to punctuate quotations is so that when you use them in your writing, they will be set off in a way that lets the reader instantly know that these are the words actually spoken. Some children avoid using dialogue in their writing because they are not sure how to punctuate it. Other children include dialogue without any special punctuation. When you teach children to revise by adding dialogue, you are teaching them how to make their writing come alive. Teaching children how to punctuate the dialogue they add lets you teach mechanics and editing in a meaningful way. After several mini-lessons and practice, most children will comfortably add dialogue and quotation punctuation to their writing.

Teaching Grammar through Revision by Replacing

Look at the example on page 88. Notice that the words replaced in this example included boring nouns, verbs, and adjectives. Just as you can teach adverbs in a way that is useful to children by tying it to the adding revision strategy, you can teach nouns, verbs, and adjectives by teaching replacing lessons in which you only look for one particular kind of boring word. Here is a mini-lesson on revising that helps children focus on verbs.

Write a piece for your mini-lesson in which you use "overused verbs," such as said, ran, and walked.

Playing with My Puppy

Today, I came home from school, and my puppy came to see me. He came up to me and licked my face. I put the leash on him, and we went outside. He walked. He saw some other dogs. We went back home. We played with his toys. We played fetch with his bone. I like to play with my puppy.

When you finish writing it, tell the children that you are going on a hunt for boring verbs and would like their help replacing those verbs with more powerful, more vivid ones. Read each sentence with the children and underline all of the verbs.

Playing with My Puppy

Today, I <u>came</u> home from school, and my puppy came to see me. He <u>came</u> up to me and <u>licked</u> my face. I <u>put</u> the leash on him, and we <u>went</u> outside. He walked. He <u>saw</u> some other dogs. We <u>went</u> back home. We <u>played</u> with his toys. We <u>played</u> fetch with his bone. I <u>like</u> to <u>play</u> with my puppy.

Read the paragraph again and have the children help you replace some of the verbs with more powerful verbs. Notice that all of the verbs can't be replaced and that some verbs are already powerful verbs.

Playing with My Puppy

Today, I came home from school, and my puppy ~~came~~ to see me. He ~~came~~ up to me
ran *jumped*
and licked my face. I ~~put~~ the leash on him, and we ~~went~~ outside. He ~~walked~~. He
placed *hurried* *jogged down the street*
~~saw~~ some other dogs. We ~~went~~ back home. We played with his toys. We played fetch
noticed and barked at *jogged*
with his bone. I ~~like to play~~ with my puppy.
enjoy playing

Do several more mini-lessons on replacing verbs. You may want to once again choose a passage from a popular author who uses wonderful verbs to use as an example. Instead of writing it first with boring verbs and having the children find and replace these verbs, you may want to reproduce the paragraph from the book on a transparency and have children locate all of the verbs and replace them with the boring verbs that might have been there in this wonderful author's first draft.

Remember, teach everything you want to teach about writing through mini-lessons, but children also need opportunities to apply what is taught to their own writing. After several boring-verb mini-lessons, partner your children so that children with similar writing abilities are together, and have them hunt in their own writing for boring verbs and replace them. Just as in the adding lessons, "spy" on the partners as they revise and be on the lookout for good examples to share with everyone when you gather together as a class at the end of the writing time.

The series of mini-lessons and partner work just described for boring verbs can also be used for boring nouns and adjectives. Here are the original and revised versions of a noun and adjective replacement lesson:

Boring Nouns

Playing with My Puppy

<u>Today</u>, I came <u>home</u> from the <u>store</u>, and my <u>puppy</u> came to see me. He came up to me and licked my <u>face</u>. I put a <u>rope</u> on him, and we went outside. We walked down the <u>street</u>. He saw some other <u>dogs</u>. We went back <u>home</u>. We played with his <u>toys</u>. We played fetch with his bone. I like to play with my <u>puppy</u>.

Replace the boring nouns:

Playing with My Puppy

Today, I came home from the ~~store~~, and my ~~puppy~~ came to see me. He came up to
(supermarket) (collie)
me and licked my ~~face~~. I put a ~~rope~~ on him, and we went outside. We walked down
(cheek) (leash)
the ~~street~~. He saw some other dogs. We went back home. We played with his ~~toys~~.
(boulevard) (fetch) (bone and ball)
~~We played fetch with his bone.~~ I like to play with my ~~puppy~~.
(collie)

Boring Adjectives or Too Few Adjectives

Playing with My Puppy

Today, I came home from the grocery store, and my puppy came to see me. He came up to me and licked my face. I put a leash on him, and we went outside. We walked down the street. He saw some other dogs. We went back home. We played with his ball and his bone. I like to play with my puppy.

Use better adjectives to replace the boring adjectives and add more adjectives:

Playing with My Puppy

Today, I came home from the (crowded) grocery store, and my (new, little, furry, brown) puppy came to see me. He came up to me and licked my (hot, sweating) face. I put a (bright, blue) leash on him, and we went outside. We walked down the (quiet, narrow) street. He saw some other dogs. We went back home. We played with his (bright, new) ball and his (big, white) bone. I like to play with my (precious new) puppy.

Just as for verbs, use examples from some of your children's favorite authors. For variety, you may sometimes want to rewrite the author's work, changing descriptive nouns or adjectives to boring nouns and adjectives. Then, have the children identify the boring words, change them to better ones, and compare that to the real author's text. For other lessons, duplicate the actual text from the published book, then have students identify the nouns or adjectives and imagine less descriptive nouns or adjectives that might have been in the first draft of the book. Realizing that some of their favorite authors probably replaced words to make their books even better fosters students' positive attitudes toward revising.

Teaching the Revising by Reordering Strategy
Revising by reordering is not a common revising strategy, and for that reason, it should not be taught until students can revise by adding and revise by replacing. Moreover, children cannot learn to revise by reordering until they have a firm sense of sequence and logical order, a sense that probably not all of your children will develop until third grade.

Teaching the Revising by Removing Strategy
Just as children like to add because it makes their pieces longer, they don't like to remove things because they worked hard to write them and it shortens their pieces if they take things out. Students are usually more willing to replace something than to just remove it. This is the reason why removing is the last of the four general revising strategies taught.

Often, however, when you finish writing something, you realize that something you included does not really add anything to your writing or distracts the reader from the points you are trying to make. No one likes to delete the wonderful words she's written, but deleting or removing off-topic or distracting sentences or paragraphs is an essential revising strategy. Teach it like you teach the other general revision strategies, with mini-lessons and guided practice with partners.

CAUTION: DEAD END!

Four-Blocks Zone

Don't have students revise every first draft. That is a DEAD END that will seriously erode students' willingness and enthusiasm to revise. Knowing they are going to have to revise them dampens struggling writers' enthusiasm for writing first drafts. Students are much more willing to write and then engage in revision and take it seriously if they do not have to revise every first draft. Teachers who have students write at least three first drafts for every one they revise end up with students who are more willing to revise, and that revision does not dampen the interest in writing first drafts. Moreover, if each student gets to choose which of three or more first drafts she will take through the writing process, she will be more motivated to work hard on it than if the teacher were to choose it for her.

Teaching Students to Revise While Writing

So far in this chapter, revising has been presented as something writers do when they look back at their writing. Writers do revise after finishing first drafts, but they also revise as they write. Older children need to watch you revising as you write—particularly adding or replacing words or phrases. The need to remove or reorder and the need for a better beginning or ending are usually not apparent until a piece is finished. You learned in Chapter 2 to do a lot of "thinking aloud" as you write during mini-lessons.

"I know how to spell this word now, but this is how I probably would have spelled it when I was your age," spoken as the teacher stretches out and writes **resteraunt**.

"I am at the end of my sentence now, so I will put a period here."

"I have written about the different kinds of turtles, and now I want to tell about the body parts of all turtles. So, I will indent and start a new paragraph."

You may also think aloud about small revisions you make as you write.

"I shouldn't say **dog**. I wasn't walking just any dog. I was walking a poodle. I will cross out **dog** and write **poodle**."

"**Big** is one of those boring, overused words, and the dog we encountered on our walk was huge. I will cross out **big** and write **huge** instead."

"I was frightened when the huge dog came toward us. In fact, I was really frightened. I will put a caret (^) and add the word **really** so that the reader will know I was not just a little frightened."

"Part of the reason I was so frightened is that we were walking on a very lonely street. I will add the words **very lonely** just before **street**."

Doing some simple revising as you write and thinking aloud to explain the reasons for your revisions will teach your students that they don't need to wait until they are finished writing to think about how to make their writing even better.

At the end of the writing time on some days, ask children if anyone did any revising while he was writing, and have children volunteer what they revised and why. Before too long, you will see most of your children making small, but important, revisions as they write their first drafts.

Depending on the age and writing sophistication of your students, you may want to teach only some of the revising strategies—probably the easier ones of adding and replacing. Regardless of what you decide is appropriate to teach, you should post a chart to remind students what they know about revising.

Tips on Revising

- Look again at your writing. Pick a friend to look with you.

- Use special revising pens or scissors and tape.

- Add: Words that make the writing more vivid or clearer

             Dialogue that makes the writing come alive

             Missing information

- Replace: Boring Words

             Telling with showing

             Beginnings that don't grab the readers' attention

             Endings that don't answer the readers' questions

- Remove: Sentences or paragraphs that don't stay on topic or that distract the reader

- Reorder: Sentences or paragraphs that are not in the right sequence

- Revise while you are writing.

Revision—A Time to Focus on the Meaning of the Piece

Everyone knows that the most important part of any piece of writing is its meaning. Having a separate revision stage of the writing process is extremely helpful to developing writers for two reasons. It helps them learn to write better because it gives them an extended time to reread and rethink what they have written while focusing on the meanings, rather than on mechanics and conventions. It also helps them because it allows them to think about how the sentences and parts of their pieces all fit together and support each other, rather than how one sentence follows from the previous one.

Writing Cycle 3

1. Write or choose a first draft.

2. Get a suggestion from your teacher or a partner of something to revise.

3. Revise your first draft.

4. Confer with your teacher to have your revision approved.

5. Use the Editor's Checklist to edit your revised draft alone or with a partner.

6. Confer with your teacher to have your corrections approved and to fix things not yet on the checklist.

7. Publish your piece!

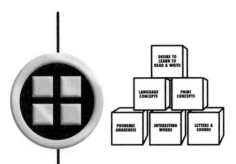

Building-Blocks Variations

Building Blocks is the program for kindergarten. It shares many similarities with Four Blocks, but there are also important differences. Most of the writing kindergartners should be doing is first-draft writing that they share with others. Revising is NOT something most kindergarten classes would profit from.

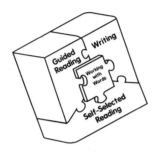

Big-Blocks Variations

Big Blocks is the program for upper grades. Revising is especially important for children in upper grades, and all the suggestions in this chapter are appropriate for both Four-Blocks® and Big-Blocks classrooms.

Chapter 6
Conferencing—
Whatcha Got for Me?

You do not prepare for writing conferences like you prepare for a writing mini-lesson. For experienced Four-Blocks® teachers, these words are not terrifying because they know that the "preparation" for conferences has its roots in both the mini-lessons presented and previous conferences held with students, rather than being a separate lesson. Drawing on both mini-lessons and previous conferences allows the teacher to respond to the current piece of writing much more easily than if either or both were missing from the Writing Block.

The Kinds of Writing Conferences

All kinds of talk about writing goes on in classrooms in which students write daily. Children talk with one another, and the teacher talks with children. Some of these "conferences" are more readily identified as conferences than others. The kind of conference, and who is involved, is sometimes a "teacher decision" and sometimes not. The duration of the conference and the topic are not always predetermined, since students confer with one another, too. Those student-led conferences aside, there are two major types of teacher-led conferences: over-the-shoulder and scheduled.

Over-the-Shoulder Conferences

Over-the-shoulder conferences occur in the initial weeks of the school year before scheduled conferences begin. They also occur throughout the school year in the few minutes the teacher wanders the classroom prior to beginning scheduled conferences. Even once scheduled conferences have begun, some teachers like to spend an occasional writing period on over-the-shoulder conferences instead of having scheduled conferences that day. The teacher may set aside every 10th day, for example, and do quick, over-the-shoulder conferences.

An over-the-shoulder conference lasts no more than one minute per student (and some are shorter), the teacher never sits down, and its purpose is to respond to the work in progress. The teacher stops at each student's desk, leans over, and checks in with the student.

The following three vignettes demonstrate some typical over-the-shoulder conferences:

T: How's it goin'? (to a student whose head is down on the desk, his pencil loosely drawing rings on a piece of paper)

S: I don't know what to write about. (still drawing circles)

T: Where's your "What I Can Write about When I Don't Know What to Write" list?

S: I already looked at it. There's nothing good there.

T: Try this. I'm setting the timer for three minutes. Take a piece of paper for notes and go around the room and look at what others are writing. See if you can get some ideas there. Don't bother them, just read over their shoulders. I'll be back when the timer goes off.

The teacher does three more over-the-shoulder conferences while the timer is ticking and returns to the first student after the timer goes off.

T: What topics are people writing about?

S: Jana's writing about worms, like she always does. Maria is telling about her birthday party. Felipe is writing about when his dog got lost. Then, I started thinking about when we lost my little brother at Target®. That's what I am going to write about.

T: Good for you! Isn't it great how many ideas there are for writing and how you can find ideas from your friends? I'll check with you later to see how it's going.

Would allowing students to wander the room looking for ideas work if they didn't have preparation for doing that? Not likely. This teacher had already done a few mini-lessons on where to get ideas and modeled several strategies, including reading the titles and first few sentences of others' writing to look for ideas. After those mini-lessons, this teacher felt confident in allowing the student to use this particular strategy.

Another typical over-the-shoulder conference is shown here:

T: How's it goin'?

S: Great, except how do you spell **which**, you know, not the person **witch**, the one like **which one**?

T: You know I don't spell words for you when you are writing a first draft. But, if I were you, I would look at the Word Wall, and that might solve your problem!

S: Okay.

A third typical over-the-shoulder conference is:

T: Whatcha doin'?

S: Arrgh! I can't figure out what to do next! Read this. It's not right, but I don't know how to fix it.

The teacher reads aloud the part the student is struggling with.

T: I'm not sure if this is what your problem is, but I wondered right here (pointing to a sentence) how he knew that Carmen had done what she did. He accuses her of being guilty, but she denies it, and he has no proof to show her. How did he know she took the cookies?

S: He probably saw crumbs on her skirt. She had on corduroy or something that stuff sticks to. And, he saw her leaving the kitchen right before the mom yelled about the cookies being gone.

T: What a great way to solve your problem! I knew you could do it!

Over-the-shoulder conferences allow the teacher 1) to monitor student progress toward writing more often than just through scheduled conferences, 2) to identify possible topics for mini-lessons by seeing what students are struggling with, 3) to remind students to use previously introduced mini-lesson concepts, 4) to introduce new information that has not been shared with the class when a student is ready to learn it, and 5) most importantly, to "ooh" and "aah" about what students are writing! Over-the-shoulder conferences are a powerful part of the writing teacher's arsenal.

CAUTION: DEAD END!

Don't sit down for an over-the-shoulder conference. Sitting down signals to the student (and to you!) that the conference will last more than a minute. If a student is in need of a more extensive conference, note the student's name and schedule a one-to-one, five-minute conference for the next day or arrange a peer conference that day.

Always begin the year with over-the-shoulder conferences. Scheduled conferences begin after students have accumulated a number of pieces in their working portfolios and are writing willingly enough to be left on their own to write while you conference with individuals.

A scheduled conference is the most obvious kind of conference and the one that the most has been written about. It is the conference in which teacher and student meet, one-on-one, for three to five minutes, to discuss the ideas in a particular piece of writing or to discuss getting the writing in final shape for publishing. Here's one kind of conference:

T: Whatcha got for me?

S: I'm writing about Cinderella. You know, one of those kind you're reading us where they change some of the stuff, but it's really the same story. In my story, Cindy lives in the city, and her dad is the super for the building they live in. Her stepmother makes her clean up all of the trash that the renters in the building throw into the basement. The president's son is having a big party and wants all of the girls to come, but Cindy isn't allowed to. This bag lady, who is like her fairy godmother, makes her a dress out of duct tape and trash bags so that she can go. My

sister said that she read in the paper that somebody at the prom made a dress like that, so that's where I got that idea.

T: Sounds as if you do have this story in good shape. What is left at the dance for the president's son to find? How will he find Cindy again?

S: That's the part I don't know too well. See, on my plan I wrote that she would leave a glass shoe, but it didn't sound right when I wrote it in the story. See, read this.

T: (after reading the section) Hmm. I see what you mean. You know what I wondered? I wondered how Cindy could have a glass slipper. I mean, it's not like the bag lady is a real fairy, or is she? If she is, you have to let your reader know that earlier so that she can do magical stuff and people won't be surprised. If she isn't a fairy, you have to make everything seem real, as if it could happen. Like the dress out of trash bags and duct tape—you know that can be done. The bag lady didn't need to make a dress appear by magic. So which one is it? Fairy or not fairy? Once you know that, I think you can choose the right kind of shoe for Cindy.

S: If the bag lady isn't a fairy, I could have her find a pair of shoes in the trash bags she has. 'Cause, you know, bag ladies have lots of stuff to pick from.

T: Yes, you could do that, but think this through. If something is in the trash, it belonged to someone else. Wouldn't the son have more than one person who could wear the shoe? How would he know it was Cindy who came to the dance if the shoe fits two girls?

S: So I have to have the bag lady make her shoes. Ohh! Ohh! I know! Out of duct tape and trash bags! Yeah! The bag lady makes the shoes, too, and she puts heels made from chunks of wood on the shoes. That would work, wouldn't it?

Tip

Carry 4" x 6" (10 cm x 15 cm) index cards, one per student, attached with a metal ring, as you conduct any writing conference. Make notes about each student's writing on a dated line. Use only one line per conference—use key words (not sentences) and write small if you need to!

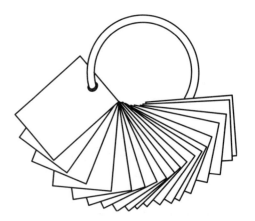

One-to-one conferences also allow the teacher to help students get pieces ready for publication. The kind of editing and the kind of publishing will vary by grade level and even within the grade level throughout the year. Here is an example of a teacher working on a piece with a student:

T: Whatcha got for me?

S: I'm done with my ants article! I just need to fix the spelling and stuff. Then, we can put it into the class newspaper.

T: You already revised it? Who helped you revise?

S: Ming did. Well, and you did, last week when we had a conference. But, Ming and I met on Monday, so that gave me two days to fix the ideas.

T: So, you are ready to edit it? What have you already done?

S: I checked the Word Wall to see if any words were there. Then, I went into my spelling dictionary for more. And, I checked to see if I have periods and stuff. You know, I used our checklist. (pulling it out from the pocket in the writing folder)

T: So, this is the final edit you want me to do?

S: Yeah.

T: Okay. Let me read it over one more time for ideas. (teacher reads)

Good job! I didn't know ants could live underwater. Now, let me do a few edits we haven't put on the checklist yet. (She reads the piece aloud, fixes a few spellings and does a few editing things the piece needs before it is published. She does this quickly, talking aloud about what she is changing but not going into a long explanation of things not yet taught.) Now, you can make your final copy on the special paper we use for the newspaper and do your illustrations in the space left. You're almost there! People are really going to learn a lot about ants!

Tip

Students can learn to prepare for scheduled writing conferences just as they do for Self-Selected Reading conferences. In a mini-lesson, teach students how to come prepared. They need to bring current work-in-progress, any checklists they are using to guide them, and questions they need help with. Post a schedule or sign-up sheet of students who will conference each day.

Conversations, Not Interrogations

When you design mini-lessons that systematically focus on the skills that particular class needs assistance with, when you review notes in the childrens' writing folders, and when pieces of writing are before you, what you need to talk about with students becomes clear. Starting each conference with an open, "Whatcha got for me today?" begins the conversation.

Conversations demonstrate to the student not only that the writing is valued by the teacher for the opportunity it provides for additional teaching, but that the value of the writing is even greater for celebrating the student as an emerging author. Teachers set the tone for conferences by the way they talk with students. Teachers can send a message that student writing is the important communication of ideas or that writing is an assignment to complete. Compare the following two snippets of conferences to see what tone is communicated.

T1: Okay. Let's get started. Did you try to use today's mini-lesson on making characters more interesting?

S: Uh. No. I was writing about worms.

T1: Oh, right! No characters there! (small chuckle) How many details did you include? Let's count them. One, two . . . hmm. Only two? Don't you know more about worms? I'm not sure you can write a paper that only has two details in it. Can't you find one more? How about this? I read once that worms have five heart arches. You could put that in.

S: Okay. Or this one . . .

T2: Whatcha got for me today?

S: I'm writing about worms. Did you know that if you cut off one end it grows back?

T2: You're kidding! Show me that part in your paper.

S: Here. "When you cut off a worm's back end, it can grow back. Then, the worm can crawl again and dig through the dirt."

T2: That is the kind of interesting fact the kids are gonna love learning. What else did you tell them? What can I help you with?

S: Well, I only found two facts in the book I read. Do you have any more books I can use?

Teacher 1 is controlling the student's writing so much that the student loses a sense of ownership. With loss of ownership, writing becomes much more difficult for the student to write and for others to enjoy reading. Teacher 2 begins the conference in a more open way, inviting the student to share what he did. When there is ownership, students are much more likely to request assistance because they already have confidence in what they are doing.

Or, compare the following snippets:

T1:   So, you're writing about worms again. Is there anything new this time?

S: I found out how worms move through dirt. They have really strong muscles, and they move those ring things, sort of like scrunching up. It's kinda hard to describe.

T1:   Yeah. (reading text) I see what you mean. This isn't very clear at all. And have you been checking your punctuation? Right here you need a period. And, a comma would make this part easier to read. Be sure to go through and fix those right now before you forget what I said.

T2:   Whatcha got for me today?

S: I'm writing more on my worm book.

T2:   Wow! You are our room's worm expert! I have learned so many things from you about worms. Read something to me.

S: "Do you know how to tell a worm's head from its tail? The head end of a worm is more pointy. That makes it easier to dig through the dirt, sort of like it's poking through. So now, when you pick up a worm, you'll know which end you're holding, and that's important because worms poop dirt."

T2:   Were you listening to yourself reading that? When you read this sentence (points to second sentence) and this one (points to last sentence), your voice was pretty excited-sounding. Do you remember a mini-lesson on that? What could you put there to show how you read it?

S: Oh! I know! Those whatchamacallits, the excited marks. Yeah! I could put those in here.

T2:   Right! Exclamation points will remind you how to read this to the class, and when they read your worm book, they will know how you want them to read those sentences. The exclamation points tell them to read it just like you read it.

The two teachers contrasted in the above snippets demonstrate two different perspectives on conferencing. The first teacher is a teller, dictating what to do, how to do it, and when to do it. There is no "joie de vivre" in the conference. The teacher is performing a perfunctory meeting with the student, presumably because someone told her to have conferences to improve student writing. There is no conversation; communication is one-way.

The second teacher is a coach, helping the student discover how to apply what he already knows but hasn't used. The teacher's reactions, comments, and questions demonstrate an interest in the student's topic, even though it sounds as if the kid could be fixating on worms! We've all had a student like this, but this second teacher finds the power in the student's topic. After all, people get doctorates in worms! Surely there is plenty for this second grader to discover about worms. The dialogue is two-way. The teacher and student are having a conversation about this piece of writing.

CAUTION: DEAD END!

It is so easy to fall into interrogations. Sharing writing requires a willingness to expose yourself and what is important to you to others. Whenever you do that you are taking a risk. Children's writing that doesn't take risks is dreary to read. Keep your initial comments open with questions like, "Whatcha got for me?" and "How's it going?" With openers like these, you communicate that you are more interested in the students' ideas. Letting your conferences become interrogations is a DEAD END!

The Three Purposes for Conferences

The conference part of the Writing Block serves many purposes, but three very important ones are to develop better writers, to develop a particular piece of writing, and to use the time for teaching/reteaching students beyond the mini-lessons presented to the class. Since conferences are no longer than five minutes, the teacher cannot do everything at the same time. Focusing on one aspect of one of the following purposes will give better results than trying to do all three purposes within the same conference.

Conferences Develop Better Writers

The more students understand about the writing process and its various components, the better able they are to implement the components. Now, that is not to say that understanding always translates to better writing immediately, but, as a basic learning principle, understanding generally precedes application. For example, many people would love to write novels that would win a National Book Award. They read these books and know why they were selected. Readers can identify the elements that make that particular novel an award winner, but a person may try to write an award-winning novel, only to end up with pablum issuing from the word processor. It is frustrating to know what good writing is and not be able to produce it!

However, elementary students are not to that point yet. They still need to learn what the elements of excellent writing are. This is one reason why reading to them at least once a day from quality literature is critical. It is also one reason why many mini-lessons are built around identifying the elements of excellence in quality literature. Before you can write it, you have to know what it is.

In a writing conference that focuses on developing better writers, the teacher addresses those elements with the purpose that understanding of the elements can translate into improved writing for not just the current piece, but for future pieces as well. You are striving for a metacognitive understanding of the element, not just a specific application. Here is an example:

T: Whatcha got for me today?

S: I've been writing about worms, and I have all of this neat stuff I've learned.

T: Yeah, I know. When we had our over-the-shoulder conference yesterday, I was pretty impressed with all of those facts. Let me see how it begins. Why do you think I want to read that part?

S: Umm. Because it has to be interesting in the beginning?

T: Does it? Why should it be interesting in the first sentence?

S: I don't know. I just know you said so in a mini-lesson.

T: Have you ever started to read something and wondered if you should keep reading it? Here, let me read two bits to you. (Teacher reads the first sentence from a book on bees and the first sentence from the class's science textbook.) Which sounded more interesting? The book on bees or the science book?

S: The book on bees.

T: Why? How was it different?

S: Well, it had a question, so you started wondering about bees right from the beginning.

T: Think about having an opening like that, one that causes people to wonder right from the beginning. Using questions is one way to do that. Another is to find the strangest fact and put it in the first sentence. That causes people to think, too. Is there a really great fact you could make into a question or put in the first sentence?

When a student understands the purpose of an opening that grabs the reader's attention, the student is more likely to be able to write great openings no matter what the piece of writing is about.

Conferences Help Develop a Piece of Writing

Over-the-shoulder conferences focus on developing a particular piece of writing, and some scheduled conferences do, as well. In order to develop their writing, students need to know genre and writing elements very well. When they know those two things, it is pretty easy for them to identify what is missing or needs further development. A writer sent off a children's mystery story manuscript and received a rejection notice from the publishing company that stated, "It wasn't very mysterious." Well, what makes a mystery mysterious? How do you build suspense? How do you leave clues for the reader that don't seem like clues until near the end? How do you throw suspicion onto other characters, rather than on the one who was actually guilty? You see, the more you know about mystery, the better able you are to find what is missing or needs development.

By the same token, a personal experience narrative that doesn't focus on a "small moment" (Calkins and Oxenhorn, 2003) can ramble and lose its impact. A question to ask a student is, "Why this small moment? What caused you to pick it from all of the other small moments that didn't affect you in some way?"

A personal experience narrative (PEN) shouldn't be a dreary accounting of events that constitute the majority of our waking moments. Rather, a PEN often led to some insight, affected the writer emotionally, or made a difference to the writer or to someone else. In other words, there is impact. Does the writer convey the emotional reaction through appropriate word choice or through an organizational structure that builds to the insight? Does the reader feel what the writer felt? What is the tone the writer wanted to create, and how did the writer's voice show that? One major problem with PENs is that we have allowed children, for too long, to tell only what they did, not how they felt about what happened. When you get a piece of writing like this:

I went to Target last night. I got a toy.

you need to ask a lot of questions to help the student develop the above PEN. "What toy did you get? Why did you want that one? How did you feel on your way to the store? How did you feel after you got the toy? How do you feel about the toy now? Why?" There was a reason the student picked that small moment. A good personal experience narrative helps others to understand why.

Another way to develop a better piece of writing is to focus on revision or editing during the conference. And, you have to pick which one and which part of the one you picked. Again, choose an aspect of revision or editing that has implications for future pieces of writing while still keeping the focus on this piece. When editing, expect the child to have self-edited or peer edited for the things on the Editor's Checklist. Do whatever other editing the piece needs to make it readable to everyone else. Tell the child what you are adding, changing, etc., but don't do a long, individual lesson on this. If you notice several children needing the same kind of editing help, and it is not yet on the checklist, plan some mini-lessons on that topic and add it to the checklist.

Revision and editing are clearly two very separate events. For those of you familiar with the Six Trait Analytic Scale, five traits are about revision; the only trait focused on editing is Conventions. That might help to clarify what you do in a conference. First, you make the body healthy, then you do the plastic surgery.

Revision work in a conference is about strengthening the foundation of the writing. After you have the ideas, organization, words, tone, and flow of the writing right, you can make it "pretty" by ensuring that the punctuation, spelling, handwriting, capitalization, and so on, are worthy of the piece and are appropriate to the grade level of the student.

It is easier to have editing conferences than revision conferences because print conventions are so obvious. Misspellings, inaccurate or missing punctuation, and inappropriate capitalization are much easier to spot and to fix than are writing elements, such as organization.

Always have brightly colored markers, scissors, tape, and extra paper available at scheduled conferences to show students how they can cut apart a piece of writing and move around sections to improve organization or how they can add additional details by creating space. The students love doing revisions this way. Of course, the more access students have to computers, the more easily they can make revisions and edits. Some teachers hold scheduled conferences with students in the computer lab, so the pieces of writing can be manipulated very easily. Having students sit in the same row allows the teacher to wheel back and forth on a chair to assist multiple students at the same time.

Conferences Extend Mini-Lessons into Specific Pieces of Writing

T: Whatcha got for me?

S: I've been working on this thing about trains. See, there are like a jillion kinds of train cars, and trains go all over the place. They go to all of the places for different reasons, like to leave cars, or take trees to be cut up, or take people to work.

T: So, you are having trouble with . . .?

S: Well, everything I just said, I told right here. Now what?

T: It sounds like you are looking for a better way to organize your writing. Do you remember a couple of weeks ago I did a mini-lesson on vegetables? I showed how I put vegetables into different groups. Once they were in the groups, then I told more about each group.

S: Yeah, but that was vegetables . . . and I still don't like spinach!

T: So you said! The point is that anything that can fit into groups can be done the same way I did the vegetables. So, what are your groups here in this part?

S: You mean like some trains move things and different trains move people?

T: Yes, and trains also move animals and produce to be made into food for the grocery store, and other trains move already-made food in cans or in refrigerator cars to take to grocery stores. Separate out the different kinds of train cars and make each one its own section. Once you have separated the sections, you can tell more about each one. You could have quite a long piece!

Mini-lessons are only an introduction, no matter how many times you repeat the lesson focus. If mini-lessons don't show up in student writing, why bother doing them? One way to ensure they show up is to look for connections you can make between mini-lessons and current pieces of writing. Conferences increase your instructional time by allowing you to connect mini-lessons to current writing and to extend mini-lessons for students ready to stretch, as shown in this conference example:

T: Whatcha got for me?

S: I wrote about my dog and all of my friends.

T: How are your friends connected to your dog?

S: Well, they all like her, mostly. Some are afraid of her.

T: I see here that you are telling what your dog is like, what her name is, what she eats, and what her toys are. Then, here you start talking about your friends. You don't have the part about some being afraid of her.

S: I just now remembered that.

T: Do you remember when I did the mini-lesson on coming up with story ideas? Where I said I get my ideas?

S: Uh-huh.

T: (Teacher whispers) I am going to give you secret information that I didn't tell the other kids in that lesson. I am giving you this secret information because you are ready for it, and this writing shows that. Are you ready?

S: (Student leaning toward the teacher and whispers.) Yeah.

T: (Teacher whispering, too) Sometimes, I find out I have too many stories in one story. When I do, I separate out the different stories, and then I can write two of them!

S: (Continuing to whisper) Do I have two stories in mine?

T: (Whispering back) At least two! You may even have three or four! Here is one. Tell all about your dog, what she's like, where you got her, what you do together—stuff like that. Then, you can tell a story about a friend who is afraid of her. What happened that time? How does your friend feel about your dog now and why? And then a third story could be about what you and your friends have done with your dog, like this part where you talk about going down to the frog pond with her and they are all yelling for her to go into the water.

S: Wow! I didn't know I could do more than one story about my dog.

There is never enough teaching time. Extend your mini-lessons into conferences where you can.

Short and to the Point

Think of fresh celery pieces—crisp, short, and appealing, leaving you wanting more after one bite. That is a metaphor for a good writing conference. The alternative, that bunch of celery left in the back of the refrigerator, limp and long, is very unappealing. The limp celery seems to be pointing somewhere, but you'll notice it is a curve rather than a straight line.

In a good scheduled writing conference, the teacher knows each student's writing well enough to know what the struggles and strengths are for that student. This teacher knows the writing process (plan, revise, and share) and writing essentials (organization, word choice, and voice) well enough to know where the student is bogging down. Teachers who hold good conferences also know the genres well enough to teach the elements in mini-lessons and to help students incorporate those elements into their writing.

Another feature of holding quick conferences is having students move in and out of the conference area quickly and smoothly. One teacher seats all students who are conferencing that day at a horseshoe table where they remain the entire time, working on writing while waiting for the teacher's attention. One other advantage to this arrangement is that the teacher can give support, move to another conference, and then come back to that student to follow up in five minutes.

Another way to speed up the transitions among conferees is to seat them at an adjacent table, and signal each one to get ready 30 seconds before you are finished with the student seated beside you. Many students listen in on other students' conferences, so they hear all sorts of information they can use in their own writing.

Keeping conferences short and to the point has many advantages, one of which is that students can pay attention for a short time to a small bit of information. When conferences last too long, students lose track of what the most important thing is.

Also, find out what students are doing right. Conferences that focus only on what is wrong with the writing leads the student to think that he can't write, even if he can. Celebrate an inclusion of a mini-lesson concept, "ooh" and "ahh" over a character description, and laugh when something is intentionally funny in a story. Be genuinely positive, and it will pay off in student risk-taking.

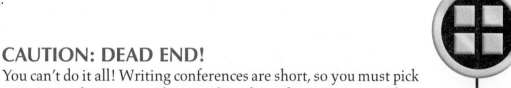

CAUTION: DEAD END!

You can't do it all! Writing conferences are short, so you must pick one or two facets to work on with each student. Any more than that is overwhelming for the student and takes longer than the time you can allot each student. Pick the one or two elements that will pay off most, either by making this particular genre stronger or by working on some aspect that crosses genres, like word choice. Remember, this isn't your only conference with a student. You will have a year of conferences to work on elements that need attention. And between over-the-shoulder and scheduled conferences, you will be meeting with each student dozens of times over the year.

Keep the Rest of the Class Writing

A question that always comes up is how to keep the rest of the class writing while you are conferencing with other students. One of the simplest responses is to make sure you don't begin scheduled conferences too soon! You will notice that while you are holding over-the-shoulder conferences and are out and about in the room, there is more focus on writing than when you are sitting across the room in a conference. This is the "police car syndrome" applied to the classroom. When you are driving around town and a police car pulls up behind you, you slow down, even if you were already going the speed limit! There is something about the presence of authority!

In your classroom, this same "propinquity factor" works to keep students writing (or seemingly writing and at least not bothering other students) as you move around the room, feet and eyes roving so that you can be in more than one place at a time. Before you remove the propinquity factor, make sure that students know what they are to be doing and that they are experiencing successful writing on a regular basis. Each student's working portfolio or writing folder ought to include several pieces, with at least three to five good pieces. "Good pieces" are those that are substantive and developed appropriately for the grade level and for that student's writing ability. When students have been able to produce three to five pieces with just mini-lessons and over-the-shoulder conferences, they should be able to sustain their writing while you meet with other students in scheduled conferences. Periodically, pick a day for no scheduled conferences and just do over-the-shoulder ones. This will provide additional support for those students needing a more frequent touchstone.

Never skip sharing the writing, even on a busy day. It is important that students have multiple audiences for their writing, both in oral sharing and in publishing on paper. Sharing helps students build an awareness of audience and realize that it is audiences we write for. When they understand that, and realize that they have things to say that others want to hear, the writing flows (most days).

An alternative way to share writing is to have multiple small groups sharing writing simultaneously. In this way, each student shares every day. This is a great way to build in accountability for each day's work, since students know they must talk with peers about what they accomplished. The teacher sets a timer so that each group is paced through the sharing at the same time. The teacher wanders from group to group, listening in on the writing talk, making notes about student topics, ways of sharing, and participation level. These comments can be referred to during the conference to clear up misconceptions or to extend learning.

Teachers who have implemented Writing Workshop classrooms tell us that they could not go back to how the daily assigned writing is paced through the writing process. Through conferences, children learn that they can become capable writers with messages that others are interested in. A major goal of school writing, as with school reading, is not just to create students who can write, but to create lifelong writers who are confident in their abilities to express written ideas in a variety of genres and for a range of audiences.

Tips on Conferencing

- Remember to have two kinds of conferences: sit-down and over-the-shoulder.
- Converse with children about their writing; don't interrogate them.
- Conference for three purposes:

    To develop a better writer

    To help the student develop a piece of writing

    To extend mini-lessons within a student's own writing
- Hold short, focused conferences that have a point and a structure.
- Keep the rest of the class writing while you conference.

Building-Blocks Variations

Building Blocks is the program for kindergarten. It shares many similarities with Four Blocks, but there are also important differences. Building-Blocks teachers do a lot of over-the-shoulder conferencing when children begin to write. They do not spell words for children but help children stretch out words and listen for sounds (which helps develop phonemic awareness), and then represent those sounds children hear (use what they know about phonics). Building-Blocks teachers **do** sit down and have "coaching conferences" where they coach their young writers one-on-one. In these conferences, the teacher encourages children to tell her what they know about their topics, and shows children how to "write" what they say. The child does the writing, but the teacher leads them through the steps. "You said, 'I like my sister.' Can you write I on your paper? Good! Your next word is **like**, what do you hear at the beginning of **like**? Great! Write that next on your paper. What other sounds do you hear in **like**? I and k . . . good job. Write those two letters next to the l you have already written. Let's read what you have written so far. 'I like.' Your next word is **my**. What letter will you put down first for **my**? Say **my** again. What letter comes next?"

Most of the writing kindergarten children do should be first draft writing that they share with the class. These children need coaches more than editors, so over-the–shoulder conferences and coaching conferences are what we think kindergartners need to develop into young writers who **like** to write!

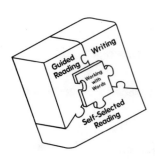

Big-Blocks Variations

Big Blocks is the program for upper grades. Conferences are especially important for students in the upper grades and all of the suggestions in this chapter are appropriate for both Four-Blocks and Big-Blocks classrooms. Usually the older the students are, the longer the pieces they write, and the more children there are in each classroom. This means that students may have fewer conferences with the teacher (Certainly everyone in a class of 28 cannot have a weekly conference with the teacher!) but the conferences will also take longer periods of time. Students in the upper grades can often help each other, and teachers should take advantage of this. Compliments from their peers are important, as are their classmates' opinions. Teachers need to work with their older students on just how to conference, as well as what they can (and cannot) do and say in conferences!

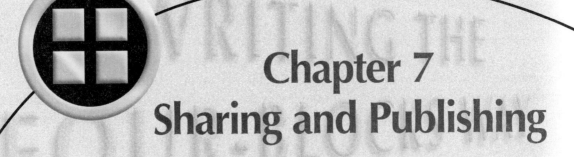

Chapter 7
Sharing and Publishing

Writers revise (make it better) and edit (fix it) so that they can publish (go public). Sharing students' writing and publishing are important parts of the Four-Blocks® writing program. Sharing is an important part of writing instruction because it shows respect for the writing and the writer. Publishing, or "going public," is important because it gives children a real reason to learn to edit, revise, and rewrite their pieces. There are many ways to share and publish in elementary classrooms, and each has its time and place. In this chapter, you will learn several of the most popular sharing and publishing procedures used in Four-Blocks classrooms.

Sharing

Sharing begins as soon as writing begins in most Four-Blocks classrooms, and writing begins the first week of school, if not the first day. The first sharing is usually just "circling them up" and letting the students who want to read or talk about their writing that day. The teacher usually begins by saying, "Tell us what you have written about today." So, the youngest writers don't have to read their pieces if that is uncomfortable or hard for them; they can simply talk about what they have drawn and written that day. When teachers let students share what they have written, it shows respect for the writers, but sharing also benefits the audience. When students share their personal writing, classmates have an opportunity to hear what they have written about; they also get to hear ideas and topics they, too, may know something about and can write about. This happen in Four-Blocks classrooms every day. One student writes about going fishing with his grandpa, and it reminds another student of a time when he went fishing off a pier with his dad. Another student remembers the time he went out on a boat with his grandparents; how he learned to put the worm on the hook and pull the fish in after it bites. When he goes back to his seat after sharing time, this young student adds "fishing" to his "List of Things I Can Write About." A young girl might share her writing about grocery shopping on the way home from school, and it can remind several children about a time they went either grocery shopping, to the shopping center, or to the mall. Sharing writing with peers is much more interesting for students than just writing for the teacher. Children know of many topics that interest friends and other students their age, but not as many topics that interest teachers.

Teachers in Four-Blocks classrooms let students share their writing in many ways. Early in the year, the easiest way to share daily writing is to circle the children up and have each one do a quick share, telling her classmates what she wrote about that day. As the children have more to say, the teacher will still circle them up, but now he tells the students they only have time for a few to share each day. This change is made because the students have more than a sentence or two to share and the sharing takes longer. The most common sharing procedure in Four-Blocks classrooms is probably Author's Chair. Teachers also use Pair and Share, especially with older students, as well as some other whole-group sharing techniques.

Circle Them Up and Have All Students Do a Quick Share

Early in the year, sharing is usually quick, and every child who wants to share has an opportunity to share. Each student gets to read or tell about what he wrote about that day. Students do not write a lot the first few weeks of school, and the sharing that follows writing is quick and informal. The Writing Block ends with children having time to share what they have written that day. Each child has the opportunity to share a sentence or two about his picture or read something he has written to date. The sharing often sounds like this:

"This is my cat, Tommy." (Grade 1)

"I went to the grocery store. I went with my dad." (Grade 1)

"After school, my Aunt Michelle takes me to soccer practice." (Grade 2)

"I wrote about my favorite football team. They played at Erickson Stadium on Sunday, and I went to the game with my family. We sat at the 50-yard line!" (Grade 3)

Circle Them Up and a Let a Few Students Share

As the days pass and students are writing more, the sharing will take a little longer, and all of the students cannot share their writing every day. The teacher continues to circle the class up and then selects a few students to read or tell about their writing each day. Hopefully, every student who wants to share will have an opportunity every few days or once each week. It is still early in the year, and sharing continues to be quick and informal. After children write, the teacher gives several students time to share what they have written about during a brief (5–10 minutes) period at the end of the time allotted to writing. Each child reads or tells a sentence or two about her picture or writing.

A first grader sharing for this driting might sound like this:

"This is my family. My dad's name is Joe, my mom's name is Christine, and this is me."

Young writers usually tell more than they write as they share their writing. Here are some second graders telling what they have written about:

"This is my dog, named Aussie. He likes to sleep under the back porch when it is hot. "

"Yesterday, I went to the grocery store. I went with my dad. We bought some grapes. I like green grapes!"

"I planted tomato plants with my mother. I watered them all summer. I picked the bugs off them. Now, we have lots of tomatoes. We give them to our friends."

In third grade, most students are writing paragraphs, and as the number of minutes allotted to writing increases, they can often write more than a paragraph each day. The better your students read and write, the faster sharing is, but the writing often leads to questions from classmates. Here is the sharing of two different students in third grade:

"I like to read about bears—brown bears, polar bears, panda bears, any kind of bear. I watch bears on television when they are on the Discovery Channel®. In this paper, I will tell some interesting facts I have learned about bears. Bears come in many sizes and shapes. The biggest bear is the . . . ."

"I like football games except when it is cold. My favorite part is watching the cheerleaders. I like their outfits, but I wonder if they are sometimes cold at night games. I think when the cheerleaders are cheering it helps to keep them warm. I watch the cheerleaders closely and remember the routines. When I get home, I practice the cheers. I hope to cheer for the Tiny Packers next year. I want to be a high school cheerleader when I grow up."

CAUTION: DEAD END!

As the year goes on, students write for longer periods and sharing takes longer. The children enjoy sharing, but be sure they don't see sharing as more important than writing. Children in any classroom, at any grade level, should spend more time writing than sharing.

Author's Chair

Once the children are in a daily routine of mini-lesson, writing, and then sharing, the Author's Chair can be introduced. In Four-Blocks classrooms, the children are often divided into five groups (sometimes labeled Monday, Tuesday, Wednesday, Thursday, and Friday). On their allotted day, all of the children in one group get a chance to read their writing and ask for comments and questions. Each student knows which day is her day to share and on that day usually spends some time during the writing period thinking about what she will say, or reading, rereading, and practicing her piece. Teachers often help those children that need a little extra help as they practice and prepare for the Author's Chair so that it will be a successful experience for all.

What exactly is an "Author's Chair"? The Author's Chair can be just a student's chair placed in the front of the classroom, but more often, it is a special stool, special chair, or even a rocking chair. Some teachers buy an inexpensive plastic lawn chair, decorate it with paint and glitter, and write "Share Chair" or "Author's Chair" in attractive, bright letters on the back. Each day, the designated students take turns sitting in this chair and sharing things they have written, while the rest of the students listen quietly and then respond. The writing shared in the Author's Chair does not have to be pieces that have been revised, edited, and published. The writing may be first drafts, finished or unfinished, or final products. After a young author reads his piece, he asks for comments and then questions.

The first day that Author's Chair is introduced, the teacher spends time during the mini-lesson talking about what will happen during Author's Chair each day. The teacher and class talk about "nice comments" and the old saying, "If you can't say anything nice, then don't say anything at all!" The rule for sharing is that you cannot just say it is "good." You must tell what you liked about it, why you liked it, or what you learned from it. After two or three nice comments, the students may then ask questions. Some teachers say, "Give the stars before your wishes!" which means several students say two or three things they liked about a student's writing before students may ask about the things they wish they knew more about. Early in the year, the teacher models the types of thoughtful questions students should learn to ask each other; for example, is there something the children want to know that the author did not tell? The children soon learn how to ask these questions by themselves.

Author's Chair is a time when children can listen to what their classmates are writing about, think about what they are saying or trying to say, and learn to respond to the writing appropriately. Comments let children know what they have done well; questions help them know what they left out or could say better when revising. When a student reads a piece that is not published, the focus of the Author's Chair is on what the classmates liked and what they would like to know more about. Answers to these questions might make the writing clearer or better. Questions could lead to revisions (adding on or changes) during the writing period the next day. Here is an example of sharing in the Author's Chair. Matthew is a beginning second grader who writes about his new cousin.

I have a new boy cousin. His name is Cooper Hunnicutt. He is four months old and has red hair. My other two cousins are girls. My sister is a girl. I am glad my Uncle Ryan and Aunt Suzanne had a baby boy. I got to hold him when I went to visit him.

Comments:

"I liked your story about your new baby cousin, Cooper. I have a baby cousin, too."

"I like your cousin's name. My brother's name is Cooper."

"I liked the way you told us that all of your other cousins are girls. I have boy and girl cousins."

Questions:

"You said you visited your baby cousin. Does he live near you?" (The author replies that his baby cousin lives in another city, and it takes three hours to drive there. Matthew goes on to explain that the new baby lives near his grandmother and grandfather.)

"Do you see the baby often?"(Matthew explains that he will see him on holidays and every time he visits his grandparents. From those two questions, Matthew decides he has more to tell, and with the teacher's encouragement, he decides to add this information to his writing the next day.)

When a student sits in the Author's Chair and reads a published piece, students need to understand that asking questions won't help the writing or writer, so the teacher should help classmates focus on comments about what they liked or what they learned from the piece.

Here is an example of comments to young authors after reading published pieces:

"I liked the way you told us all about playing ball in Little League. Your family was very busy with both you and your brother playing at the same time!"

"I liked your story about mountain climbing with your mom and dad. I have never climbed a mountain. Is it hard?"

We have seen children enjoy sharing in the Author's Chair no matter what their writing ability. The secret seems to be the "nice" comments they receive after reading their pieces. These positive comments encourage children to share and help each child feel good about writing. If this is new to your students, model nice comments. You will be surprised how quickly young students follow your lead. When each child hears something positive about her writing, it will encourage her not only to write, but also to share her writing.

Tips for Author's Chair

Decide who will share each day and set up a schedule. Many teachers have one-fifth of the class share each day. Divide your best and struggling writers across the days.

When sharing an unpublished piece or a "work in progress," have two or three children tell something they liked, then let two or three children ask a question.

You may want to model then post some response starters:

Stars:

"I really liked how you . . . ."

"What I thought was most interesting . . . ."

"What I liked best . . . ."

Wishes:

"What else happened when . . . ?"

"I didn't understand how . . . ?"

"I wish you would tell us . . . ."

"Tell us more about . . . ."

For published pieces, tell the authors what you liked best or what you learned.

Pair and Share

Pair and Share can be done quickly and easily at any grade level. Anything done with twos is twice as much fun! When school weeks are cut short by holidays or bad weather and end up being just two days long, some children worry about not getting their sharing opportunity that week. Pair and Share can be the answer! Students get in twos or pair with neighbors close by and share what they are writing about with their partners. Once the teacher pairs them, they can use the same partners again (unless two children do more talking than sharing!). Students will have more success if they not only know who to share with, but also what to do when sharing and where to share. So, the teacher tells who will share together, how they will share, and where they will share.

Some teachers have students share with the partners sitting beside them and they stay in their seats. Other teachers let students go quietly to special spots in the room. (A chart helps students understand what pairs sit where in the classroom.)

What does the teacher do during this time? He "spies" on the students; that is, he wanders around the classroom; monitors the partners; and stops to visit with several pairs, helping, praising, or just listening to their sharing. When classes know what to do in the Author's Chair, they find Pair and Share easy.

Here is another Pair and Share format, called Stars and Wishes, that can be done quickly and that allows everyone in the class to have a turn. Partner one reads his story to partner two. Partner two gives (tells) a "star" (compliment) to partner one, mentioning something she liked

Conference

about his writing. Then, partner two reads her piece, and partner one compliments her piece with stars. Eventually, after time passes and students understand this procedure, the teacher can add "wishes" (what the children wondered or want to know). It will take a few tries before most children know the procedure and have learned to be respectful and interact appropriately with each other. Teachers should model the behaviors they expect their students to adopt.

Tips for Pair and Share

- One of the partners reads or tells what he has written about.
- The other partner says something she liked about the writing.
- If the partner has a question or wants to know something about the writing, the question(s) follows the "nice" comments.
- Finally, partners change roles and share, comment, and question again.

Small Group Sharing

Anything that can be done in twos can be done in small groups! The idea is that the teacher assigns students to small groups. (One possibility is that the Monday children get together, the Tuesday children get together, etc.) Each group has a leader who makes sure that everyone has a chance to share and that the procedure is followed. (Students read their pieces, then call for "nice" comments, and finally ask for questions). Once again, your students will have more success if they not only know who to share with, but also know what to do when sharing and where to share. So, the teacher tells who will share together, how they will share, and where they will share. Small Group Sharing is more successful if students have used Author's Chair and partners first.

What does the teacher do at this time? She "spies" on the groups; meaning she wanders around the class-room, monitors each small

group, and stops and visits the groups, praising when deserved, giving extra help when needed, and joining a group if necessary to guarantee their success.

Another sharing format is "Four Square Share." This procedure is also used for Self-Selected Reading. Four students work together in a group with their desks pushed together in a square.

Child 1—reads his writing

Child 2—restates or tells what Child 1 read

Child 3—compliments the writer

Child 4—asks a question of the writer

Child 2—reads her writing

Child 3—restates or tells what Child 2 read

Child 4—compliments the writer

Child 1—asks a question of the writer

Child 3—reads her writing

Child 4—restates or tells what Child 3 read

Child 1—compliments the writer

Child 2—asks a question of the writer

Child 4—reads his writing

Child 1—restates or tells what Child 4 read

Child 2—compliments the writer

Child 3—asks a question of the writer

Small groups work well as students get older. They like working with their peers and don't need the close monitoring that individual sharing provides.

Publishing

If you have students who have had opportunities to write daily since kindergarten, you may have students that not only like to write, but can write quite well. If you have students who have NOT had many opportunities to write or who have only written to story starters or prompts, you may have students who DO NOT like writing. It is hard to produce a good final piece each day on a teacher's topic, especially if students are beginning writers! Teachers in all grade levels usually have students on a variety of writing levels and with a variety of attitudes toward writing. Some students, when publishing, actually get excited about writing and appreciate knowing the mechanics and techniques that will help them become better writers.

Visitors to Four-Blocks classrooms often ask how teachers have time to publish all of the books. The publishing—editing, revising, copying or typing into the skeleton book, and illustrating—all happen in that 20–30 minutes (approximately) of writing time that occurs each day after the mini-lesson and before sharing. When a child has three to five good finished pieces, he chooses one to publish, edits it using the checklist, revises and edits with the teacher, and then publishes that piece. When students are working on publishing, they are not writing any new first drafts on those days. Once a piece is published, the child starts producing first drafts again, and the cycle begins again. During the daily 20–30 minutes of writing time, different children are at different stages of the writing process. Keeping children all on the same stage of writing is a difficult task; letting children progress at their own rates is easy once you begin.

CAUTION: DEAD END!

Trying to publish everything a child writes is a DEAD END. It is too much work for the children and way too much work for the teacher! Once publishing begins, most teachers set a minimum number of good pieces—three, four, or five—that each child must write before picking one to publish.

In Four-Blocks classrooms, there are variations in the way to publish students' writing. Publishing may include individual books, class books, pieces published in school newspapers, and publishing on Web pages. Individual pieces can become part of small "all about" books, alphabet books, accordion books, predictable books, storybooks, informational books, chapter books, or theme books. We often see a topic or genre being studied by the class during guided reading, then modeled by the teacher during writing mini-lessons. Finally, the students' writing is turned into books and published pieces. Students at all grade levels need to know that not everything they write will be published, so they will not need to revise and edit everything they write. A quick edit is a good daily habit for students to make sure that their first drafts say what they wanted them to say. Students need a reason to take their writing through the whole writing process, however, and that reason is publishing. Publishing can be done to make a class book or individual books.

Publishing Class Books

Class books are the easiest way for a whole classroom of students to publish at any grade level. Each student contributes her writing on a topic, and the class set is bound together to make a class book. For example, in first or second grade, everyone in the class could draw a picture of herself and write a sentence or two. After you edit the sentences with your students and the students make the corrections, you can bind the pieces into a class book that the children can look at, read, and enjoy.

Some teachers realize how captivating class books are and use them to review each theme or unit studied during the school year. A teacher starts the class book by doing some focused writing lessons related to the science or social studies topics being studied. He models how to narrow the theme, how to write about the chosen topic, then how to revise, edit, and publish a piece. The students, following their teacher's lead, write, revise, edit, rewrite, and illustrate their pieces. This writing is compiled in a class book, and the class book can be added to the material available for the class during Self-Selected Reading time. Children love reading class books at any grade level! A focused writing lesson often takes a week or more from start to finished book.

Here is an example from a class doing a study of China in second grade.

Day One
The teacher thinks aloud, the class brainstorms, and the teacher creates a web.

The teacher tells the class that since they are studying about a country in the East—China—they are going to take a week off from their individual, Self-Selected Writing to make a class book about China. Together, they brainstorm all of the things they have learned and could write about. The teacher writes what the students tell her on a web. She writes China in the middle, and on spokes around the center, she lists what students tell her about location, the geography, the climate, the cities, the food, the people, dress, work, and school.

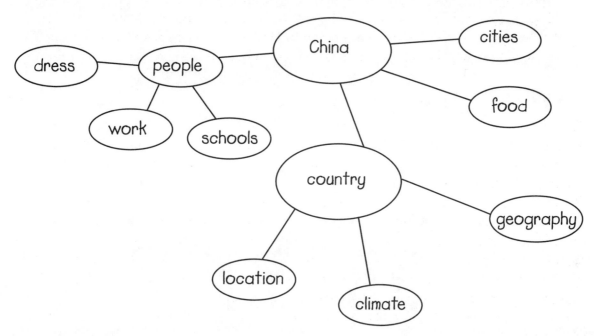

Days Two and Three
On the second day, the teacher thinks aloud and writes using the web, and the children help her. The next day she adds to the writing.

The teacher writes the introductory piece about China with the children's help. She begins her writing using the web created during the mini-lesson on the second day. She ends her lesson by doing a "quick edit." When the children return to their seats on the second day, each one is asked to begin an individual piece about China. They know to look at the topics on the web and choose things to write about that they learned about China that interested them. The third day, the teacher continues writing about China in her mini-lesson and ends with a quick edit. The children will continue writing and adding on to their pieces the third day, as well.

Day Four
For her mini-lesson, the teacher reads her piece, adding and changing a few sentences, and then does a quick edit using the Editor's Checklist and the children's help. The teacher reminds the children that when they finish writing, they need to reread their pieces, make any changes

that would improve their pieces, then use the Editor's Checklist to check for writing errors.

Day Five

The teacher rewrites her introductory piece and illustrates it with a map of China. She explains that when everyone is finished revising, editing, rewriting, and illustrating his piece, she will bind all of the pieces together to create a class big book.

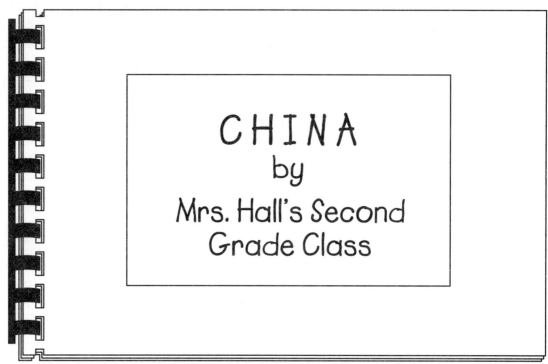

Social studies and science themes contain lots of topics for class books. Your students' stories can be put in a class book also—and you will have a collection of short stories! How-to-make things and recipes are other popular elementary topics for class books. A class cookbook makes an excellent, as well as inexpensive, present for students' parents for holidays (Christmas, Hanukkah, Mother's Day, Valentine's Day, or Father's Day). Young children also like to tell about how they think things are made. Sometimes these stories make the local newspaper because their directions are very entertaining! Teaching mini-lessons on writing directions can help children focus on ordering events. In a mini-lesson on directions, for example, the teacher and children can make peanut butter and jelly sandwiches for a snack. After making and enjoying their sandwiches, the teacher and class might compose directions for it. The following day, children may work alone or in pairs to write recipes for favorite sandwiches. This can be done with cookies or favorite vegetable snacks, too. (Before completing any food activity, ask families' permission and inquire about students' food allergies and religious or other food preferences.)

Publishing Individual Books

Most visitors marvel at both the writing and publishing of young children in Four-Blocks classrooms. They often ask, "How do you do it?" and "Where do you get the books?" Children write daily, so publishing flows naturally as each one finishes several pieces and chooses one to revise, edit, and publish. Students do not usually edit and publish the first few weeks of school, but some children are ready to start soon after that. Because writing is naturally multilevel, let the children show you when they are ready to publish. When most of the class has published books, help those who haven't published yet to publish one. Some children publish four or five books each year; some publish 20 or more!

During writing in Four-Blocks classrooms, teachers help students learn to "tell about" the many things they know or are learning about. They tell about ideas, friends, dreams, favorites, secrets, fears, etc. They learn to write stories, poems, letters, biographies, informational pieces, and more. Grammar, mechanics, organization, voice, and genres can be taught in the context of real writing, so the students actually understand what you are teaching them! They learn to write to take a piece through the writing process, to "make it better" by revising, to "fix it" by editing, and then to publish it. The best advice for teachers is: Do not have your students go through this publishing process if you will be the only one to read their work. Publishing gives students a reason to write and a reason to take their writing through the writing process!

Since most or some (depending on grade level) of students' writing time is spent on self-selected topics, you should decide how often they should publish. Some teachers publish after the students have three pieces completed, while others wait until they have five pieces—you know your class and what is manageable. The teacher's time, which has been spent circulating and encouraging children in their writing, is now allocated primarily to writing conferences in which she helps children revise, edit, and publish. The students should decide which self-selected pieces they would like to publish.

Once Author's Chair and publishing begins, drawing is not usually included each day. Many teachers let each child draw a picture to go with the one piece of writing she plans to share that day in the Author's Chair. Of course, illustrations are drawn to go with published books. Once publishing begins, not all children are writing first drafts during the writing time each day. Some children are working to produce the three good pieces that will allow them to pick one to publish. Other children are conferencing with the teacher and preparing to publish. Other children are copying or typing and illustrating their published pieces. Once publishing begins, the teacher also changes how she uses her time while the children write. Instead of "circulating and encouraging," teachers spend longer periods of time "conferencing and editing" with children who are ready to publish. How do you begin to publish? Once again, you model it! Here is an example of a teacher modeling the publishing procedure around the end of the first quarter of the school year:

First Day of Publishing
The teacher shows the class three pieces she has written, thinks aloud, and says:
"I have written many pieces this year. I have written about the things I like to do, the places I have gone with my family, and the things we are studying about. Today, I am going to look at three of the pieces I have written and decide which one I want to publish. When we publish in this class, we make a book. We put the books we make in the book baskets so that everyone can read them. At the end of the year, you will get to take the books you have published home. Let's look at the three pieces I think are my best." The teacher then puts three pieces on the overhead projector (or shows three pieces from the chart tablet).

The teacher reads and discusses each of the three pieces:

One by one, the teacher displays and reads each of the three pieces and discusses what she likes about each piece. "I like this one about Smarty Jones, a horse that everyone wanted to win the Triple Crown. He didn't win, but lots of you watched the last race at Belmont Park in New York on television last June. I was surprised how much you knew about this horse, the jockey, the owner, and the trainer. I think it would make a good book, and I know just how I would illustrate the pages. I will need some help from a student who can draw horses to illustrate this book. I can draw some things well but not horses! I think many of you would enjoy this book because you helped me when I was writing the story and enjoyed reading the story after I wrote it.

"I really liked 'Making Cookies,' but I am not so sure everyone liked it as much as I did. I want to publish something that most of the class would like to read. Another piece I like is 'Favorite Authors.' After I wrote about a favorite author I liked, Kevin Henkes, it reminded me of several more authors I liked, so I wrote about them. That book could become a chapter book with pages on eight of our favorite authors. It is very hard to choose between 'Smarty Jones' and 'Favorite Authors,' but I think for my first book I will choose 'Smarty Jones.' When we talk about publishing chapter books, I can come back to 'Favorite Authors,' or we could make a class book on that topic."

The teacher returns to the chosen piece and revises and edits it:

"The first thing I want to do is to think if there is anything I want to change about my story. I like it, so I don't want to change too much, but read it with me one time and see if you can think of anything I left out or that would make it a little better." The children and teacher read "Smarty Jones" together and decide to change the word good to smart. The teacher crosses out **good** and writes **smart** above it. The piece has already been edited, but there are more items on the Editor's Checklist now than there were at that time. The children and teacher do a quick re-edit. The teacher circles two words that she had stretched out to spell. She then writes the correct spellings above these. "We don't worry about the spellings of words not in the room on first draft," she reminds them. "But, I will help you fix the spelling of every word when you are making a book so that everyone can read it easily."

Second Day of Publishing: Rewriting or Typing a Sentence on a Page

The first publishing lessons take more than one day to model. On the first day, you choose, revise, and edit your piece. On the second day, you model what to do next—divide the selection into the number of pages you have to write on and begin to copy your piece over in your "very best handwriting." Often teachers use a computer and printer to print the first book for students, especially if they think the author's handwriting might make it hard for other children to read. Some teachers edit with the child, and then type the text or let the child type it.

You need to do this lesson on the actual book. Bring the children up close to you so that they can see what you are doing. Let them read from the overhead or chart each sentence and watch as you write it in your book.

The teacher thinks aloud, talks, and writes the title page:

I start with my title page and write the title, 'Smarty Jones,' here in my very best handwriting. Underneath the title, I write the word "by" and then write my name, "Mrs. Hall," because I am the author of this book. You will write your names because you will be the authors of your books. Write one sentence, in your best handwriting, on each page. (Children with 10 sentences can make 10-page books. If someone has 14 sentences, help her decide how to put 2 sentences on some pages. Most teachers usually don't go over 10 pages for individual books.)

Smarty Jones is a racehorse.

Many people watched him win the Kentucky Derby.

People got excited when he won the Preakness.

If he won at Belmont Park, he would win the Triple Crown!

I watched the race on television. I was excited.

Many people thought he would win.

He led for a while, then Birdstone passed him in the final stretch.

It was a sad day for Smarty Jones, but he didn't know!

Third Day of Publishing: The Teacher (with Help) Illustrates the Book
The teacher turns to each page, thinks aloud about what she might draw, then draws a picture that goes with the text on the page. She has a student who draws horses well help her on some pages.

Smarty Jones is a racehorse.

"On this page, I will have Joey draw Smarty Jones. He needs to use blue for his colors! On the next page, I will draw a television set with people, really just heads, watching . . . ."

Fourth Day of Publishing: The Teacher Makes the Cover, Puts the Book Together, and Reads It
Write the title and author on the cover and illustrate it. Talk about the complete book and how carefully you copied every page. (Some children will write the final draft just like they wrote the first draft, so this part needs to be stressed—copy the edited copy! Keep some correction fluid on hand if children write final copies in pen. If they publish on the computer, remember to check it before they press "Print.")

Fifth Day Publishing: The Teacher Writes the "All About the Author" Page
The teacher tells the class a little about the "author" by writing a page about herself.

Mrs. Hall teaches second grade. She has two daughters and a grandson. She likes to read and take care of Cooper. She likes to write books, too!

Let the children know that you will interview them and write this page when they publish their books. In third grade and above, students may be able to write this page on their own.

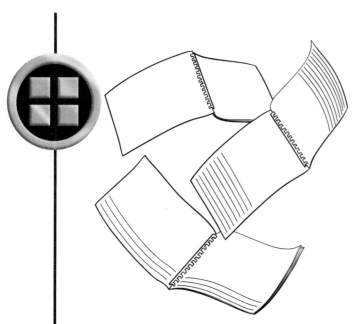

Blank Books for Publishing

It is always helpful to have wonderful parent volunteers at your school. At some schools, these volunteers make blank books for the teachers and students to use. The books are made by cutting packages of plain white paper in half and using half sheets of standard size colorful card stock as the front and back covers. The books used to publish in first and second grades usually have eight pages. Those pages include: a title page, a dedication page, five lined pages with a space to draw at the top of each page, and a page where the teacher writes "About the Author" as the child dictates something about himself. The books made later in the year in second grade and those made in third grade need more space for writing, so more lines are added to the pages and more pages are added to the books. The books are usually turned lengthwise and "bound" with a commercial bookbinder or stapled together. Teachers keep a supply of books in various colors in their classrooms. When a child is ready to do a final copy, she has a book that is ready to write in.

Sometimes children type their final copies on the computer, then cut apart the sentences and paste them on the pages. Sometimes the children copy their stories into the books in their best handwriting. In first grade, the first books are usually rewritten or typed by the teacher or a parent volunteer. Early in the year, not every child in first grade can write legibly, so writing for the children helps until formal handwriting can be taught and practiced, and everyone has a book to be proud of and which classmates can read.

After the books are written, the children illustrate them. Many Four-Blocks classrooms have a publishing table or center where you will find crayons, markers, correction fluid, scissors, and all of the materials the children need to copy over, illustrate, and finish their books.

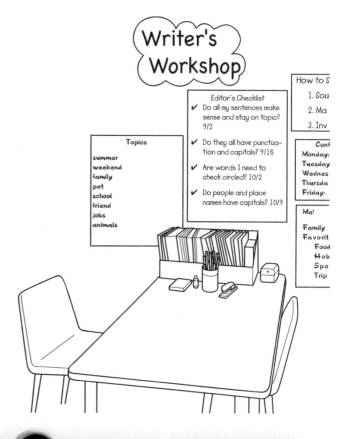

As children get older, they either want to publish everything or nothing. When they want to publish everything, they need to begin to think more critically and ask, "Which is my best piece?" "Which piece would my classmates like to read?" When they want to publish nothing, then you need to ask yourself, "What can I do to set this student up for success?" Once students have published some good pieces and gotten some positive feedback, they are usually willing to write and publish again.

One Third-Grade Teacher's Story

"My class has just begun our revising/editing/publishing process during the Writing Block. My rule is that students can sign up to publish when they have three good first drafts. Each day, as we begin writing in our Writing Block, I gather the children who think they are ready to publish. The number varies each day, but the procedure is always the same. Each student brings me his writing notebook, shows me his three first drafts, and indicates which one he has chosen to publish. I look quickly to make sure each child does have three "good" first drafts. Some children really want to publish everything, so they write one good first draft and then dash off two others to try to fool me. I inform them that I have been teaching third grade since before they were born, and I know 'three good pieces' when I see them. I tell them that I understand they want to publish everything they write, but that rules are rules, and they must write three good pieces and then pick one. I send them back to their desks and tell them I look forward to seeing them again soon when they have three good first drafts. Of course, what is 'good' for one child differs from what is 'good' for another, but a teacher can still tell when a reasonable effort has been made—and when it hasn't.

"Those who have three good drafts, including revising and editing their pieces, are then ready to choose partners with whom they will revise and edit again. When working with partners, our class uses the mnemonic TAG to help the children remember what helpful partners do. In fact, I have a poster on which I have written:

> Tell what you liked.
>
> Ask questions about what you didn't understand.
>
> Give suggestions for making the published book terrific.

"As each child reads the piece aloud, his partner listens carefully and then tells something she liked. The children are encouraged to say things like:

'I liked how you made it funny by telling how your mom tricked you.'

'I liked the part where you realized this was a surprise party for you.'

'I liked how you ended it.'

Next, the partner asks a question if there was anything unclear or something else she would like to know:

'How did your mother keep this a surprise if all of the stuff was set up in the dining room?'

'How many kids came to the party?'

'What did you get for presents?'

Next, the partner tries to give a helpful suggestion:

'Maybe you need to do more at the beginning with the setting, like describe the dining room set for the party and then describe how you were grounded.'

'Why don't you name the kids as they are quietly sneaking in the back door?'

'You could use better words to show how mad your were about being grounded—like furious or really bummed out.'

"After the partners give their revising suggestions, the students make any revisions needed. I always have them write on every other line in their notebooks so that they have space to add things, cross things out, and indicate where they were going to insert longer chunks. I have also shown them how to write any new parts on separate sheets of paper, ready to insert in the correct place. After revising their pieces, the partners edit for the things on the current checklist. We have been adding these gradually, and I have been modeling how to help a friend edit. Currently, our Editor's Checklist looks like this:

Editor's Checklist

1. Do all the sentences make sense?

2. Do all the sentences start with caps and end with punctuation?

3. Do all people and place names have caps?

4. Do all the sentences stay on the topic?

5. Does the piece have a beginning, middle, and end?

6. Are words I need to check the spelling of underlined or circled?

"Now, it is my turn to work with the children who have written three good pieces and who have revised and edited their selected pieces with partners. The children are now ready for me to play "editor-in-chief." I give the piece a final edit, and then the child goes over to one of the classroom computers and types and formats the piece. Adding the illustrations is the final step. Some children draw by hand, but others like use the computer drawing tools and find the appropriate clip art to illustrate their pieces.

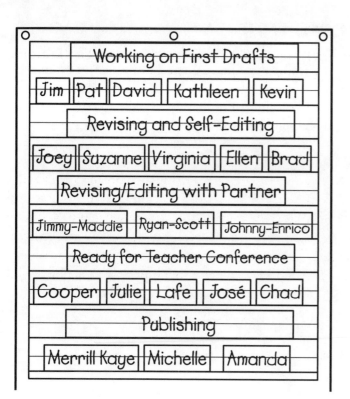

"Currently, my students are in all different stages of writing, revising, editing, and publishing. A few have finished their first published pieces and are now back to writing another three good first drafts. I keep up with where they all are by having them put their cards in the appropriate slots of my writing steps pocket chart."

Another Publishing Option

While many teachers find the just described, "pick-a-piece-out-of-every-three-to-five" procedure quite workable, other teachers prefer to work with a third of their class each week. These teachers divide the class into thirds, including one of their most able and least able writers in each third. In week one, children in the first third edit and publish pieces while the other two-thirds of the class work on as many first drafts as they can in a week. In week two, when the first third of the class has published pieces, they go back to first-draft writing while the teacher works with the second group. In week three, the final third (who have been producing first drafts for two weeks and may have a lot to choose from) get to publish pieces. Week four finds the first third back into their revising/editing/publishing cycle.

Regardless of how you structure the revising/editing/publishing process, it is important that children spend more of their writing time doing the difficult, but important, work of first draft writing. It is during this first draft that children do a lot of the "mental work" that moves them along in reading and writing. As they use the Word Wall and other room resources to spell words and stretch out the spelling of longer words, they are applying their word and phonics strategies. They also apply their comprehension strategies as they learn to keep their writing on topic, to put things in the right sequence, and to decide if what they write is going to be "real" or "make-believe."

CAUTION: DEAD END!
In the early grades, most children do not write real stories. They write "all-about stories" by telling all they know about their dogs, their friends, or events they attended. Their writing is more descriptive and personal. Publishing all-about stories is fine when that is the stage of writing your children are in.

Some Popular Formats for Publishing Books

Accordion Books

Alphabet Books

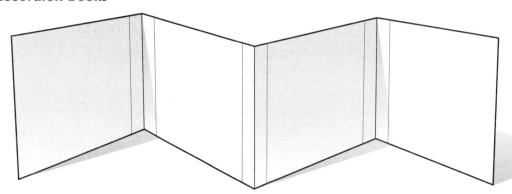

Insect Alphabet
by Jon N.

Aa
Ants are busy insects.

Machine-Bound Books

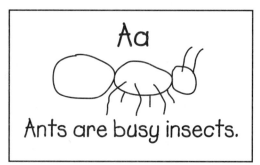

Summer Fun
by
Susie Mortimer

ME →

Stapled Books

Fun with
Grandpa

My Friends

Shape Books

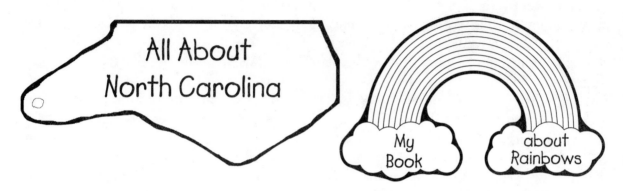

All About
North Carolina

My
Book

about
Rainbows

Publishing Writing in a Class Newspaper

A class newspaper is the perfect place to publish young children's stories. You can publish just a page or two of children's writing even more easily since you do not have to develop a wide variety of subjects in a newspaper. It takes time to publish either a newspaper or a page of story sharing. However, it allows your students to not only share their writing with their classmates, but also to share with their parents as well. If you have Writer's Workshop up and running, then you will regularly have finished pieces. With a parent volunteer to type the text (remember, older children can do almost everything parents can do!) and copy any illustrations for each piece, then you can easily send home a page or two of the latest and greatest stories on a regular basis. For those teachers who don't have this kind of parental/volunteer support or who don't have the computers available for their students to write on, then one class newspaper published near the end of the year would be a better choice.

Publishing Writing on a Class Web Site

If you have a class computer, or several computers, students can type their final copies, then load them on the class Web site. New pieces are added and old pieces are removed as the year goes on. Children can read their work and the work of their classmates at home by visiting the Web site. When the class studies a new genre, the public can see what they are learning about and how well they are writing. There are many wonderful class Web sites on the Internet today.

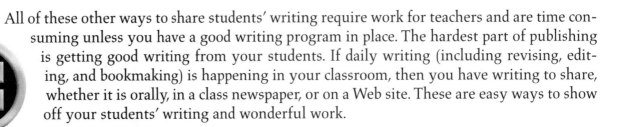

All of these other ways to share students' writing require work for teachers and are time consuming unless you have a good writing program in place. The hardest part of publishing is getting good writing from your students. If daily writing (including revising, editing, and bookmaking) is happening in your classroom, then you have writing to share, whether it is orally, in a class newspaper, or on a Web site. These are easy ways to show off your students' writing and wonderful work.

Publishing Writing on a Bulletin Board

When the youngest students in your school begin to write, you want to celebrate what they can do, not focus on what they are doing wrong. In kindergarten or early first grade, a first draft is acceptable to place on a bulletin board. However, be sure to let parents and grown-ups who visit your classroom know that this is first draft and hasn't been taken through the publishing process. Later in the year in first grade and in all other grade levels, writing that is put on a bulletin board is writing made "public," so it should go through the publishing process (write, revise, edit, recopy) before it is posted. Let the children know that when they write something that other people will see (the public), they have to make sure that they respect the readers. Let students know they will have the help of an Editor's Checklist and an editor (you) to correct their mistakes before the class and others have an opportunity to see it. Make a big deal of how you can and will help them to see that all of their mistakes are fixed, and everyone will see just their best writing. Help your students display their writing proudly. If you will put all of your students' writing on a bulletin board and the board needs to be done by "tomorrow," remind students that they won't all get a conference, but you will look at and correct all of their writing. This is better than putting, "Good Writing!" on a bulletin board that has "sloppy copy." Children are not afraid to display their work if they know it is not only good writing but that anyone who reads it will not find any mistakes!

Recording Finished Pieces for a Listening Center

Many young students who can read and write well enjoy recording their published pieces into a tape recorder or onto a CD and then placing these in a Listening Center for their classmates to hear. If the piece recorded is a story, make sure it is a "finished" story with a beginning, middle, and end. Some teachers place the published book in the listening center along with the tape. Children enjoy reading their classmates' writing, as well as hearing them read their work aloud. Let your good readers and storytellers "show off" and help by adding interesting, "original" materials to your listening center.

Links for Publishing Children's Writing

These are some of the many sites available for publishing student work on the Internet.

http://www.ucalgary.ca/~dkbrown/writings.html

http://www.discoverwriting.com

http://www.kidpub.org/kidpub/

http://www.scils.rutgers.edu/~kvander/childpublishing.html

http://www.magickeys.com/books/link-pub.html

http://teenwriting.about.com/mbody.htm

http://www.poetry4kids.com/

http://falcon.jmu.edu/~ramseyil/writing.htm

http://www.yahooligans.com/school_bell/language_arts/writing/Publishing_on_the_Web/

http://www.ecis.org/links/writing_links.htm

Classroom Publishing/Writing Programs

Many commercial companies offer software for writing and publishing, but nothing can take the place of a good writing teacher. Students like Kid Pix® where they can use clip art and add drawings to the reports and books they are publishing. Some other commercial programs for writing are:

Writing Blaster®

This is a word processor and paint box rolled into one. Writing Blaster® not only helps kids develop fundamental writing skills, but provides hundreds of ways to turn those skills into multimedia creations. Using words, pictures, sound effects, and surprises, kids of all ages and skill levels can have fun expressing themselves while publishing everything from greeting cards to book reports, to their very own storybooks.

Writing by Pro One

The writing process becomes clear and easy when students use this program by Pro One. This is a full-featured word processor with on-screen guides that teach students the writing process. Writing Basics begins with Sentences and Paragraphs, and it covers complete sen-

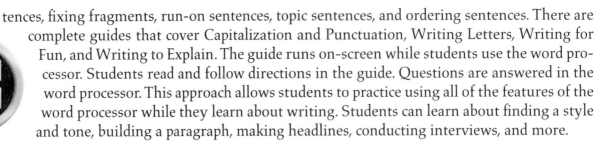

tences, fixing fragments, run-on sentences, topic sentences, and ordering sentences. There are complete guides that cover Capitalization and Punctuation, Writing Letters, Writing for Fun, and Writing to Explain. The guide runs on-screen while students use the word processor. Students read and follow directions in the guide. Questions are answered in the word processor. This approach allows students to practice using all of the features of the word processor while they learn about writing. Students can learn about finding a style and tone, building a paragraph, making headlines, conducting interviews, and more.

Writing Tutor®

A step-by-step system to help students of all ages succeed at any writing assignment. The program walks students through a 10-step process from idea development and first drafts to final edits and revisions. There are word and image databases to inspire ideas and writing tools to create cohesive drafts. Writing Tutor® has over 50 tools, including photo storyboards to create story ideas, idea wheels to create new themes, issue wheels to explore possible topics, time lines, diagrams, and checkers to check for language variety, unity and coherence, troublesome adjectives and adverbs, and more. On-screen handbooks help with grammar, common writing problems, and explain literary terms and style issues. The Writing Handbook covers The Writing Process, Elements of Writing, Types of Literature, Elements of Nonfiction, and more. There is also an index to easily find help on punctuation, grammar, and more.

Parents and Others Can Help with Publishing

Many teachers who like to publish are not afraid to ask for help from parents, grandparents, older children, or any school volunteers available to them. They have these volunteers make blank books (see page 132), type stories for young students or students that need help, reread final copy to see if all corrections were made, and get supplies for the bookmaking center. These teachers also find time to explain the writing process to parents so that parents aren't writing for children, spelling all of the words, or doing too much of the work during writing, revision, or editing with students. Students need help, but not someone to do it for them! Parents are valuable in getting books and supplies ready. Besides binding blank books, volunteers can make sets of accordion books, shape books, or bound books for the teachers to use with the class.

Young Authors' Celebrations

In many Four-Blocks classrooms, the year ends with students looking at what they have published and choosing one book to read during a Young Authors' Celebration. Parents and other invited guests come to be an appreciative audience for your budding authors. Everyone savors his accomplishment and reflects upon how far he has come as a writer during the school year.

Tips for Publishing

- Don't try to publish every piece. Let children choose one out of three to five good pieces or let a third of the class publish each week.

- Start by publishing a class book. It's easy, and everyone is successfully published.

- Set up routines for publishing individual books.

- Use partner editing and/or revision before children come to you, the final editor-in-chief.

- Children should recopy or type the final books only one time.

- Use parents or volunteers to make the publishing process go smoothly.

- Use a variety of book and other publishing forms across the year.

- Except for kindergarten, published pieces should have correct spelling and be mechanically correct.

- Don't expect everyone to publish the same number of books but don't leave anyone out. Even struggling writers can publish books. (See Chapter 10.)

- Publishing should be the "frosting on the cake"—the reward for lots of hard work. Celebrate your young authors and their books!

Building-Blocks Variations

Kindergarten teachers find many ways to share and celebrate their students' writing. They circle students up and let them share their writing. Some teachers use Author's Chair later in the year. Students are ready to publish their writing in kindergarten when they can write with phonics spelling, know letters and sounds, and how to form letters. The goal is one published book for each child in your kindergarten class. Published writing in kindergarten is NOT perfect writing. Most teachers allow children to write with "phonics spelling" so that children can remember what they have written and be able to read it to the class. If everything is corrected, many children cannot read their own writing. Kindergarten children need a cheerleader more than they need an editor. When publishing in kindergarten, teachers coach children to write five sentences about a topic. Sentences should begin with capital letters and have punctuation at the ends. Phonetic spelling is accepted in kindergarten. Often the child, the teacher, or a teaching assistant will type the story. The printed or typed sentences are cut apart, and then each sentence is pasted on a page and illustrated. The teacher discusses each illustration with the student. The book has a Title Page and Dedication Page at the beginning and an "All About the Author Page" at the end of the book.

At the end of the year, children enjoy sharing their "books" and reading them to classmates and parents at a Young Authors' Conference or Tea.

Students are ready to publish when they can publish.

Big-Blocks Variations

Sharing happens more with partners and in small groups, as well as the Author's Chair in Big-Blocks classrooms. Teachers talk to their students about writing in conversation, just as they would like students to talk to each other. In conferences, teachers listen to the writer and the writing and ask the kind of questions that will enable writers to think about what they have written and what they want to do next. To have a good writing program, teachers need to put editorial concerns in the proper place, which is after the content is written and revised. Self-editing and peer editing are part of publishing in Big-Blocks classrooms. In the upper grades, the first editor of any piece should be the writer himself. Students can work with partners or small groups to get help. Then, the teacher edits during a publishing conference, and the teacher and student have a conversation about the writing. The teacher makes sure that the revision, self-editing, and peer editing didn't miss anything, and that the writing is well developed and has good punctuation and grammar. Students can help each other and should be able to work more independently in the upper grades, but they need the teacher to make sure they have done their best work. Students never outgrow the need to publish their writing. Older students can write and publish books, including chapter books, and should do more writing to topics to prepare them for middle school and high school, where they will be asked to write in most content areas. Upper-grade students can often do anything the teacher can do, so good students mean Web sites and class newspapers are possible with help on their part and yours. There is no limit to what older students can do with sharing and publishing!

Chapter 8
Genres—
What Kinds of Writing Do Children Do?

This chapter focuses on students' understanding and control of genre elements. There are many different genres or types of writing, and each one must be learned separately. By the time students finish elementary school, most teachers expect students to be able to produce pieces that are adequate examples of each of several genres.

Just What Is "Genre"?

"Genre" is a one-word way to say "kind of writing." State standards often list the following genres for students to learn: personal experience narrative, story, report, summary, expository essay, communications, literature response, and persuasive essay. Districts, then, typically require particular genres for specific grade levels, but they don't always specify within the genre. For example, a search for what an expository essay is will reveal many types. Which one is the one to teach? Or, do you require all of them from students?

The same thing happens with the state-mandated genre of "communications." Because of lack of specificity, students in fourth grade are taught the elements of writing a friendly letter for the fourth time. When does the "letter to the editor" get introduced? How about letters requesting information? Notes? Thank you's? Memos? E-mail messages? All of these are common forms of communication.

Additionally, teaching genres is not as simple as listing genres. Not only do teachers need to know which genres to teach, but they also must understand the elements within each of those genres. When students are learning how to produce writing of a particular genre, they usually learn how to control a few salient genre elements first. To help them learn the genre at a more complete and sophisticated level, it is usually necessary to focus on the particular elements most students still need to learn.

Within genres are subgenres. "Communications," a commonly listed state expectation, is one example. Communications has multiple subgenres, such as E-mail and thank-you letters. Just within the story genre, there is fantasy, science fiction, historical fiction, realistic fiction, adventure, mystery, tall tales, folktales, fairy tales, legends, and so on. When a state standard lists "story," what are they expecting? Or does it even matter? It can get pretty confusing. The following list shows the kind of genres most often used in classrooms.

Typical School Writing Genres (Not Meant to Be an Exhaustive List)

Informational

Biography/Autobiography: includes personal experience narrative, memoir, diary/journal, and the story of a person's life

Report: includes research report, classroom magazine/newspaper article, book or movie review

Story

Folktale/Fairy Tale/Tall Tale: includes story innovations (retellings, extensions, parallel stories)

Imaginary Stories: both could-happen and couldn't-happen stories

Letter: includes personal (friendly letter, thank-you, E-mail) and business (memo, letter to the editor, request for information)

Poetry: includes both free and formula, or pattern, poetry

Multi-Genre: includes two or more genres within a book (for example, the *Magic School Bus* series)

Why Is Genre Important in Reading and Writing?

Learning to write genres clearly supports reading those genres. When students understand the elements of a genre, they are more likely to read like a writer of that genre so that they understand the devices used or the ways of developing the ideas. For example, students who excel at writing informational reports from experiments would be more likely to comprehend the steps of a written experiment and the findings reported. Teaching the elements of genres supports both reading and writing because students bring insights from reading the genre to knowing how to write in the genre. They also bring insights from trying to write in the genre to understanding that genre when they read.

What Are the Elements of the Genres?

Do you ever confuse a mystery with a folktale? Never! There are specific elements that define each genre to a degree that allows identification while you are reading. Before you can teach genres in writing, you must identify those elements for teaching. It helps students if you can explain the writing they will do for you (other than poetry) as either informational, didn't happen but could, or couldn't happen. In the informational category, you will have biography/autobiography and reports. In the didn't-happen-but-could and couldn't-happen categories, you will show the students how to write a variety of stories.

Informational

Biography/Autobiography

Biography and autobiography are focused on people and the events in their lives. Biography means writing about a life (someone else's) and autobiography is writing about your own life. These vary largely in length, purpose, and target audience. Both biography and autobiography may be a description of a single event (as in a personal experience narrative) or a series of significant events from a person's life (such as a story of a person's life).

Because biography and autobiography are highly personal, they tend to elicit more emotion, from both author and reader, than some other genres. The author's voice is often clearer because of the connection to the subject of the biography/autobiography.

Elements of biography and autobiography and titles of children's books to aid your instruction are listed below. Use the elements to plan mini-lessons, then show students examples in literature and demonstrate how to use one or more elements while writing.

Biography/Autobiography Elements

Biography/Autobiography includes personal experience narrative, memoir, diary/journal, and the story of a person's life. These subgenres vary largely in length, purpose, and target audience. For any of these, the author knows the person either personally or through research.

Biography

- An important person is the main character.
- The importance of the person's life is shown by describing the person's influence on others or events.
- The author typically uses chronological order to present the person and important events. If not, it is possible to reconstruct the chronological order of events from the information given.
- The author includes selected actual events and dialogue from the main character's life.
- The selected events and dialogue illustrate the reason the main character is an important person to write about.
- The author has a bias about the subject but may attempt objectivity.

Autobiography

- The author is the main character.
- The writing describes either a single "small moment" (Calkins, 2003) or a series of events.
- The importance of the event(s) described is relayed to the reader.
- The author uses selected actual events and may use dialogue.
- The author does not attempt to be objective.
- The author's personality (voice) is clearly present in the way things are expressed.

Children's Authors Whose Works Support Biography/Autobiography

Four authors have written the most intriguing and best written biographies for children:

Jean Fritz: Most people credit Jean Fritz's 1973 *And Then What Happened, Paul Revere?* (Putnam, 1996) as marking the beginning of truly authentic biography for children. Since then, she has published many biographies which have won both awards and the hearts of children including *Bully for You, Teddy Roosevelt!* (Putnam, 1991), *The Great Little Madison* (Putnam, 1989), and *Where Do You Think You're Going, Christopher Columbus?* (Putnam, 1980).

David Adler: Perhaps the best writer of "picture book" biographies for young children, David Adler has written numerous biographies. Look for his simply written and beautifully illustrated biographies about Harriet Beecher Stowe, George Washington, Abraham Lincoln, Martin Luther King, Jr., Thomas Jefferson, Anne Frank, Harriet Tubman, Davy Crockett, Louis Braille, Jackie Robinson, Rosa Parks, and numerous other well-known people.

Diane Stanley: Stanley's picture-book biographies are written for children in upper-elementary grades. Titles include *Peter the Great* (Morrow, 1986), *Cleopatra,* (Morrow, 1994) and *Leonardo da Vinci* (Morrow, 1996).

Russell Freeman: Freeman's biographies are wonderfully written and illustrated with real photographs. Among his most appealing to children biographies are: *The Wright Brothers: How They Invented the Airplane* (Clarion, 1991), *Eleanor Roosevelt: A Life of Discovery* (Clarion, 1993), and *Lincoln: A Photobiography* (Houghton Mifflin, 1987).

Report

Reports present information that a student has gathered through observation, interviews, or print or visual/auditory sources. Though it may feel this way to students, reports are not just a school task. Many adults must present various types of reports to planning teams, boards, or management. Learning to coherently present information so that others understand it requires the two special skills of summary and organization of ideas.

Reports have an undeserved reputation for being dry and dreary. That certainly does not need to be the case. Take a look at how some of the wonderful children's informational books present information—report it—in a highly engaging way. Open up your repertoire of report formats by immersing students in informational books prior to doing the reports so that students see how interesting information presentation can be.

Is there a place for the "formal research report"? Sure—in high school and college. Our perspective (as authors and teachers) is that we handicap students for later learning of the specific requirements for formal research reports by early on causing them to hate and fear presenting information to others. Let's get students to love sharing what they have discovered. Then, teachers can map onto that the specific expectations for formal reports.

One step in the process is increasing the frequency of reports of information. When students do "the report" each spring, they get little practice. Generally speaking, students like being in control of information. They come home and during dinner table conversation often start with, "Did you know . . . ?" You can capitalize on that by allowing frequent opportunities to share what they have learned. Celebrate learning and sharing information! Rather than having one report a year, have one once a month!

Another step to improving report writing is to broaden the range of options. Writing a movie review is a report of information based upon the collection of data (viewing the movie and perhaps talking with others who also saw it). Producing a classroom magazine allows students to use multiple formats (crossword puzzles, articles, cartoons, and so on) to report the information they find. Desktop publishing programs facilitate the production of alternate formats for reports.

Report Elements
Report includes research report, magazine article, newspaper article, book review, or movie review.

- There is a single important idea.
- This single most important idea is supported by lots of facts.
- The information is presented in a way that interests the reader.
- Organization is very important so that ideas flow clearly and logically.
- New ideas are clarified with examples, analogies, definitions, explanations, and descriptions.
- The voice is expert, projecting knowledge of information.

Children's Authors Whose Works Support Report Writing
Any well-written informational book that focuses on one topic is an excellent example for helping students learn to write reports. There are many such books. Here are three of the most versatile and creative authors of informational books:

Gail Gibbons: For beautifully illustrated informational books for young children, the first author to look to is Gail Gibbons. She has written about almost every animal including bats, cats, dogs, chickens, pigs, frogs, spiders, gulls, horses, wolves, grizzly bears, polar bears, and whales. Children who are more fascinated by "things" will love her books about bicycles, houses, tools, trains, and berries. Her books on weather, the moon, the planets, stars, and seasons will make science more real and exciting. Children love holidays, and she has written about almost all of them including Halloween, Thanksgiving, Christmas, and St. Patrick's Day.

James Haskins: Haskins has written over 100 social studies informational books, many of which focus on the African-American experience. Two perennial favorites of children are *Get on Board: The Story of the Underground Railroad* (Scholastic, 1993) and *The March on Washington* (Scholastic, 1991).

Patricia Lauber: Lauber has written more than 50 informational science books for children. Topics of particular interest to most children include space, volcanoes, and dinosaurs.

Story
Of all the genres, story is the most used and developed in classrooms. Teachers know the elements of story, both what could happen and what couldn't happen, and they are able to show those elements in literature and teach the elements explicitly in mini-lessons. Even so, many

teachers say they struggle with how to teach elements such as the development of the problem into its logical solution.

An additional complication with story is the variety of story subgenres. While all stories share some specific elements, within the subgenres great differences emerge. You would never confuse a folktale with a contemporary, realistic fiction story. Teachers need to explicitly identify those differences to help students produce the types of story they are working on.

Some story elements appear in all stories. These general story elements and the specific elements of folktales, fairy tales, legends, and mysteries are listed here. You can brainstorm a similar list with your students for the specific elements in story subgenres you teach in your room. Remember to read aloud and have students read many examples of a specific subgenre before you brainstorm your list or expect students to write in that subgenre.

Story Elements
Story includes folktale, fairy tale, tall tale, story innovation, mystery, realistic fiction, and more.

- There is a problem to be solved.
- There is a distinct beginning, middle, and end.
- There is a logical solution to the problem (perhaps multiple attempts at solving it), or it becomes clear why the problem cannot be solved.
- The time organization or progression may be linear, circular, flashback, etc. If it is not linear, it is possible to reconstruct the chronological order of events.
- The characters are connected to the problem and/or solution.
- The setting (time and place) may or may not be critical to the plot.

Subgenre of Story: Folktale
Folktale Elements
Folktales were originally told to show societal expectations before people could read rules.

- Common people or animals are used as main characters.
- Magical elements may be present.
- The plot line is simple.
- There are few characters, with little character development. The story relies on stock characters.
- Most culture groups have used a number for characters and/or events that fit their belief systems. (For example, European folktales use three; Navajo folktales use four.)
- The bad or foolish are punished, and the good or wise are rewarded.
- The purpose is to teach a lesson about breaking rules or how to behave in certain situations.

Subgenre of Story: Mystery
Mystery Elements

- A mystery has a problem to be solved and a culprit to be identified.
- Some mysteries are crimes, and some are not.
- The setting is very important, almost like another character.
- The problem to be solved is more likely to be an intended crime than the problems in other stories.
- A mystery usually leads people to at least one false conclusion.
- It is not usually obvious "who dunnit."
- If it is obvious "who dunnit," it is not obvious how or why.
- The mystery solver is someone who is smarter than others around.
- The mystery solver has some special ability or talent that is used to solve the mystery.
- The culprit is (almost) as smart as the solver.
- The clues are all there to be figured out.
- To figure out the mystery, you have to pay attention to details.
- The mystery solver often uses the scientific method to figure it out.

Subgenre of Story: Fairy Tale
Fairy Tale Elements

Traditional fairy tales illustrated desirable characteristics that the ruling class expected in preliterate societies.

- Royalty and magical beings are used as main characters.
- Common people or animals that talk are used to show how one can rise above one's station.
- The story often involves the element of wish fulfillment for peasant or emerging middle classes.
- Magical elements or events are always a part of the story and how the problem is solved.
- The plot line is simple.
- The characters are stock characters with little character development.
- Most culture groups have used a number for characters and/or events that fit their belief systems. (For example, European folktales use three; Navajo folktales use four.)
- The bad or foolish are punished, and the good or wise are rewarded.

Subgenre of Story: Legend
Legend Elements

- The story focuses on a single character who is someone to look up to, who is memorable, or who is larger than life.
- Some legends have a basis in fact, but even those that don't are assumed to be about real people.

- The story is meant to take place within human history with qualities that make it seem real.
- The story is always associated with a particular place or time in history.
- It may have originally been told orally (as with folktales) or originally written down.
- It may be viewed, like myths, as teaching a lesson that has meaning for the group from which the legend comes.
- True legends can have no events that couldn't actually happen or have been perceived to happen.
- Some stories taught as legends are actually tall tales or myths.

Showing children clear examples of the type of story you want to write will not only help them understand the basic elements that all stories share, but will also provide examples of how story subgenres vary. For example, realistic fiction is a very different type of story from a folktale. A starter kit of some story titles is listed here. Start a class list of story types and add to this chart all year. That way, students will understand the subgenres even better since they will be searching for them as they read or as you read to them.

Children's Stories and Authors Whose Work Supports Story Writing
The following stories have very clear story structures so that you have models to read to children in preparation for teaching the genre elements.

Folktales/Folktale Variants
The Three Little Pigs
Goldilocks and the Three Bears
The Little Red Hen
The Three Billy Goats Gruff

Fairy Tales/Fairy Tale Variants
Cinderella
Snow White

Legends/Legend Variants
Johnny Appleseed
Paul Bunyan
Anasi the Spider

Realistic Fiction (Stories That Could Happen but Didn't; Have All Other Story Elements)
Many of the picture books teachers read aloud to children and the "chapter books" popular with children today are realistic fiction. Here are five well-known authors.

Eve Bunting: Bunting writes beautifully illustrated books on sensitive and difficult subjects. Some of our favorite titles include *The Wednesday Surprise* (Clarion, 1989), *Night Tree* (Harcourt, 1991), *The Wall* (Clarion, 1990), *Fly Away Home* (Clarion, 1991), *Smoky Night* (Harcourt, 1994), and *Going Home* (HarperCollins, 1996).

Betsy Byers: In 1971, Byers was awarded the Newbery Medal for *Summer of the Swans* (McGraw Hill). Children also enjoy reading her more recent series of books about Bingo Brown and The Blossoms.

Beverly Cleary: Cleary created the popular *Ramona* and *Henry Huggins* series which are still popular books with children. *Dear Mr. Henshaw* (HarperTrophy, 2000) is popular with slightly older readers.

Katherine Patterson: Among other wonderful realistic fiction titles, Patterson wrote *The Great Gilly Hopkins* (Avon, 1978) and *Bridge to Terabithia* (Crowell, 1978)

Cynthia Rylant: Rylant has written a wide variety of realistic fiction for young readers including the very popular *Henry and Mudge* books.

Vera Williams: Williams writes beautifully illustrated books for children which tackle contemporary problems in a positive and nonthreatening way. Favorites include *A Chair for My Mother* (Greenwillow, 1982); *Music, Music for Everyone* (Greenwillow, 1984); and *Cherries and Cherry Pits* (Greenwillow, 1986).

Mysteries
Mysteries are one of the most popular types of story for children. Many of children's favorite mysteries are series of books including the *Nate the Great* mysteries by Marjorie Sharmat, the *Cam Jansen* mysteries by David Adler, and the *Encyclopedia Brown* mysteries by Don Sobol.

Circular Stories (Story Comes Back to Where It Began)
Circular stories are fun for children to write because when you know the beginning, you also know the ending. Laura Numeroff's *If You Give a Mouse a Cookie* (Harper Collins, 1985), *If You Give a Moose a Muffin* (Harper Collins, 1991), *If You Give a Pig a Pancake* (HarperCollins, 1998), and *If You Take a Mouse to School* (Harper Collins, 2002) are the best known examples. *One Fine Day* by Nonny Hogrogian (Aladdin, 1974) is another wonderful circular book.

Parallel Stories (Two Related Stories Run Side by Side with Similar Events Perceived Differently, Different Characters, or Different Events)
Meanwhile, Back at the Ranch by Trinka Hakes Noble (1992, Puffin)

Letter
Even in our visually oriented society, written communication is still a critical skill for children to master. We all write fewer letters than we used to, and many of us have switched postage stamps for time stamps to send E-mail messages. This trend is growing, so you must address with students how E-mail messages are constructed and what "netiquette" rules to follow. There are conventions and expectations with the various message formats that go beyond the traditional friendly letter.

Letter Elements
Letter includes personal (friendly letter, thank-you, E-mail) and business (memo, letter to the editor, request for information).

- The writing has a focus, a reason for the message.
- The format varies depending upon the type of communication, purpose, and familiarity with the recipient.
- The writing includes the date it was completed.
- It also includes who it is to and from.
- A request includes "please" and "thank you."
- E-mail conventions include not using all caps, since that is like shouting.
- All communications, even ones in which you disagree with the person, should have respectful tones.
- The content is organized into paragraphs with a topic and related details.

Unlike most of the writing students do in school, letters have personal and emotional content. When they write to E-pals from another school, the purpose for the writing is obvious to them. When they are talking about things important in their own lives, the topics are selected. And because communication is a basic human need, there is less difficulty with this genre than others in the areas of attitude, interest, and motivation.

To avoid the problem mentioned earlier of the same content being taught over and over (for example, "the friendly letter"), schools can decide which communication forms are most appropriate for each grade level. Certainly, various grade levels could have students write friendly letters, but the main instruction could occur in just one grade level.

An interesting format for story using communication that might appeal to some of your students appears in some of the books in this list. The characters tell the story through letters sent back and forth. *Dear Mr. Blueberry* (Simon James, 1996) and *The Jolly Postman* (Ahlberg, 2001) are two examples of this subgenre. Your students might tell a story through E-mail notes they write both parts for or that they co-author with other students.

Children's Books to Support Letter Writing

The Armadillo from Amarillo by Lynne Cherry (Voyager Books, 1999)

Arthur's Pen Pal by Lillian Hoban (HarperCollins Children's Books, 1982)

Click, Clack, Moo, Cows That Type by Doreen Cronin (Simon & Schuster, 2000)

Dear Mr. Blueberry by Simon James (Aladdin, 1996)

Dear Mr. Henshaw by Beverly Cleary (HarperTrophy, 2000)

Dear Mrs. LaRue: Letters from Obedience School by Mark Teague (Scholastic, 2002)

Dear Peter Rabbit by Alma Flor Ada (Aladdin, 1997)

Flat Stanley by Jeff Brown (HarperTrophy, 2003)

Giggle, Giggle, Quack by Doreen Cronin (Simon & Schuster, 2002)

The Jolly Postman by Janet and Allan Ahlberg (Little, Brown, 2001)

Messages in the Mailbox: How to Write a Letter by Loreen Leedy (Holiday House, 1991)

Never Mail an Elephant by Mike Thaler (Troll Communications, 1994)

Yours Truly, Goldilocks by Alma Flor Ada (Aladdin, 2001)

Poetry

Poetry may be the most difficult of all genres to read and to write. Poetry looks different on the page and uses economy of language to express ideas. The look of poetry on the page may be intimidating to students who are puzzled by all of the white space and the non-conventional punctuation usage. Also, where a novel may use a couple hundred words to describe a sunset, a poem may use 10. That economy of language presents special challenges to students.

Poets must have an extensive vocabulary and be highly aware of how words sound with one another. They use words to create images through rhythm, rhyme, or figurative language. Reading "golden orb, eclipsed by cerulean edge" is very different from reading a novel's more extensive description of an ocean sunset. Even more than other genres, writing poetry must first be preceded by years of reading and listening to poems. There is music to poetry that children need to develop an ear for. Cadence is critical.

Poetry Elements

Poetry includes free poetry and formula, or pattern, poetry.

- Word choice is the single most important feature of poetry. Each word is chosen because it is the best one for that spot.
- Poetry is arranged on a page differently from stories or informational writing.
- Poetry always has rhythm and may have rhyme. The author may repeat sounds or words for effect.
- Poetry creates images for the reader through figurative language.
- Poetry sounds good when read aloud.

Children's Books to Support Poetry Writing

There are so many poets writing wonderful poetry for children, it is almost impossible to choose just a few. Any teacher who wants good poetry models for children will want to look at the poetry of Eloise Greenfield, Nancy Larrick, Myra Cohn Livingston, Eve Merriam, Jack Prelutsky, Shel Silverstein, and Jane Yolen.

Multi-Genre Literature

Some selections are clearly and purely in one genre, but others are hybrids. These are called multi-genre pieces, and they are becoming more and more common. Especially with informational books, blending genres can make the message more memorable.

One obvious and well-known example of multi-genre literature is the *Magic School Bus* series by Joanna Cole. There are three levels of text in each of these books (making them tough read alouds!). One level, and the most prominently placed level, is the text that flows as does the text in most books. The words are written in sentences and account for most of the print on most pages. This is the part that you would, in a typical book, read aloud to students. This level of text supplies the main information for the book, though the information is conveyed through a story structure.

A second level of text appears in the speech bubbles. Poor Arnold has a hard time with the adventures Ms. Frizzle involves the class in! He expresses those concerns in the speech bubbles. Other characters respond to Arnold and add to this level of text. Some information is conveyed here, but the main purpose of the speech bubbles is to provide the emotional impact of the adventure. The Frizz NEVER has a speech bubble.

The third level of text appears in what we like to call "factoids." Factoids are the boxes you may have seen in newspapers or magazines. The factoid box provides pure information. In the *Magic School Bus* series, the factoids pull key ideas from the experience and highlight them on posters along the margins or the classroom wall in order to ensure that the key ideas are clear.

Another example of multi-genre literature is on the book list for letter writing models. *Dear Mrs. LaRue: Letters from Obedience School* by Mark Teague (Scholastic, 2002) has text consisting of newspaper articles and letters only from Ike the dog to his mistress, Mrs. LaRue. There are two types of pictures on each page. One type depicts what he describes in his letters; the other is what is really happening and contradicts the other type.

In multi-genre books, if a book is heavier on the history or science than the fiction, the purpose of the book has shifted from story to information dissemination. An example of this kind of blended book for adults caused quite a furor in the literary world when Edmund Morris wrote a biography of Ronald Reagan in which he inserted himself as a character!

In order to determine the predominant and secondary genres of multi-genre literature, you must first identify the author's purpose. If the purpose of a biography is largely to entertain with a tale, then the book is story; if the biography is largely to inform or explain, then the book is informational. Tricky? Sometimes it is. The good news is that you don't need to get it down to the "gnat's derriere" with students. Mostly, you are going to show them how to write within a genre rather than blending genres. Once they have learned the genres, teaching them to blend them is easier. Here are some descriptions of the elements of multi-genre literature and books you can share with children which demonstrate multi-genre writing formats and content.

Multi-Genre Elements
Multi-genre includes two or more genres in the same selection (*I Was There: Discovering the Ice Man* and the *Magic School Bus* series, for example)

- Two or more genres are present with most of their elements.
- One genre is primary; the rest are secondary.
- The primary genre seems to have been written before the secondary genres were added.
- Each genre makes a contribution to the total meaning without redundancy.
- The different genres are integrated so that the reader is not confused about which is which.

Children's Books to Support Multi-Genre Writing

The Magic School Bus series by Joanna Cole and books by Loreen Leedy are multi-genre books. More and more children's authors are using this. Other titles include:

Dear Mrs. LaRue: Letters from Obedience School by Mark Teague (Scholastic, 2002)

I Was There: Discovering the Ice Man by Shelley Tanaka (Scholastic, Inc., 1997)

How Do You Teach the Genres?

The short answer to the question is: show them in books and show them in your mini-lessons. Teaching mini-lessons is such a powerful way to make clear what you want students to focus on. Margaret Mooney showed us how to teach through modeling and guided practice when she wrote *Reading To, With, and By Students* (1990). That structure for how to organize reading instruction works for writing as well. The Writing Block of Four-Blocks clearly is writing to (modeling with mini-lessons), writing with (guided practice and conferences), and writing by children (independent application). That is the framework suggested for helping students learn any new writing skill or process. Specifically, this chapter will talk about those in relation to genre.

Writing to, with, and by students describes the kinds of things both students and teachers do during writing. The lesson examples here show how to conduct a "Read To-Write To" lesson and how to conduct a write to, with, and by lesson. Both formats can be used with many elements, not just genres. One difficult aspect of the Writing Block, unlike with Guided Reading, is that students see a lesson demonstrated but may not practice the information presented in the lesson until weeks later.

Once you know the elements that make up a genre, you can teach those elements in mini-lessons, provide a writing scale for teaching students how to evaluate their own papers for whether the elements are present, and use that same writing scale yourself to evaluate some of their papers to determine the degree of proficiency students demonstrate with the genre.

Where Does It Break Down for Reluctant Writers?

Knowing the elements of a genre builds students' confidence in writing in that genre. Before beginning to teach genre elements, however, it is critical to immerse students in the genre through read-alouds and guided reading selections. Immersion scaffolds instruction for students, sort of like building shelves in their brains to store information on. When you read aloud or students read a particular genre, you talk about the elements you see there. Then, mini-lessons on those genre elements are easier, because you can say, "Oh, remember the folktales I have been reading to you and that you've read in Guided Reading? I was wondering, how do we know it IS a folktale? I started thinking about it and jotting down some of the things I noticed. The first thing, of course, is that a folktale is a story, so it has a problem and solution, characters connected to the problem and solution, a setting, you know, all of those story elements that we listed on the wall a while back. But, this isn't like *Holes* (Louis Sachar,

2000) that we read together. All of the folktales have things that are alike. Let's see if we can think of some."

After having identified the elements in advance to ensure they aren't missed, write some of them in front of students and elicit additional elements from them. If they miss some on your list, you can always tell them that you just thought of another. If students still have trouble identifying elements, go back to reading more and having them read more in that genre. They, and you, will be frustrated in trying to write in a style they are unfamiliar with.

Tips for Genres

- Before children write in a genre, they must have read and/or listened to many examples of that genre.
- Children's skill in writing a specific genre will lag their understanding while reading or listening to that genre.
- Each genre has specific elements that define it. When you understand the genre elements, you can teach them to students.
- Successful writing in a genre requires an understanding of the genre's elements.

Building-Blocks Variations
Building Blocks is the program for kindergarten. It shares many similarities with Four Blocks, but there are also important differences. Most of the writing kindergartners do should be Self-Selected Writing. While teachers read to kindergartners from a variety of genres, they are not expected to learn to write in particular genres.

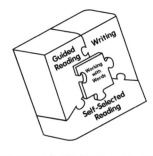

Big-Blocks Variations
Big Blocks is the program for upper grades. Learning to write in a variety of genres is especially important for children in upper grades, and all of the suggestions in this chapter are appropriate for both Four-Blocks® and Big-Blocks classrooms.

Teachers in the upper grades need to read many different genres to their students during teacher read alouds. They also should choose several genres to work with each year during their Guided Reading and Writing Blocks—preferably working on the same genre at the same time in both Blocks with focused writing lessons following the reading of the genre.

Chapter 9
Focused Writing

It is useful to highlight the distinction between self-selected writing and focused writing. These two general ways of teaching students how to write better are both required during the elementary grades if all students are to become good writers. Focused writing occurs occasionally in K–2, but the real benefits of focused writing cannot be realized until after the children have acquired the basic writing abilities and attitudes that only years of self-selected writing can teach them. In writing the Four-Blocks® way, the first three writing cycles rely on self-selected writing, while the fourth and fifth writing cycles rely on focused writing.

Focused Process Writing

Like self-selected writing, focused writing has two versions—a process version (Writing Cycle 4) and a single-draft version (Writing Cycle 5). Unlike self-selected writing, the single-draft version of focused writing instruction is more challenging than the process version. This is because, in self-selected, single-draft writing (Writing Cycle 1), there are no standards other than a willingness to write independently and positive response to peers' writing during sharing. In focused writing, however, students always have standards to meet in their final drafts, so it is easier for them to meet those standards in multiple steps or phases than in a first draft that is also a final draft. It is only toward the end of elementary school writing instruction that most students can reasonably be expected to produce first drafts that are also reasonably proficient final drafts (Writing Cycle 5).

There are a number of important differences between self-selected and focused writing. In self-selected writing, students devise their own topics and how to write about them; in focused writing, the teacher usually gives the class a prompt that limits their writing choices in one or more ways. In self-selected writing, the time before students begin writing their first draft is spent on individual planning—deciding what to write about and how; in focused writing, students also do some individual planning beforehand, but students additionally are taught background knowledge for the ingredients of the prompt (topic, role, audience, genre, and/or starter sentence) that are specified by the teacher. In focused writing, the students may also be guided to do some inquiry or research on the topic, role, audience, or genre before beginning to write.

In self-selected process writing, there is an emphasis on having students learn to revise and edit so that they will acquire individual writing skills and strategies and produce more sophisticated final drafts. In focused process writing, that effort continues, but the emphasis shifts to having students learn how to evaluate their own papers as instances of the specific genres they are learning how to produce. And, in focused writing, there is also the expectation that students are gradually developing automaticity with basic writing skills and strategies so that they will eventually be able to produce more sophisticated and mechanically correct first drafts.

What is the "focus" that gives focused writing its name? Once students have learned what self-selected process writing is designed to teach them, the main purpose of elementary writing instruction becomes to teach the particular knowledge and strategies needed to produce good examples of specific genres of writing, usually beginning with friendly letters or imaginative narratives of some kind. During a focused writing program, you achieve that purpose by using (1) prompt-based writing sessions that are each built around different well-crafted prompts, (2) genre-based writing scales that students use to evaluate their own first drafts, and (3) student revisions guided by their writing scale self-evaluations. All three instructional activities focus your students on how to produce the specific genres of writing that instruction beyond self-selected process writing is designed to teach.

Prompt-Based Writing Sessions

In focused writing, as in self-selected writing, the writing process cannot begin until the student has a first-draft to take through the process. During a focused writing program, students generally produce their first drafts during a prompt-based writing session.

Planning and Teaching Prompt-Based Writing Sessions

During self-selected writing instruction, the objectives are general objectives. That is, almost everything you try to teach during the first few years of writing instruction is important for almost every genre a person will ever write.

In focused writing instruction, some of the objectives are still general, but many are specific to particular genres of writing. As a result, in focused writing instruction, you must move the students beyond self-selected writing and into prompt-based writing to ensure that they learn how to produce the particular genres that focused writing instruction is designed to teach them. Fortunately, students who have had adequate amounts of well-taught, self-selected process writing instruction no longer need much self-selected writing in order to overcome background knowledge and motivation problems. Their background knowledge has increased through their Self-Selected Reading and subject-matter learning, they have learned how to draw on any relevant knowledge they may have when writing, and they have developed enough self-confidence and intrinsic motivation in writing to persevere through whatever problems in writing do arise for them.

To teach students how to produce good examples of the specific genres you are teaching them to write, you must place them in supportive writing situations where they will attempt the targeted genre, will likely be successful at producing it, and will gain knowledge and learn strategies that transfer to other writing of that genre. Use well-crafted prompts and prompt-based writing sessions that are each built around one of those prompts in order to place students in those supportive writing situations.

The Prompt-Based Writing Session Frame

Prompt-based writing sessions include the following phases and steps:

I. Prewriting Phase

   Step 1: Teach or review background knowledge for the prompt.

   Step 2: Present the prompt and answer students' questions about it.

   Step 3: Have students engage in inquiry or research. (optional)

   Step 4: Have students individually plan their writing.

II. Writing Phase

   Step 5: Have students write first drafts.

III. Sharing Phase (Optional)

   Step 6: Have each student share her first draft with at least one other student.

At first it may not seem so, but there is tremendous flexibility in this prompt-based writing session frame. For example, Step 1 (teaching or reviewing background knowledge) can consist of an entire Guided Reading lesson that would ordinarily stand alone. In this way, you can integrate reading and writing by using the Guided Reading lesson as the background knowledge step of the prompt-based writing session. During Step 3 of this integrated lesson, the students can work together in inquiry groups to discuss what about that piece of literature made it so interesting, beautiful, inspiring, gripping, etc. In Step 4, students can be led to plan individually what each will do to make his attempts at that genre of writing interesting, beautiful, inspiring, gripping, etc. Many other variations in the steps of a prompt-based writing session could be presented.

Well-Crafted Prompts

The heart of a prompt-based writing session is the prompt. A prompt is simply a brief, written statement of the writing assignment. Constructing a good prompt is the first thing a teacher does when planning a prompt-based writing session to elicit a first draft from the students. The prompt that is given to the students in Step 2 determines what background knowledge needs to be built for the class in Step 1, what inquiry or research, if any, students do in Step 3, and what planning tactic individual students apply in Step 4.

A good prompt and good decisions about what to teach at each of the four mandatory steps and two optional steps, make for a successful prompt-based writing session. The more prompt-based writing sessions you plan and teach, the better you and your students will become at doing them. Once you become proficient at crafting good prompts and teaching successful prompt-based writing sessions based on those prompts, you will have a powerful tool to help your students learn how to write better.

Analyzing your prompts. Your ability to construct good prompts will come from trial and error, as well as understanding your particular students. It will also help you to think critically about each prompt you construct if you analyze it before using it with your students. Analyzing each prompt you have constructed before you teach the prompt-based writing session based on that prompt will also help you plan each step of that session. Analyzing a prompt simply consists of breaking it down into its ingredients.

A prompt may have as many as five ingredients:

Audience = to whom the writing should be directed

Role = who should seem to be "speaking" the words that are written

Topic = what the piece of writing should be about—its content

Genre = the overall form the piece of writing should take

Starter Sentence = the first sentence the writing should have (Sometimes only the first part of the first sentence is given.)

A writing assignment only has to have one of these five ingredients to be a prompt. In self-selected writing, students are asked to write without being given a role, audience, topic, genre, or starter sentence. The students are free to choose any role, audience, topic, genre, or first sentence they care to. Focused writing, however, uses a prompt to specify or narrow at least one of these five ingredients, and all five may be specified or narrowed by the prompt.

CAUTION: DEAD END!

Four-Blocks Zone

How many of the five ingredients should ordinarily be specified or narrowed by the prompt? There are two DEAD ENDs to avoid. First, it is not necessary to specify all five ingredients in a prompt, since only one will be the instructional focus anyway. It is easier to plan prompts when you don't feel obligated to include every ingredient. Students also have more room for creativity and ownership when they write if the prompt does not limit all five dimensions of their pieces. So, CAUTION: feeling that you must include all five ingredients in your prompts is a DEAD END. However, the opposite tendency is an even bigger problem. Focused writing builds on years of successful self-selected writing by focusing on specific writing abilities that the students still need to acquire, especially that of knowing how to produce good examples of the major genres. Students also need to learn how to write from other perspectives (roles) than their own and how to address different audiences than themselves, their teacher, and their peers. Most importantly, focused writing helps students learn how to write to someone else's specifications, an essential writing ability that future schooling, employment, and issues of life will require from all students. So, CAUTION: feeling guilty about limiting children's freedom in third grade and higher by including more than one ingredient in your prompt is a DEAD END. It prevents focused writing from building on self-selected writing to achieve the essential goals that only it can achieve. In short, feel free to specify or narrow one or all five ingredients in an occasional prompt, but most of your prompts should include two to four of the five ingredients. If some students are not paying close attention to the prompt but instead are trying to continue with the kind of writing they did in self-selected writing, it is better to specify more of the ingredients in your prompts. If most students are attending carefully to the prompt when they write, it is better to specify fewer of the ingredients.

A prompt may also contain written specifications as to how long the piece of writing must or can be and when it is due, but these are not really considered ingredients of the prompt. Students may also be informed in writing as to what will be done with the drafts after they are finished (for example, shared, taken up and graded, self-evaluated, and/or filed in working portfolios/writing folders), but that information is not considered an ingredient of the prompt, either. At first, most prompts used in focused writing instruction (Writing Cycle 4) have two characteristics. First, they usually specify the genre. Second, they rarely specify the exact topic, although they may narrow it quite a bit. Early on in Writing Cycle 4, student papers written in response to a prompt all share the same general topic (for example, a pet), but they will vary in their specific topics (for example, a goldfish, a dog, or a cat). In that case, each student still can decide what specific topic she will write about, based on her background knowledge and interests.

Imagine that you have constructed the following prompt for your third-grade class:

> Write a letter to a friend. Tell your friend what you hope you'll get for your birthday.

Now, let's analyze this prompt into its ingredients:

audience = a friend of yours

role = yourself

topic = what you hope you'll get for your birthday

genre = a friendly letter

starter sentence =

When analyzing a prompt, try to put every important word in one of the five ingredients. Try not to put any word from the prompt in more than one ingredient. If one or more of the ingredients are not specified or narrowed in the prompt, just leave it blank. Since the students will never see the ingredients broken out separately, it is not necessary to word the ingredients in complete sentences. (Do not show students your analyzed prompt because they must learn to write to integrated prompts. Moreover, writing to an integrated prompt is easier than writing to an analyzed one. The analyzed prompt is only to help you, the teacher, decide whether it is likely to make a well-crafted prompt for eliciting first drafts and decide how you could plan each step of a prompt-based writing session to maximize the success and learning your students would experience from writing to that prompt.)

Evaluating your analyzed prompt. After you have analyzed a prompt you are considering for use with your class, it is time to evaluate that prompt. Evaluation of an analyzed prompt you have constructed can lead you to simply accept or reject the prompt, but often the evaluation will lead you to revise it. There are four criteria on which you should evaluate a prompt for use in focused writing instruction.

First, examine the ingredients of topic and genre in your analyzed prompt to determine if the prompt has the characteristics an early prompt has. Decide whether it is likely that all student papers written to your prompt will be of the same genre. If not, revise your prompt to make it clearer what genre the students are to try to produce during the session. It is usually best to be direct in your wording: "Write a letter," or "Write a poem," or "Write a fairy tale." Next, decide whether it is likely that all student papers written to your prompt will have the exact same topic. If so, it may be too sophisticated for students at this time. At first, a successful prompt may narrow the topic, but it probably shouldn't specify it. For example, if your prompt asks students to write about taking a vacation to Disney World®, it is specifying the topic in a way that is usually inappropriate for early focused writing instruction. On the other hand, if your prompt asks students to choose the places they would most like to take vacations and to write about those places, the prompt can be effective because different students will write about different places. Why does it matter? Because during early focused writing instruction, you will still make it possible for students to choose something they know and care about to write on, even though they have much less leeway about their topics than they did during self-selected writing.

Second, if your prompt contains a starter sentence, examine that starter sentence to determine whether it implies an exact topic or a different audience, role, or genre than the prompt otherwise specifies. Starter sentences can help children get started with a draft, but starter sentences can also present problems of interpretation and continuity to children. It is essential that any starter sentence included in a prompt be consistent with the rest of the prompt. If your prompt consists entirely of a starter sentence, make sure that your prompt narrows but does not specify the topic unless your students have done a lot of focused writing. For example, "My favorite restaurant is not too far from where I live." Also, be sure that the starter sentence makes it clear what genre students are to write, unless you do not care what genre they write during this session. For example, "The story of my life began when I was born." If you have a specific topic or genre in mind, it is usually best to tell students directly and not rely on them correctly interpreting the starter sentence.

Third, examine each ingredient in your prompt to determine what background knowledge you will need to build if all of your students are to understand the prompt, have confidence they can write to it, and be able to successfully write to it. This third principle for evaluating your prompt is where you decide what the instructional focus of the prompt is.

Imagine that you have a prompt you have just composed for possible use with your class. You have analyzed it into its ingredients and find you won't need to build any background knowledge for any of the ingredients. You are sure you could just hand out a printed copy of the prompt, and your students' planning and writing would be as successful and enjoyable as if you had done background building (Step 1) and required student inquiry or research (Step 3). What is the instructional focus of that prompt? It doesn't have one! What are students expected to learn from preparing to write and then writing to that prompt? Apparently, nothing specific. Prompts requiring little or no background building should either be discarded or modified to introduce an ingredient of instructional focus.

On the other hand, imagine that you examine each ingredient of your prompt and find you will have to build extensive background knowledge for two or even three ingredients. Again, that probably means your prompt doesn't have an instructional focus because almost everything about the prompt requires instruction. Prompts requiring extensive background building on several ingredients should also be discarded or modified to achieve an instructional focus.

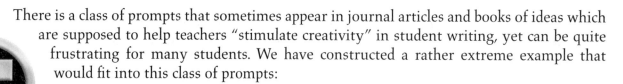

There is a class of prompts that sometimes appear in journal articles and books of ideas which are supposed to help teachers "stimulate creativity" in student writing, yet can be quite frustrating for many students. We have constructed a rather extreme example that would fit into this class of prompts:

> You are an animal from South America who was abducted by aliens from outer space. They were unable to speak or understand your animal language. Write a story telling us how you were able to communicate with them and persuade them to bring you back home. Begin your story with this sentence: "I was resting after eating a big lunch."

Analyzing this prompt into its ingredients yields:

audience =

role = an animal from South America

topic = how, when you were abducted by aliens from outer space who were unable to speak or understand your language, you were able to communicate with them and persuade them to bring you home

genre = a story

starter sentence = "I was resting after eating a big lunch."

The background knowledge that should be taught, or at least reviewed, to prepare elementary students for this "creative" prompt would probably include the following areas:

- the essential elements of a story
- how to write in character
- animals from South America, including what and when they eat and how they rest
- aliens from outer space
- abduction by aliens from outer space
- nonverbal communication
- persuasion

Obviously, this prompt lacks instructional focus for any class of elementary students you have ever known or could conceive of. You would either discard or modify it. How could it be modified to give it an instructional focus?

This prompt could be modified so that the instructional focus would be on an important part of good writing, rather than on subject matter or general information. To that end, eliminate all aspects of the prompt requiring any area of background knowledge in the list other than the first two ("the essential elements of a story" and "how to write in character"). Eliminate the topic-building items of background knowledge in the list because the time spent building knowledge for those topics would not help your students become better writers in general or of a particular genre. Eliminate "persuasion" because it is generally beyond what can be taught successfully to most elementary school students. That would leave you with the choice of modifying the prompt to focus on either "the essential elements of a story" or on "how to write in character." Either of these would be appropriate for a focused writing session.

Arbitrarily choosing "how to write in character" as the instructional focus, you could "modify" the prompt as follows:

> You are the pet of a boy or girl in the third grade. Tell your owner what you wish he or she understood better about you.

Now, let's analyze this modified prompt into its ingredients:

audience = a boy or girl in the third grade

role = a pet you have or would like to have

topic = what that pet might wish

genre =

starter sentence =

If you compare the ingredients of the revised prompt with the ingredients of the original, you see that in modifying the original, you really ended up discarding it and replacing it with a completely new one. The process of thinking about it as a modification, though, probably helped to produce a better prompt than just starting over from scratch would have done.

There are four different types of background knowledge that could be built for a prompt, depending on which of the five possible ingredients the prompt contains and which one of those ingredients is the instructional focus of the prompt. When you find yourself having to build extensive background for the role, the audience, or the general topic, that prompt might be appropriate for writing to learn (writing across the curriculum) but may be of limited value in learning to write (during the Writing Block). On the other hand, a prompt requiring you to build extensive background for how to take on a role in writing other than being oneself, how to write effectively for an audience, or how to write about a familiar topic in an unfamiliar way, can be of significant value in helping your students learn to write better.

Fourth, examine the ingredient of topic in your prompt to decide if that ingredient permits students to write about something most of them are intrinsically interested in. Prompts that do not include the ingredient of topic always provide students with the opportunity to write about something they are intrinsically interested in. Prompts that narrow the topic provide students with one or more general topics of varying interest. It is these general topics that must be scrutinized to determine whether they are likely to be of interest to the majority of your students. It is too much to ask that every general topic contained in a prompt be intrinsically interesting to all of your students. However, by having some prompts that do not include topics and by trying hard to choose interesting topics for your prompts containing general topics, you hope that most of your students are writing about things that are interesting to them most of the time.

Background Building

Once you have a good prompt with an instructional focus that is likely to be interesting for most of your students to write to, you are ready to plan the background knowledge building you will do in Step 1 of the writing session built around that prompt.

The background building you do is directly related to the ingredients of your prompt. There are two kinds of background knowledge for a prompt that students need in order to write successfully to it: knowing about (declarative knowledge) and knowing how-to (procedural knowledge). Knowing about is knowledge that can be "declared" or stated, orally or in writing. Knowing how-to is knowledge that must be shown or demonstrated. For example, if your prompt specifies a role (for example, the President of the United States) your students must take on when writing, you have to make sure they have the two kinds of knowledge necessary to write to that role: (1) knowing about that person and role and (2) knowing how to write from a point of view that is not their own. These two kinds of knowledge are also necessary when your prompt specifies a target audience for the writing: (1) knowing about that person or group of persons and (2) knowing how to write with a particular audience in mind.

Most prompts in focused writing specify the genre, and this ingredient of the prompt is usually the instructional focus of the writing session. Being able to produce a particular genre requires knowing how-to rather than knowing about. When a prompt contains a general topic as an ingredient, students need knowlege about that general topic. When your prompt contains an ingredient requiring procedural knowledge that some of your students may lack, you need to make sure they have that knowledge before planning and writing to that prompt. Likewise, when your prompt contains an ingredient requiring declarative knowledge some of your students may lack, you need to make sure they have that knowledge before planning and writing to that prompt.

Declarative knowledge can be told to students by the teacher or by other students who know it. That is why the background building step (Step 1) of a prompt-based writing session often includes a well-prepared teacher explanation or teacher-guided discussion.

Procedural knowledge always has to be demonstrated or modeled for students. A mini-lesson is always included in Step 1 of every prompt-based writing session during focused writing instruction. This mini-lesson often models some aspect of producing the genre that will be specified in the prompt presented in Step 2. If not, it models some other aspect of writing to the prompt or a strategy for improving the mechanics of the piece of writing.

CAUTION: DEAD END!

In traditional writing instruction, the most common DEAD END to avoid is giving students knowledge about when what they need is knowledge how-to. Telling students what a biography is does not teach them how to write one. A mini-lesson in which your model writing a brief biography will be much more effective than you telling students what a biography is. Show, don't tell!

Presenting the Prompt

The prompt must be presented to the students in written form. The analysis of the prompt into its ingredients should not be given to students. If you present the prompt by handing out a copy to every student, require students to keep them out and open on their desks while they write. If you present the prompt by writing it on the board, every student in the room must be able to see and read it from her seat. If you present the prompt on the overhead projector, every student in the room must be able to see and read it, and there must be enough light in the room for the student to be able to see to write without discomfort. Unless students can easily refer to the prompt while they plan and write, they are more likely to wander into writing that deviates from it in one or more ingredients.

Inquiry or Research

This step (Step 3) of the prompt-based writing session frame is optional. The purpose of this step is to help students overcome a lack of declarative knowledge about the role, audience, topic, or genre in the prompt they will write to. Step 3 is important to add when the background building done in Step 1 for one of those ingredients is not likely to be sufficient for the class. Because Step 3 always involves the students in individual or small-group study, it has the potential to provide deeper background knowledge for a prompt ingredient than Step 1 can build. The trade-off is that the prompt-based writing session takes quite a bit longer to teach when it includes Step 3.

Every teacher is aware of the tradition of having students write about something where their only source of information is an article from an encyclopedia. Many of these papers are thinly paraphrased copies of parts of that article. Step 3 of a prompt-based writing session avoids this traditional trap by guiding individuals or small groups to consult multiple sources of information or to conduct investigations. During focused writing instruction, research and inquiry in Step 3 of a prompt-based writing session is usually done in mixed small groups while the teacher moves around to monitor and offer advice.

Individual Student Planning

Steps 1, 2, and 3 of a prompt-based writing session, if included, are done in order to achieve the maximum possible conformity of background knowledge and understanding of the prompt among the students. There is nothing in any of these steps that encourages students to differ from one another when they write. Step 4 is where student individuality is fostered.

During Step 4, there is no group activity at all. Having students plan in small groups or as a whole class really just means that more background is being built, and students are not given time or guidance to plan individually how they will approach writing to the prompt. This step is frequently skipped or turned into a group activity, but it should not be because it has the potential of making students better writers and making their writing more unique and interesting to them and others.

At the least, to plan, students need some time in the privacy of their own thoughts when they are not permitted to talk with anyone or begin writing. Beyond this minimal encouragement and opportunity to plan, teachers can improve the likelihood and quality of individual planning by imposing a required planning tactic on the students.

There are many planning tactics that teachers can require students to use. Some of the most effective ones are:

- Webbing
- Filling out a story diagram (before writing an imaginative narrative of some kind)
- Brainstorming important words that probably will be used in the writing
- Writing the sentence that probably will be the last one of the paper

Student use of a planning tactic before beginning to write should be timed. Two minutes should be the minimum amount of time allowed for individual planning. Five minutes should ordinarily be the maximum time allowed. Teachers should move around to monitor and support the planning but without doing the planning for a student.

In the experience of many teachers, requiring students to use a planning tactic does help many of them plan better what they will write. It also gets them into the habit of thinking about what they are going to write before they begin.

CAUTION: DEAD END!

The first four steps of the Prompt-Based Writing Session Frame comprise the Prewriting Phase of the session. Step 1 and the optional Step 3 ensure that students have the declarative and procedural background knowledge that they will need to understand and write successfully to the prompt. Step 2 ensures that the students are familiar with the prompt and have had an opportunity to ask questions about it in case they find anything about it confusing or unclear. Step 4 ensures that the students take some time to plan how they will individually approach the writing before beginning. The steps of this teacher-directed phase of a first-draft writing session are crucial to students' success and learning during focused writing.

Unfortunately, there is a student-centered school of writing instruction that thinks teachers are barely necessary, and a teacher-centered school that thinks students learn to write primarily from having their papers marked and graded. Followers of either school are apt to give students the writing prompt to read on their own, without teaching them Steps 1–4. CAUTION, this is a DEAD END! In either case, the students are expected to teach themselves how to write, either just by writing or by later reading the teacher's comments on their papers. In contrast, when teaching writing the Four-Blocks way, it is the Prewriting Phase (Steps 1–4) of the Prompt-Based Writing Session where the teacher teaches students how to write first drafts that conform to the teacher's well-crafted prompt.

First-Draft Writing

During all writing instruction, it is important that students have a comfortable, well-lit, and quiet place to write. All students should have paper and writing implements ready before any of them begin to write. It is also important that they not be allowed to interrupt their writing to ask how to spell words or other questions of the teacher or each other. Focused writing instruction includes process writing, so there will be time later for conferencing, revision, and editing. None of these should be allowed to take place during first-draft writing, however, or the length and students' sense of ownership of first drafts will suffer.

Sharing

This step (Step 6) of the prompt-based writing session frame is optional. Over the years, many teachers have found it helpful to distinguish between "sharing" and "conferencing." While both include having a student allow someone else to hear or see what she has written, conferencing is always done with the purpose of helping the writer improve the draft she shares. During sharing, a writer may receive some feedback, but no systematic attempt is made to make sure that the writer makes use of that feedback during a revision of the draft. On the other hand, conferencing is always part of the preparation for revision. Step 6 of a prompt-based writing session is sharing, rather than conferencing.

Step 6 of the prompt-based writing session frame exists to be used whenever a number of students seem to be writing for the teacher rather than for each other to read. Nothing works better to change a student's sense of audience for writing than having her share her first drafts soon after writing them. Because first drafts have not yet been edited, sharing during Step 6 of a prompt-based writing session should ordinarily be done orally, unless the students have demonstrated the ability to ignore spelling and other mechanical errors in the papers of others they read.

Preventing and Solving Problems during Prompt-Based Writing Sessions

Once you are comfortable with it, the prompt-based writing session frame is a powerful tool for teaching the students who are ready for it how to improve the quality and length of their first drafts. Still, there is always the potential for problems to arise. One common problem with prompt-based writing sessions is pacing: either sessions may become boring or get off-track because one or more steps take too long, or sessions may become frustrating or ineffective because one or more steps are done too quickly. Another common problem is the difficulty some children have transferring what they have learned in reading to their writing. To maximize the effectiveness of prompt-based writing sessions, it is important to prevent or to solve these problems.

Consider the Time Each Step of Your Prompt-Based Writing Session Is Taking

Students who are ready to benefit from focused writing instruction should be able to sustain their writing on a new first draft for at least six or seven minutes, depending on whether the prompt would require that long to complete the assignment. Many third-, fourth-, and fifth-grade classes have done enough writing in previous years, so they are comfortable writing on a first draft for 10 minutes or even longer.

Except for instances when students are required to do extensive research or inquiry, it is important that each prompt-based writing session be completed in one sitting. The maximum benefit will accrue if all of the steps follow one after the other until completion of the session.

If, say, 35 minutes is the allotted time for writing instruction in your daily class schedule, and if you have decided that your class has no need to share first drafts, you want to make sure that you plan the prewriting phase of your prompt-based writing session to take no more than 20 minutes. That ordinarily should be no problem. The exception is when you expect your students to engage in research or inquiry.

Often, the inquiry you have your students do will consist of 10 or fewer minutes of work in small mixed groups. In those cases, you can still usually complete your prompt-based writing session in 35 or 40 minutes. When Step 3 takes longer than 10 minutes, it usually becomes necessary for the session to be spread over two days. It is important to point out that, while optional, having students engage in small-group inquiry groups prior to writing can be a powerful addition that justifies the extra time it takes, even when it spreads the prompt-based writing session out over two days.

The important insight here is for you to pace prompt-based writing sessions so that students get acclimated to staying on task. Do not reward those who procrastinate, spend their time distracting each other, or try to get you or others to tell them what to write or spell words for them. When you give students extra time to complete a step of the session because some did not take it seriously and use their time wisely, you make it even more likely that students will not apply themselves in the future. It is better to "apologize" to them for not giving them enough time and stick to the original time allotment than to give more time.

Integrating Focused Writing with Guided Reading

Because there are so many links between reading and writing, reading can promote children's writing development, and writing can promote their reading development. The materials children read provide models for the drafts they write. Writers benefit from Guided Reading lessons that help them make the most of these models. Likewise, when students learn to control a particular aspect of writing, they are usually better able to process that same aspect when reading. In fact, because writing beyond Self-Selected, Single-Draft Writing instruction is ordinarily more difficult than reading, writing is "overlearning" for reading. In other words, to gain control over an aspect of writing means to learn it better than reading requires that aspect to be learned. Consequently, writing instruction leads to fluency in reading in the areas taught during writing. For example, phonic spelling in kindergarten and first-grade writing help children benefit from their phonics instruction better than they would without it (Clarke, 1988). Also, sentence-combining instruction in writing often leads to improved sentence-comprehension ability in reading (Levine, 1977; Straw and Schreiner, 1982).

In a complete and balanced reading program, writing instruction is really another method of teaching reading. Some children will learn how to read better from good writing instruction than they will from any other reading instruction method. All children will transfer some of their increased writing ability to their reading.

In a complete and balanced reading and writing program, Guided Reading instruction that emphasizes comprehension will help some children understand how writers write and motivate them to want to be authors themselves. All children who are writing regularly will transfer some of their increased reading ability to their writing.

In addition to the general cross-fertilization that will inevitably occur between reading and writing in a successful literacy program, there are special lesson frames that strengthen the mutually supportive relationships between reading and writing.

Reading-Writing Lessons

A reading-writing lesson (Cunningham and Cunningham, 1987) is simply a Guided Reading lesson followed by a prompt-based writing session that builds on or extends that activity or lesson. Here are the parts of the prompt-based writing session that would require special planning during a reading-writing lesson.

Prewriting Phase

Step 1. Teach or review background knowledge for the prompt. The Guided Reading lesson can be seen as synonymous with this step. If the Guided Reading lesson that the prompt-based writing session is based on took place one or two days ago, aspects of that lesson to be built on should be quickly reviewed.

Step 2. Present the prompt. The prompt must be crafted to build on or extend the Guided Reading lesson. For example, if the Guided Reading lesson consisted of completing a discussion web after reading a piece of literature, then the prompt must have a clear and direct link to that web.

Step 3. Have students engage in inquiry or research (optional). If the Guided Reading lesson left students with unanswered questions about the selection they read, the focused writing part of the reading-writing lesson can use this step to have them try to go beyond the original selection to answer those questions. The answers they find would then be included in the writing they produce in response to the prompt. For example, if the students read a nonfiction selection during the Guided Reading lesson, they could do further research on the Internet on the topic of that selection. The writing they do would include some of the new information they gathered during this inquiry/research step of the prompt-based writing session.

Of course, the prompt-based writing session that is the second part of a reading-writing lesson can target genre rather than topic, but that would require the Guided Reading lesson that is the first part of the lesson to target some aspect of the genre or the author's craft, rather than the content of the reading selection.

Writing-Reading Lessons

A writing-reading lesson is simply a prompt-based writing session followed by a Guided Reading lesson. The most common reason for a writing-reading lesson is to increase student interest in the reading they will be asked to do during the Guided Reading lesson. For example, if students were going to read a story set in the arctic or antarctic circle or an article about one or both of those regions, a prompt-based writing session could serve to pique the students' interest in that story or article. The prompt-based writing session could have this prompt:

Explain why you think some people choose to live in the coldest places on Earth.

The background building for this prompt should probably include using a globe to teach the concepts arctic circle and antarctic circle. It should also include teaching less important but more intriguing concepts, such as the 30-30-30 Rule ("When it is 30 degrees below zero Fahrenheit, and the wind is blowing 30 miles per hour, human flesh freezes solid in 30 seconds."). Such a writing session has value for improving writing, but it can also prepare students to read with more interest and curiosity during a Guided Reading lesson than they might otherwise do.

The Focused Writing Process

Prompt-based writing sessions provide students with as much instruction and support as possible in producing first drafts with the ingredients specified in the prompt. Once students have attempted to write to a prompt, however, they always benefit from revising and editing their first drafts in separate steps that allow them to concentrate on just one dimension of their papers at a time.

The editing part of the focused writing process (Writing Cycle 4) is the same as it was in the self-selected writing process (Writing Cycles 2–3), except that students learn how to proofread and correct their own papers for more sophisticated spelling words and writing rules. However, the revision part of the focused writing process (Writing Cycle 4) differs significantly from the way it was done in the self-selected writing process (Writing Cycle 3). In focused writing, students begin revision by using a set of questions or criteria to self-evaluate their own first-drafts. Then, they revise their drafts to bring them into line with those questions or criteria.

Revision during Focused Writing

In the focused-writing process, student revision is guided by having students self-evaluate their first drafts using a writing scale. Writing scales to guide student revision can focus on any ingredient of the prompt or any aspect of good writing related to content, organization, or theme. In the elementary grades, however, the writing scales Four-Blocks teachers train students to use to guide their revisions are always genre-based. This approach eventually leads students to internalize the elements of each genre in a unique way that dramatically increases the effectiveness of their writing.

Genre-Based Writing Scales

A writing scale is a list of questions to answer or criteria that students are taught to use to evaluate their own papers. Each question or criterion receives a "yes" or a "no," depending on whether the paper is judged to answer the question or meet the criterion. A writing scale for a genre is a list of yes/no questions or criteria that concentrate on the key elements of the genre. Developing a writing scale for a genre is tantamount to making explicit what you, as the teacher, look for in deciding whether a particular piece of student writing is a good example of an assigned genre. Providing students with a writing scale based on a genre is the only way to effectively teach them to self-evaluate their writing as instances of that genre. Through repeated self-evaluations, they will eventually internalize a sense of the genre so that they will be able to produce conventional examples of the genre on first draft.

Tips on Rubrics and Scales

There are two important differences between a writing rubric and a writing scale. First, writing rubrics are usually instruments that lead to a grade or holistic score on a three-, four-, or five-point scale being placed on the paper. As such, writing rubrics may be used by teachers and the results shared with students or their parents. In contrast, a writing scale leads to a "yes" or "no" being placed by each question or criterion on the scale. There is no overall score or grade computed for the paper.

Second, writing rubrics usually take account of every major aspect of the paper, including spelling, handwriting, and other mechanics. In contrast, a writing scale is focused on only one aspect of the paper—in this chapter, whether the first draft conforms to key elements of the genre that was specified in the writing prompt.

Writing rubrics are fine for teachers to use but are too complex for most students in the elementary grades to use well. Because a writing scale has a few very specific "yes or no" standards of competence concentrated on one dimension of the paper, even students in grades 1–3 can learn to use a writing scale to self-evaluate their own first drafts. An Editor's Checklist is a writing scale that even first graders can begin learning how to use to proofread and self-correct their own papers. Most third-grade students can usually begin learning how to use a genre-based writing scale to self-evaluate and revise their own papers in order to produce acceptable examples of a genre the teacher is teaching them to write. A writing scale also has the advantage over a writing rubric in that it can be taught to students gradually and systematically because they evaluate their own papers for just one question or criterion at a time, rather than try to assign a grade or score to the paper based on multiple criteria considered simultaneously.

The first criterion or question on a genre-based writing scale should help students learn to address the topic in the prompt when one is specified. While the topic ingredient of the prompt is different from the genre ingredient, a writer is not proficient with a genre unless he can produce it without changing the topic, if the prompt specifies or narrows one. Here is a question that gets at whether the student's paper addresses the topic as well as the genre:

1. Does *my* paper have the same topic as the prompt?

When teaching students how to use a writing scale, it helps to show them papers from another year's class, with the names removed, that have or do not have the same topic as the prompt that students were writing to. This should include papers where the topic was the same as the prompt at the beginning of the paper but where the topic changed at some point in the paper. Help your students understand that writing well to a prompt always includes having the same topic as the prompt.

The remaining questions/criteria on each genre-based writing scale are tied to the elements of the genre on which the scale is based. These elements were presented and discussed in the Genres chapter. In addition to the key elements of a genre, it is always important for students to study how each genre of writing usually begins and ends. These two concerns are also reflected as the last two questions/criteria in the genre-based writing scales used in writing the Four-Blocks way.

The following three genre-based writing scales illustrate how straightforward it is to construct a genre-based writing scale from a list of key genre elements plus the three additional questions/criteria included in each scale.

Writing Scale for a Folktale

1. Does my paper have the same topic as the prompt?
2. Does my story have just a few characters?
3. Are the main characters either animals or common people?
4. Does my paper tell a simple story?
5. Does my story teach a lesson?
6. Does my paper begin like a folktale?
7. Does my paper end like a folktale?

Writing Scale for a Biography

1. Does my paper have the same topic as the prompt?
2. Does my paper have one main character?
3. Does my paper explain why the main character is important enough to write about?
4. Does my paper include several actual events from the main character's life?
5. Do the events I include show that my main character was important?
6. Is it easy for a reader to determine the order in which these events happened?
7. Does my paper begin like a biography?
8. Does my paper end like a biography?

Writing Scale for a Report

1. Does my paper have the same topic as the prompt?
2. Does my paper have one most important idea?
3. Does my paper support the most important idea with lots of facts?
4. Does my paper present the facts in a way that would interest the reader?
5. Does my paper use examples, analogies, definitions, explanations, or descriptions to introduce new ideas?
6. Do the ideas in my paper flow clearly and make sense?
7. Does my paper read like an expert is speaking the words?
8. Does my paper begin like a report?
9. Does my paper end like a report?

Teach students how to use a genre-based writing scale to evaluate and revise their own first drafts. Once you have a writing scale for a genre you want to teach students how to write, it is time to craft some prompts that specify this genre. After you have analyzed these prompts and eliminated or modified any that need it, it is time to plan first-draft writing sessions based on the prompts. Step 1 of each of these prompt-based writing sessions should focus on the genre you are teaching students how to write. Students should read, and hear you read, selections in this genre and should participate in Guided Reading lessons on selections in this genre. More importantly, students should participate in mini-lessons where you write brief pieces in this genre as you think aloud about how you're doing it. End each of these mini-lessons by discussing with students how you went about writing in this genre and answering any questions they ask about that. Step 3 can be used to have students work in small mixed groups to inquire together about one or more short examples of this genre and discuss what makes it unique. Each first draft a student produces during these prompt-based writing sessions is then revised by him using some of the questions/criteria on the writing scale for this genre.

Introduce the writing scale based on this genre by giving students a copy of the first question or two and showing them how to use it to evaluate something you have written. Make sure that what you have written gets a "no" on each question on the writing scale that you are introducing to them. Then, have them help you decide how you would revise your piece so that it would get a "yes" to each question.

Next, students should be given only the first question or two to answer about their draft, and they should probably work with partners to answer it for each other's drafts and then for their own. Do not add more questions to the writing scale until the class is comfortable and accurate in answering the first question or two. After one or two more questions are added, it must not be assumed that the first questions have been mastered. Now students should use all of the questions taught so far to evaluate each other's and then their own drafts. Eventually, students will be able to self-evaluate their first drafts using all the of questions on the scale. During this time, when you respond to the genre ingredient of a student's draft, you should use the same questions on the writing scale that the students are currently using. Having students rewrite papers to get "yes" answers to all of the questions on the writing scale to that point helps them understand and internalize the characteristics of that genre. The first two or three times with a particular genre-based writing scale, the students work with partners to revise their first drafts. After that, they work independently.

Students repeatedly write to prompts that specify the genre, use the genre-based writing scale to self-evaluate their own first drafts, and revise their first drafts until they receive a "yes" on every question/criterion on the scale so far. As you introduce another question/criterion for them to be responsible for as they self-evaluate and revise their first drafts, it helps if you also emphasize that element of the genre in Step 1 of your prompt-based writing session for a time or two. Show them some selections of that genre that illustrate the element the new question/criterion deals with. In your mini-lesson, stress your writing of that element in your piece. For example, the last two criteria on our genre-based writing scales deal with how the genre usually begins and ends. There are seldom rules or formulas for these two questions/criteria. Rather, you have to show students examples and model writing beginnings or endings for them until they have a feel for how to begin and end a piece in the genre.

This process continues with the same genre until no revision is necessary on several first drafts in a row. When that happens, students have internalized the elements of the genre represented on the scale. This process usually takes a long time, with many first-draft and revision sessions, before all students become adept at producing good conventional examples of a particular genre. Consequently, it is best if you teach a genre for a while, move to another genre for a while, return to the first genre for a while, and so forth. In other words, you and your students will maintain your interest in focused writing much better if you work on two or three genres alternately throughout the year, rather than if you try to teach one until you're done with it before going to the next one. Also, you still should have students periodically do some self-selected writing and focused writing that is topic- rather than genre-focused so that you and your students do not become bored.

Editing during Focused Writing

In the focused writing process, editing operates very much as it does during self-selected writing, with two exceptions. Students are generally ready to learn to proofread and correct their own revised drafts for more sophisticated writing rules. Students are also usually ready to learn to use dictionaries to check and correct the spelling in their revised drafts.

Focused Writing the Four-Blocks Way

The focused writing program mainly consists of two complementary approaches that help students learn how to write specific genres. The first approach is prompt-based writing sessions based on well-crafted prompts that specify the genre the students are to write. Prompt-based writing sessions maximize the instruction and support students receive to increase the likelihood that they will produce good conventional examples of the genre specified in the prompt.

The second approach is focused student revision of first drafts written during prompt-based writing sessions. The revision is focused by having students self-evaluate their first drafts using a genre-based writing scale before they begin revising. The genre-based writing scale asks students to examine their first drafts for the presence of key elements of the genre specified in the prompt. The main purpose of students' revisions is for them to bring their revised drafts into line with the questions/criteria on the writing scale so far. The teacher has systematically taught the students to understand and use the writing scale, so they are able to use it to evaluate and revise their own papers for elements of that genre.

By providing the instruction required to make these two approaches successful, Four-Blocks teachers are able to teach all of their students how to produce the major genres of writing in their curriculum. In addition, the students learn how to produce these major genres while continuing to learn how to proofread and self-correct their own revised drafts for increasingly sophisticated spelling words and writing mechanics rules.

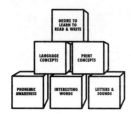

Building-Blocks Variations

Almost all of the writing kindergarten children are asked to do should be self-selected writing. Even when they are asked to write about a topic (for example, science demonstration, classroom event, field trip, or class visitor), they should decide what aspect of that topic they will write about and how they will write about it. In other words, kindergarten students are not ready to benefit from focused writing.

Big-Blocks Variations

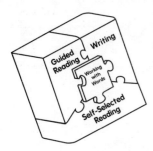

While all of the activities and principles of this chapter are appropriate for upper grades (4+), there are variations that Big Blocks teachers will want to consider. First, Writing Cycle 5 helps students prepare for the writing they need to do when there will be no time or provision for process writing to improve the first draft. In Writing Cycle 5, students are expected to produce adequate first drafts. Of course, this does not mean perfect first drafts. All writers, even the most famous and respected, benefit from or even require multiple drafts to write as well as they can. Writing Cycle 5, however, puts students in the situation where they try to have perfect first drafts since there won't be time to revise or edit the drafts in a separate step. Writing Cycle 5 has students use a genre-based writing scale or self-evaluate their first drafts in preparation for writing other first drafts to other prompts with the same genre. Second, students should be coached to reread each sentence after they write it and edit it for capitalization, punctuation, grammar, etc., before writing the next sentence. This "editing on the fly" is what mature writers usually do and does not disrupt writers with automaticity in basic writing mechanics the way it does most writers in K–3.

 © Carson-Dellosa • CD-104103

Chapter 10
How Do You Provide Extra Support for Struggling/Reluctant Writers?

"I don't like to write. It's hard and it hurts my brain to think so hard."

"When I have to write, I'm thinking about being done because I really don't like to write."

These two quotes come from some struggling writers and sum up the attitudes of many struggling writers. (Tompkins, 2002)

For many children, writing is the most difficult school task they encounter each day. According to the National Assessment of Educational Progress National Center for Education Statistics (1998), 16% of fourth graders could not write at the most basic level. Throughout this book, teacher modeling and scaffolding to help all children become better and more enthusiastic writers has been emphasized. If your daily writing instruction follows the design of the writing instruction outlined in this book, you will have fewer children who view writing as "just one more task to be completed for the teacher."

Some children and some classes of children present special challenges as you teach them to become the best writers they can be. Sometimes, your entire class is composed of struggling or reluctant writers. In the first section of this chapter, you will find two plans for beginning the year if almost all of your children approach writing with dread or ignorance. The Five Steps is appropriate for starting the year with kindergartners or first graders. Can't Stop Writing can be used with older children.

Even if most of your children are making good progress in writing, you will have some children who require extra support if they are going to reach their writing potential.

Tolstoy's famous quote that "All happy families are alike. Each unhappy family is different in its own way" could be paraphrased to contrast good writers and reluctant writers: "All good writers are alike. Each struggling writer is different in his own way."

Because writing is complex, there are many factors that can result in a child—and others—deciding that he is not a good writer. Some children don't consider themselves good writers because of the way their papers look. Handwriting may be barely legible, and there may be numerous spelling, mechanical, and usage errors. Other struggling writers may have reasonable handwriting and some fluency with spelling, mechanics, and usage, but produce mediocre pieces because of their limited world knowledge and vocabularies. Many struggling writers call everything they write a "story" and have no notion about different writing forms and genres. Others lack a sense of audience and purpose as they write. They write for the teacher and because the teacher told them to write! Many children are poor writers because they have a "once and done" approach to writing. Once they finish writing, they consider the pieces done and have neither the strategies nor the inclination to revise. Some children have physical disabilities that make it very difficult for them to write using pencil and paper. The second section of this chapter will describe some remedies for some of the most common writing difficulties faced by writers.

Children who are learning English face some special challenges in writing. Specifically, vocabulary and syntax are almost universal problems for children learning to write as they learn a new language. The final section of this chapter suggests some ways of approaching writing with English language learners.

Getting Them Started When Most of the Class Are Reluctant Writers

You learned in Chapter 3 to always start the year by having children write unedited drafts on topics of their choice. The procedure described in that chapter should get everyone off to a good start in writing—including your reluctant writers. If you have a class of mostly reluctant writers, you may need to build more structure into your Self-Selected, Single-Draft Writing. The Five Steps and Can't Stop Writing are highly structured ways to achieve the goals of getting all children to a successful start in writing. The Five Steps is an approach used by some kindergarten and first-grade teachers. Can't Stop Writing is a success-oriented way to begin writing in upper grades when many children have had negative experiences with writing and are unwilling to write.

The Five Steps

The Five Steps is a modification of The Four Steps (Fisher, 1991). The Five Steps are:

1. Think.
2. Draw a picture.
3. Write something.
4. Write your name.
5. Copy (or stamp or get an adult to write) the date.

Your first mini-lessons in The Five Steps teach children what the five steps are and how to do them. Model this using an overhead projector (or chart) placed so as not to obstruct any child's view.

Begin the mini-lesson with a blank transparency or a piece of drawing paper with no lines on it and say something like this:

"Boys and girls, in a few minutes I want you to do The Five Steps. So you will know what I want you to do, I am going to do The Five Steps and let you watch me. Before I do that, repeat after me what The Five Steps are:

1. Think. (They repeat as you raise one finger.)

2. Draw a picture. (They repeat as you raise another finger.)

3. Write something. (They repeat as you raise another finger.)

4. Write your name. (They repeat as you raise another finger.)

5. Stamp (or copy) the date. (They repeat the one you say as you raise a fifth finger.)

"So, what's the first step? (Several of them should say "think.") All right, the first thing I have to do is think about what I will draw today. Have I seen anything interesting in the past few days? Have I done something interesting that I would like to draw for you? Let me think."

At this point, you should pause and then mention one or two things that you have done or seen lately that you might draw. Make sure they are things that the children can relate to. An example might be for you to say something like:

"I know. We have a new baby in our neighborhood. I went over to visit her when they brought her home from the hospital. Maybe I'll try to draw her asleep in her bassinet."

After mentioning a couple of examples like this one, decide out loud to the class which one you will draw. Then, say something like:

"I've thought about what I'm going to draw. Now, it is time for me to do the second step. What is the second step? (At least a few of them should say "draw a picture.'") All right, now I have to draw my picture."

Pick up a colorful marker—any bright color but black—and begin drawing. Be careful to draw a very simple and primitive picture that will not intimidate the children into thinking they must be artistic to do this step. (Some of us who are less artistic won't have to be careful to do that!) While drawing, tell students what you are trying to draw. You might also say something like:

"I won't draw my picture too big because I need to leave room to write something later."

It is important that you not take too long drawing your picture. When you have finished drawing, put down your colorful marker. Then, say something like:

"I've thought, and I've drawn a picture. Now, it is time for me to do the third step. Does anyone remember what the next step is? (At least one of them should say "write something"; if not, just tell them.) Now, it is time for me to write something about my picture."

Using a black marker, print something about the picture you have drawn, such as:

> We have a new baby in our neighborhood.
>
> This is my new car.
>
> I went to see a baseball game.

At this point, explain to the students that, if they aren't sure what letters to use to spell the words, they should write some letters they know how to write. The children are told that whatever they try to write will be okay. Model for the children what their writing might look like by writing a few letters or squiggles near what you have printed.

Say something like:

"It is time for me to do the fourth step. Does anyone remember the next step after we write something? Now, it is time for me to write my name."

Write your name somewhere on the paper. Tell the children that it is okay if they cannot write their names. They should just put any letters they think might be in their names. Model this by putting one or two letters from your name under or near where you have already written your name.

For the fifth step, model for the children how you want them to get their papers dated after they have finished the first four steps. Many teachers use a date stamp, which the children love using and which brings some finality to their work as they "stamp" the date. In kindergarten, if you do not have a date stamp or don't think your children can use it, have students raise their hands so that you or another adult can stamp or write the date on their papers. First graders can usually stamp the date or copy the date off the board. For the fifth step, model the way you want them to get their paper dated.

Immediately after this mini-lesson, give the children unlined paper and crayons and tell them to begin doing The Five Steps at their seats. Be sure to turn off the overhead projector (or remove your drawing paper) so that the children will not just copy what you drew or wrote. Again, have them repeat The Five Steps aloud chorally after you. For a few minutes at the beginning, tell them they are to think about what they will draw today. The first time or two they do The Five Steps, do not let anyone start drawing until everyone has had time to think. After a minute or two, tell everyone to begin drawing her picture. Walk around the room, encouraging individual children as they move through the steps. From the time the thinking step begins until you end the activity should be about 15 minutes. At the end of each Five Steps lesson, make sure that you can read the name and date on each child's paper. If either is illegible or simply missing, turn the child's paper over and write the name and/or date on the back.

After The Five Steps is over, the children will want to show you and any other adults in the room what they drew and wrote. Take a few minutes and look at what they produced. Encourage everyone but be sure to single out the children for praise who completed all five steps. Circle up the children and let them tell about what they have drawn and written.

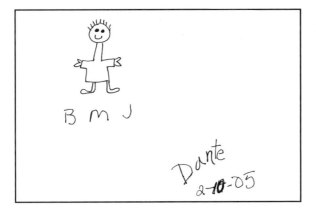

The Five Steps is a variation of driting. Just as when you use driting to introduce writing to young children, teach mini-lessons on how to look around the room to find letters or words to write and how to do sound spelling. Just as in driting, don't give children topics or spell words for them during The Five Steps. Model thinking aloud about what to write about before you begin your writing and "ooh" and "aah" about topics the children have chosen. You should also help them stretch out words and point them to places in your print-rich classroom where they can find words.

It is not unusual for a few children at first to spend all of the writing time working on their pictures, so they only complete the first two steps in the time allotted. It is important not to allow extra time for these children to complete the steps, but rather, encourage them to try to complete all five steps the next time. If you allow The Five Steps to drag on for the children who spend a long time drawing, you will find that they quickly tire of it because it takes so long. The Five Steps lesson works best if it is limited to 15 minutes or so. Help the children gradually spend less time on their drawings so they have time to complete all five steps. How can you help them accomplish this? One way has already been set up by your mini-lesson and the implements you handed out to the children. Having the children draw with crayons or markers that aren't black allows you to have the children raise their hands as they complete their pictures so that you or another adult can quickly walk over and exchange the crayons or markers for pencils. As you make this exchange, you can give them words of praise or pats on the shoulders for having completed their drawings. This practice has the added benefit of helping children to understand that writing is different from drawing. Children will gradually learn to monitor their drawing time by noticing that other children are finishing their drawings and exchanging their drawing implements for writing ones. The personal attention that children receive by exchanging implements is also something that many will complete their drawings in order to receive.

The Five Steps is a successful way to get kindergarten and first-grade children to write early in the year. It apparently succeeds because young children are more willing to decide what they will draw than what they will write. Yet, the beauty of The Five Steps is that once the child has independently chosen her topic for drawing, she has also independently selected her topic for writing.

CAUTION: DEAD END!

If you choose to start your year with The Five Steps, resist the temptation to change the order of the steps. Tradition is so strong that you may be tempted to have the children do steps 4 and 5 before the other three steps. By asking children to write their names and the date on their papers first, we immediately invite resistance from the children who don't feel they can write or who want to be able to write everything perfectly before they will try to write. By having children begin by thinking about and drawing pictures, we ease children into being willing to write for us. Changing the order of the steps is a DEAD END.

Also remember from Chapter 3 that spelling words for kids or telling them what to write about early in the year are both DEAD ENDs. Point out places in the room where they can find words and help them stretch out words. Use some of the ideas from Chapter 3 to help everyone think of what he wants to tell, but resist pleas for you to tell him what to write.

Many teachers post a chart in the room like this one to remind children of the five steps.

```
                    The Five Steps

            1. Think  .。o ⟨?⟩

            2. Draw   🌷✍

            3. Write  I like flowers.

            4. Name   Tracy

            5. Date   March 14
```

Can't Stop Writing

Can't Stop Writing (also called Sustained Silent Writing) is a way to begin writing in grades two and above if you have many children who are unwilling or unable to write. Can't Stop Writing is a "can't fail" approach to begin the year because it has only one essential rule: You can't stop writing until the timer goes off! Can't Stop Writing is always timed. Most teachers set the timer for three minutes to begin with, and then gradually increase the time as children become more willing to write. To teach what Can't Stop Writing is and how it works, model it in a mini-lesson. Here is an example of what that mini-lesson might look like:

Begin your mini-lesson with a chart or a blank transparency with notebook-paper-like lines and margins on it. Write your name and the date at the top. Say something like this:

"In a few minutes, I want you to do Can't Stop Writing. So you'll know exactly what I want you to do, I'm going to do Can't Stop Writing and let you watch me. The first thing I have to do in Can't Stop Writing is to think of what I will write about. So, now I have to think about what I will write while you watch me. Have I seen anything interesting in the past few days? Have I done something interesting that I would like to write about? Let me think."

At this point, you should pause, then mention one or two things that you have done or seen lately that you might write about. Make sure they are things that the children can relate to.

An example might be for you to say something like:

"I know. We have a new Super K-Mart® not far from where we live. The other night we drove over there to see what it was like. It was mobbed. I could write about going to see our new Super K-Mart®."

After mentioning a couple of examples like this one, decide aloud to the class which one you will write about. Then, say something like:

"I've thought about what I'm going to write about. Now, it is time for me to do Can't Stop Writing."

You will need to have some kind of timer that you set for three minutes and then turn so that students can see how much time is left, but you cannot. Pick up a black marker and begin writing. Do not say aloud what you writing as you write. You will find that the children will pay better attention if they are trying to read what you are writing as you write it. Do not write too fast or use such big words that you intimidate them with your writing proficiency—we want them to believe they can succeed at this task. Thirty or forty seconds into your writing, without comment, begin writing,

I can't think of anything else to write. I can't think of anything else.

Then, resume writing as you were before. Your students will probably titter, but you should continue on as if nothing has happened. Perhaps do this again toward the end.

When the timer goes off, unless you are at the end of a sentence, say something like this,

"I get to finish the sentence I am writing."

Then, quickly finish that sentence and put your marker down. Read aloud to the children what you have written (omitting the "I can't think of anything to write" sentences). If the children want to talk positively about what you wrote, encourage them, but keep it brief.

Immediately after this mini-lesson, make sure the children have paper and writing implements. Tell them that it is time for them to do Can't Stop Writing at their seats. Be sure to turn off the overhead projector or remove the chart so that the children will not be tempted to copy what you wrote. Tell them that they should spell the words they know correctly and use correct capitalization and punctuation when they can but that there really is only one writing rule: you can't stop writing until the timer goes off. Tell them that the papers will not be graded for mistakes in spelling, mechanics, or usage. Tell them that, of course, they aren't to write anything that uses foul language or that would hurt anyone's feelings.

Have each student write his name and the date at the top of his paper and put down his pencil. Then, tell students that they have two minutes to think about what they will write about today. During this time, do not let anyone start writing. After the two minutes have elapsed, tell everyone to begin writing. Set the timer for three minutes and turn its face away so that neither you nor they can see how much time is left. Even though you wrote during your mini-lesson on Can't Stop Writing, you should also write again while they write. Later, you will want to circulate and encourage them by "ooing" and "aahing" about their topics and help them stretch out words they need to spell. For the first several lessons, it is probably better to stay out of their space and model writing once again.

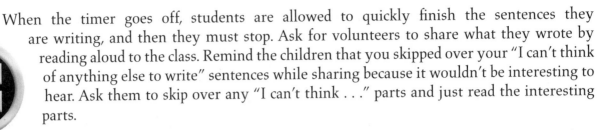

When the timer goes off, students are allowed to quickly finish the sentences they are writing, and then they must stop. Ask for volunteers to share what they wrote by reading aloud to the class. Remind the children that you skipped over your "I can't think of anything else to write" sentences while sharing because it wouldn't be interesting to hear. Ask them to skip over any "I can't think . . ." parts and just read the interesting parts.

After sharing time is over, have students check to make sure that their papers have their names and the date at the top. Take up the children's papers for filing in their writing folders or portfolios.

Staffon   2-25-05   My friends name is James. I play with him atl the time. We play basketball. he tike to play with me to. I like my best friend. We be nice. I tike to come over his house. I invite him to my birthday sometime.

Do Can't Stop Writing regularly until all of the children are sustaining their writing for three minutes. Eventually, add a minute until the students can sustain their writing for four minutes. After that, gradually add a minute at a time until the children are able to sustain their writing for six or seven minutes. How long will it take to increase a class's Can't Stop Writing time from three to six or seven minutes? It will depend on how much self-selected, single-draft writing the students did in years past, but it often takes several weeks and could take months if your children have had many negative experiences with writing in the past.

Four-Blocks Zone

CAUTION: DEAD END!

Be careful not to give rewards or pick winners. The Can't Stop Writing lesson framework for getting children to engage in Self-Selected Single-Draft Writing exists to help all of the children develop self-confidence, intrinsic motivation, and independence in writing. Consequently, you must avoid doing anything that can undermine a student's self-confidence or intrinsic motivation in writing. The quickest way to hinder the development of these essential attitudes is to give rewards and pick winners.

Rewards hinder intrinsic motivation from growing because extrinsic motivators can easily overwhelm intrinsic motivation. Only the children who already have strong intrinsic motivation to write will continue to like to write for its own sake after being rewarded for writing. The goal is for children to be willing to write without being rewarded.

Likewise, teachers who identify "winners" (the best writers, spellers, or handwriters) are implicitly, but clearly, telling the other children that they are not so good. This practice has the curious effect of building the self-confidence of those who already have the most and subtly telling those without self-confidence that they are right in not believing in themselves as writers.

Resist the temptation to spell words or give students topics during Can't Stop Writing. Do, however, model stretching out an occasional big word and how to use the Word Wall and other print in the room to help spell. Use the ideas in Chapter 3 to cope with the "I ain't got nothing to write about" problem.

Remedies for Common Writing Problems

Once you get students started writing, you will notice those for whom writing is particularly difficult. Observe them as they write and look at their writing. Ask yourself:

"What seems to cause them the greatest difficulty writing?"

Children who don't write well usually have many problems, but trying to deal with them all at once will probably not get you or them anywhere. What one problem could you tackle that would visibly improve their writing? Tackle that problem and ignore the others for now, and you will notice almost immediate improvement. Here are some common problems and do-able solutions.

Terrible Spellers

The writing difficulty most commonly observed by teachers is spelling. Children who are very poor spellers seldom write willingly or well. The third chapter discussed having a Word Wall of high-frequency words, modeling using that Word Wall while writing, and requiring that students spell correctly the Word Wall words in their writing. That will help most of your students but not students who misspell most of what they write. Children who do not spell well often spell all of the words phonetically—assigning a letter to each sound. You can usually read most of what they write. Can you read these sentences?

> I cud not wat for my berthda to cum. I wil hav a parte. All
> my frends wil cum.

Did you understand that this child is eagerly anticipating her birthday and her party? Many children write text you can read with every other word spelled incorrectly. Older writers have been doing this for years, and it is their habit. (This may happen if children are encouraged to spell words phonetically for several years without also receiving instruction in how to spell high-frequency words and common English spelling patterns. Encouraging children to invent or sound spell is only a successful beginning writing strategy if children are also given spelling instruction and expected to apply what they are learning as they write.)

Spelling is obviously this girl's greatest need. How can you help solve this problem? In years past, there would not be a simple solution to this problem, but there is today. Any good word processing program with a spelling checker will pick up most of the misspelled words and correct them. Children who have spelling as their greatest difficulty should type their first drafts on the computer and then run the spelling checker.

The spell checking program will help make the piece more readable, and if you combine this with the use of a personal Word Wall, the child will—over time—become a better speller. To make a personal Word Wall, take a file folder and grid off the inside with room for words. Leave much more space under the letters like s and t than you do for x, y, and z. Each time this child writes and runs the spelling checker, let the child select one or two words to add to her personal Word Wall. Have the child tell you the chosen words, and write them on that child's Word Wall with a permanent marker. (Do not let the child write these words herself unless you are absolutely sure she will spell them correctly and put them in the right place.) No matter how many words are misspelled, do not let the child add more than two. When the child goes to the computer to write, she should open the file folder and review the words already there. This will take some time because the spelling of some high-frequency words, such as what (**wut**), was (**wuz**), and have (**hav**), is probably automatic, but the child should be trying not to have any of these words show up when it is time to check spelling. Each time the child writes, the text written that day is spelling checked and one or two words are added to the personal Word Wall. Across many writing days, the child's spelling will improve. The child will delight in spelling have correctly and "not letting the computer catch her on that one."

My Word Wall Words

Aa	Bb	Cc
ate ask and apple	baby blue	cup candy cheese

Dd	Ee	Ff
dog down day desk drip	enter	frog funny feet

Name _____

In addition, the first draft that child chooses to publish will have many fewer spelling errors. (Homophones, such as **to/two/too** and **sail/sale**, may still be misspelled and need to be fixed by the teacher.) This will make the revising, editing, and publishing steps much less frustrating for both child and teacher, and the child's attitude toward writing will show gradual improvement.

What if you don't have a computer with a spelling checker? Surely, you can get one. Many people donate older computers to schools, and the latest model is not needed. You don't need an Internet connection or any other fancy pieces. If you decide that the computer/personal Word Wall solution will help one of your children, you can get the computer to accomplish this. Is it fair to let this child write at the computer while the others write with pencils and paper? Yes, it is, because "fair" means giving every child what she needs most, not giving every child the same thing. If you have lots of children who want to use the computer, you might get another "old" computer or two and let children rotate days on which they get to write on the computer. Perhaps your class goes to the computer lab once or twice a week. Maybe having some children write their first drafts would be more worthwhile than some of the game/worksheet activities found on computers in many computer labs.

If you have a child or two for whom spelling is the major writing problem, writing on a computer with a spelling checker will greatly alleviate that problem. Beg, borrow, or yard sale shop, and you can find the basic technology you need!

Children with Unreadable Handwriting

Some children's handwriting is so awful that you cannot read what they write. Some teachers suspect that some children use this poor handwriting so that no one can read what they write! Regardless of their motivation, children with terrible handwriting don't usually like to write, and they are almost always embarrassed to have anyone see their writing. Again, a basic computer with a word processing program is probably your best solution. (Children don't have to know keyboarding to write on the computer. One of the authors of this book "hunts and pecks" and is a very prolific writer!) Writing on the computer will not improve handwriting, but most writing in college and in the workplace is now done on computers. Children with terrible handwriting will be better writers if allowed to do first drafts on the computer. No need to develop a personal Word Wall—unless you discover that the handwriting was hiding terrible spelling. Then, you can use the procedures just described to help the child become a better speller while removing the handwriting hindrance to writing.

Children Whose Writing Lacks Any Sense of Mechanics and Conventions

Some children write with very little or no punctuation or capitalization. They also might write exactly the way they talk and use many nonstandard English structures. The writing of these children is usually readable, but hard to read, and the editing task seems enormous. Here is an example. Have you seen this kind of writing before?

> my frend and i we was walking down the stret when we seen a big black dog with a broke leg he was in pain and looked pityful we ran to the vets and told him what we saw

Clearly, the biggest problem this writer faces is the lack of any sense of sentence or punctuation. Standard written English is also a problem, but tackling that should probably wait until some sentence sense and punctuation is developed. (There are a few spelling errors, but sentence sense and punctuation are more obvious problems. Once the child develops some sentence sense, the computer spelling checker/personal Word Wall might be the next problem you tackle.) This child needs a personal Editor's Checklist that begins with the most basic rules. For children like this, you need to emphasize the positive, and the items on your checklist need to be stated affirmatively and added when the child can accomplish these.

As often as you can, preferably at the end of each day's writing, do a quick "thumbs-up" edit activity in which you read each sentence with the child and give him a thumbs-up for each sentence that makes sense. Remember, at this time, you are only reading for sense—ignoring all nonstandard English and the lack of punctuation (as hard as that is!). This piece contains three sentences, all of which make sense.

> my frend and i we was walking down the stret when we seen a big black
> dog with a broke leg
>
> he was in pain and looked pityful
>
> we ran to the vets and told him what we saw

Read these sentences with the child, stopping at the end of each sentence and giving him a "thumbs-up" for each sentence that makes sense. If, on another day, he has a sentence that doesn't make sense, give him a "thumbs-down" and help him fix it. When you think the child is able to read his piece one sentence at a time and check for sense, let him read the sentences and be his own "thumbs-up/thumbs-down" editor, and brag on the progress he is making. When the child accomplishes this most basic goal, begin his personal Editor's Checklist with a statement such as:

> 1. I can read my sentences for making sense.

This checklist can be a page in his notebook or can be taped to his writing folder.

On the day after you begin his checklist with this "I can" statement, tell him you want him to read his sentences one at a time for making sense and then check to see if there is ending punctuation at the end of the sentence. (As you were reading the sentences together for making sense, the child may have added ending punctuation without your prompting. Many children don't put ending punctuation because they have no sentence sense; they don't know where one sentence ends and the next one begins. One confused writer finished his writing each day by going down the page and systematically putting a period at the end of each line! Once in a while, he lucked out and the end of the line coincided with the end of a sentence.)

A child who is writing like this probably won't need many question marks or exclamation points, but as you are reading each sentence with him, point out any questions or exciting statements and praise him for varying his sentences! When the child can read most sentences and determine whether they make sense and include appropriate ending punctuation, add #2 to the checklist.

> 2. I can check for ending punctuation. . ? !

Continue to add items to the checklist. Beginning capitals and a capital for I are obvious next items that will improve this child's writing. Once the child develops some sentence sense, the writing will look better, and he will write more willingly. You can then decide to tackle the spelling or conventional English usage issues.

Teaching children whose spoken English is different from standard written English is a difficult, but doable, task. Some computer programs have grammar checker which will pick up common problems, such as lack of subject/verb agreement, double negatives, and incorrect or unnecessary pronouns.

You might also want to start a chart such as the following and add to it as you notice usage issues in the child's writing. Again, you need to add items gradually to the chart and not expect change to occur overnight. Most of us wrote the way we spoke when we were in elementary school. Some of us were lucky enough to have parents whose spoken English was closer to standard written English. You must be careful about telling children their speech patterns are "wrong" when these are the speech patterns the significant adults in their lives use. It is much better to make a distinction between the way we talk and the way we write.

WE MIGHT SAY ...	BUT WE WRITE ...
we was walking	we were walking
we seen a dog	we saw a dog
he ain't home	he isn't home
he don't have no money	he doesn't have any money

As you tackle any of these problems, the main traits you will need are patience and perseverance. You won't solve these problems overnight, and you can't solve all of the problems at the same time. But, if you set priorities and work toward accomplishing these priorities day in and day out, writers who lack basic mechanics and conventions will produce much more readable first drafts and feel better about themselves as writers.

Children Who Lack a Sense of Audience or Purpose

This is a very common problem if children have always been writing for the teacher. Starting out the year with Self-Selected, Single-Draft Writing and letting children share what they write will eventually alleviate this problem. When children share, model telling something you particularly liked and asking a question. Once the children get in the habit of responding that way, let them take the lead in responding to each child's writing.

It is not uncommon for some children to write very boring, "safe" text early in the year. Here is an example. Have you taught children who write like this?

I went to the mall. I went with my friend. We had fun at the mall.

Now, if this were a first grader early in the year, you would be quite pleased, but what if this child were in third or fourth grade and writing like this? Why would a child do that? My guess is that the writer of this safe, boring text has a "write what you can spell" rather than "what you want to tell" approach to writing. Notice also that all of the sentences are "safe" sentences. Not a chance that a punctuation mark other than a period or a capital letter other than for the first word of a sentence will be needed here!

A child who writes like this is writing something no teacher can find anything wrong with, but it is hard to find anything positive to say. When you have trouble making a sincere "I liked" comment, remember that you can always like the topic. Thus, your first response might be, "I liked the fact that Billy wrote about the mall because I like to go to the mall, too."

Let another child tell what she liked:

"I like to go to the mall with my friends, too."

Then, ask a question.

"Billy, who was the friend you went with?"

When Billy has named his friend, invite the children to ask questions:

"When did you go?
"How did you get there?"
"Did you buy anything?"
"What did you do there?"

Let Billy answer the questions and then comment that everyone liked what he wrote but she wishes he had told more specifics and details. If you use the procedures described for getting children to write willingly, including the informal sharing with praise and questions, children will soon start writing more interesting pieces. They now have an audience—the teacher, and more importantly, the other kids in the classroom. When children learn that what you value most in their writing is the meaning, they will gradually give up their safe, boring sentences and start writing for a purpose—to actually tell something important to them—and for an interested audience.

Children with No Knowledge of Forms or Genres
You learned in Chapter 8 that children need to write in a variety of forms and genres. As you observe the writing of your children during the first several weeks of school, you may notice children whose writing is all personal narrative or "all about me" writing. Again, this is fine if the children are first graders, but older children should have some variety of ways to write about different topics.

The first thing you need to think about if you notice this problem is what kind of writing you are doing in your mini-lesson each day. Are you doing only "all about me" writing? It is natural for us to write about ourselves and our families, pets, likes, and dislikes as the children are getting to know us at the beginning of the year, but we need to branch into some other genres fairly soon, or we will, unintentionally, give the children the idea that this is the only kind of writing we expect to see.

Before you begin teaching genres, you can model the writing of some genres in your mini-lesson:

"I love poetry. Today, I am going to write a cinquain about my cat."

"I need to write an article for the school newsletter about the field trip the third graders will take next month. I will write it for my mini-lesson, and you can help me make it as clear and interesting as possible."

"I saw many of you at the softball game last night. I am going to pretend to be a reporter and write a newspaper article about the game."

"My son has a pet rabbit. We were researching rabbits on the Internet last night. I am going to write a report telling you the most interesting facts we learned about rabbits."

Once you begin to do focused writing units on genres, all of your children will learn to write in particular genres. Before that, however, you can model writing in a variety of genres so that your children understand that you value many different kinds of writing. Be sure that when a child shares writing that is a different genre, you comment positively on that.

"I loved your poem. I am so glad to see we have another poetry lover in the class."

"That sounded like it could be a newspaper article. Have you thought about being a reporter when you grow up?"

"I loved your story, which was really a science fiction story. I bet you like to watch science fiction on TV and in movies."

Model and "ooh" and "aah" about a variety of genres, and you will be surprised at what many of your children can write.

First-Draft Only: "Once and Done" Writers
In spite of all the emphasis placed on process writing in our schools across the last decade, many children have only experienced first-draft writing. If children come to you thinking that their first drafts are the only kind of writing they will do, you need to change their minds about that. Even though you are not doing the writing process during the first few weeks or months of school, be sure children know this is where you are heading. Here are some things you can do while your children are in Cycle 1 Writing to prepare them for the writing process:

- Show some published pieces you have saved from previous years (or borrowed from another teacher).

- Invite the children to bring in books or other published pieces they have done in previous school years. How many children have anything to bring will let you know how much writing process they have actually experienced!

- Bring in a guest author and/or editor. (Suggestions for finding a local one are given in Chapter 5.) Have the guest bring some first drafts and published copies and talk about the revising, editing, and publishing steps every published piece goes through.

- Tell the children to save all of their first drafts they are working on during Cycle 1 because they might want to choose one of them for their first publication.

- Begin your Editing Checklist and explain that they will soon be publishing pieces, so they will need to learn to become editors for themselves and each other.
- Occasionally comment that one of the pieces shared would make a "wonderful book" once we get into publishing!
- Take a piece of your writing through the writing process before you begin having your children publish pieces. If you let them watch you write the first draft of the Field Trip piece for the newsletter, let them help you revise it (make it EVEN better) and edit it. When they take the newsletter home, have them brag to their parents about what they did to help you make it more interesting, clearer, and nearly perfect.

If you let the children know early on that revising, editing, and publishing are all part of writing in your classroom, most will get over their "once and done" attitudes before you expect them to begin publishing.

Children Whose Writing Lags Way Behind the Rest of the Class

In almost every class, once you begin publishing, you will have a few children whose writing is really not editable. (Like love, this is hard to describe, but you will recognize it when you see it!) Although you generally don't begin publishing until almost all of the children are writing things that are "readable," the "almost all" leaves a few children whose pieces are collections of letters with a few recognizable words and very few spaces to help you decipher the letters from the words! You might say these children just aren't ready to publish and that they should just continue producing first drafts. The message that most children would get from being left out of the publishing process is that, just as they thought, they can't write! Once you begin publishing, you need to include everyone in the process. Some children will have more published pieces than others. Some authors are more prolific than others! The goal is not for everyone to have the same number—in fact, don't count, and try not to let the children count. The goal is, however, for everyone to feel like a real writer because she has some published pieces.

Once you begin publishing, work with the most avid writers first, but when most of them have pieces published and are on their second round of first drafts, gather together the children who have not yet published anything. Help them choose pieces they want to publish and then give them the option of reading or telling what they want to say. Let the others in the group make suggestions for revision and make notes of what each child wants to write and the revision suggestions.

Then, sit down individually with each child and help him construct his piece. Get him to tell you again what he wants to say. As he tells, write his sentences by hand or type them on the computer. Once the sentences are written, read them with him several times to make sure he knows what he has said. Then, cut apart the sentences and have him illustrate each one and put them together into his book! Now—like everyone else—he is a real published author, and he will approach the second round of first-draft writing with renewed vigor—confident that he, too, can write!

CAUTION: DEAD END!

Notice that here you were willing to do something for children that you wouldn't ordinarily do for them because you don't want them to feel they can't keep up with the rest of the class, and you want them to have published pieces that are readable by the other children. However, there are two real dangers—two DEAD ENDs—that you need to beware of.

First, it is always a DEAD END to let a child dictate a first draft rather than writing it. For the first couple of years of good writing instruction, there are no standards for first-draft writing. So, every child can write a first draft if there are no first-draft standards. The only way a child can fail is to be unwilling to write.

Second, it is a DEAD END to continue to edit for a child in any area where that child has become able to take the responsibility. It is all right to do something for students they really can't do for themselves. You do that for all of your children when, after they edit their papers, you fix things they are not yet ready to fix themselves. However, when helping children whose writing isn't editable to publish, it is important to look for anything the child can edit for and have the child do that much himself. For instance, one of the first things a child can do in editing is to find and fix Word Wall words in the first draft that are misspelled. So, even if a child's first draft is not editable and during publishing you are letting the child dictate to you what she was trying to say in her first draft, when the child says a word that is on the Word Wall, have her find it and write it, type it, or at least tell you how to spell it. In other words, gradually turn over responsibility for editing to this child rather than allowing the child to depend on you. "Ooh" and "aah" at the child's every sign of independence in editing.

Children with Physical Limitations

Mainstreamed into most classrooms today are children with a variety of physical limitations that make writing difficult or impossible. Children with limited vision often cannot write with paper and pencils. Children with speech difficulties often find writing and sharing their writing arduous. Children with cerebral palsy and various other physical problems may not be able to write with pencils and paper or even with the normal computer keyboard. This is an area in which special computer devices and programs are an absolute necessity to allow these children to learn to write. It is even more critical that these children learn to write because many lack fluent speech, and being able to write gives them a way to express themselves and participate in classroom life. Here are some of the computer assistive devices and software available now. No teacher can be expected to know the specifics of all of the devices available. What you do need to know is that if you have a child with a physical disability that makes writing in the normal way impossible, there are devices that will allow this child to write. Also, by federal law, the child is entitled to have access to these devices, regardless of the cost. If you need help to make writing a reality for a physically disabled student, contact your administrator or special education coordinator. If you need support to get what you need, contact the parents and let them know what is available and that their child is entitled to have it.

Computer Assistive Devices and Software

Co: Writer (Don Johnston)

Co:Writer is a talking word-prediction program. Based on what the child has written and the first few letters of the next word, it predicts what the whole word will be. Children can click on the word, and it becomes part of the text. It also contains Flexspell which translates phonetic spelling.

Write: Outloud (Don Johnston)

Write: Outloud is a talking word processor which gives immediate speech feedback as students type words, sentences, and paragraphs. Its spelling checker includes a Homonym Checker that recognizes homonyms and offers definitions so that children can choose the correct words. Text can be read back to children. This program is particularly helpful for children with visual impairments.

Draft Builder (Don Johnston)

This program helps children organize ideas through a variety of visual maps. Speech feedback is included.

IntelliTalk II (Intellitools)

This talking word processor combines graphics, text, and speech. A variety of templates and overlays are included to produce different kinds of text.

Kidspiration (Inspiration)

Based on Inspiration, but easier to use, this program integrates pictures and writing to help children develop visual maps to connect and expand ideas. These maps, along with audio support, help children write organized text.

Special keyboards and other devices. For children who can't use a regular keyboard, there are special keyboards, switches, and eye gaze pointers that allow children with limited mobility to word process and create text.

Children with Little Prior Knowledge and Vocabulary

Some children are limited in their writing because they just don't know very much about the world and lack the vocabulary to write about what they do know. This is a problem for many children whose only language is English, but it is a particularly acute problem for English Language learners. Solutions for this problem are described in the English language learners section that follows, but remember that English only children may also have this problem, and the solution is the same.

English Language Learners

Anyone who has ever tried to learn a new language knows that the most difficult task in that new language is to write. When reading in a new language, we only have to recognize the words and language structures and think what they mean. When writing, we have to produce the words and the syntactic patterns in which they go together. Many adults who took language courses in college or high school dreaded the part of the test where they were asked to write a paragraph or two in the new language, and the attempts were often returned with many red marks! It is too bad that, in many cases, the only connected writing students were asked to do was on a test. Teachers used it to assess their understanding of the vocabulary and syntax of the language. Because it was on a test, it affected the students' grades, and it was hard to view as an "opportunity to learn!" Had students been asked to write in the new language as part of their daily learning of that language, without the pressure of a test grade, many of them would be more able and fluent in that language today. Writing is a way to learn a language. Because writing is external, it is a way for the teacher to see what misunderstandings students have and help give them helpful feedback.

Children who are learning English will learn it faster if they are encouraged to write in English. That writing, however, must be supported, and any latent "teacher" notions you might harbor that the writing should approach perfection must be put aside. Writing is hard when you are writing in your first language and extra hard when the syntax and vocabulary are unfamiliar to you. When helping English language learners write, teachers need to put on their "coach" and "cheerleader" hats, celebrate small victories, and turn a blind eye to "all of the things that need fixing." This is not easy for most teachers to do, but if you can, you will be rewarded by watching your English language learners learn to write and make more rapid progress in their mastery of English. If you want your English language learners to become English speakers and writers as quickly as possible, you will put your red pen away and your smiling face on and see writing as one more way for them to learn English. (End of sermon!)

English language learners need to participate in Self-Selected, Single-Draft Writing as outlined in Chapter 3, just as everyone else does. They need to share their writing and receive both praise and questions about what they write. When you move into Cycle 2 and begin publishing, they may need more help from you than children whose first language is English. You may want to use the suggestions listed in the Children Whose Writing Lags Way Behind the Rest of the Class section to help them produce published pieces they can be proud of.

The two most difficult areas of writing for English language learners are syntax and vocabulary. The remainder of this chapter will suggest practical strategies for supporting writers in these two areas.

Sentence Frames
Syntax is the way words go together to make a sentence. Different languages have different syntaxes. In Spanish, for example, adjectives follow nouns in sentences. The Spanish equivalent of *I have a big dog* might be *Yo tengo un perro grande* (I have a dog big).

To write in English, children need to become familiar with English sentence order and other syntactic conventions. They also need to develop English vocabulary. Using a variety of frames and models can help them to learn this. The simplest frames are sentence frames. Some examples are given here, and you will be able to come up with many frames that fit your students and your curriculum.

Basic Sentences Frames
When working with any of these frames, you will want to follow four steps:

1. Provide an experience.
2. Talk about it and create a list of words.
3. Model writing and then drawing.
4. Have the children write and then draw.

Here is a very simple example for early in the year with a class of children (of any age) who are just beginning to learn English.

Step 1

Experience—The teacher brings in a variety of fruits. The teacher and the children sample the fruits and talk about them. They use the English name for each fruit, and children may share the name for that fruit in their first language.

Step 2

Talk and List—The teacher and children talk about the fruits and create a simple web with the different fruit names and simple pictures.

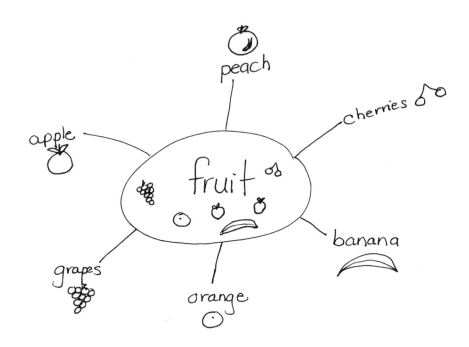

Step 3

Model—The teacher gathers the children together and models drawing and writing a sentence about one of the fruits on unlined drawing paper. She writes:

> I like bananas.

She doesn't read this as she is writing but encourages the children to read what she is writing and figure out the word bananas. After the sentence is written, the teacher and children read it together chorally. The teacher draws a simple picture of bananas and writes her name on the driting.

Step 4

Children Write and Draw—The children are given drawing paper. They copy the sentence frame:

> I like

Next, they finish their sentences with their favorite fruits, copying it from the web. They illustrate their writing and put their names on their papers.

Some of you may consider this focused writing lesson too simple, and it may be too simple for your English language learners, but it is the level that many children just learning English need in order for all children to be successful and develop positive, confident attitudes toward writing. Many teachers bind the pages each child creates into class books. Children love reading and rereading about themselves and their friends.

The basic steps of this lesson can be repeated again and again with a variety of experiences and with sentences that become more complex as the lessons go on. Here are some other examples:

1. Experience—Vegetables
2. Talk and List—Vegetables
3. Model—I like **carrots** and **cucumbers**.
4. Children Write and Draw—I like _____ and _____.
   (Simpler: I like _____. More complex: I like to eat _____ and _____.)

1. Experience—Actions (march, run, jump, etc.)
2. Talk and List—Actions
3. Model—I can **run** and **jump**.
4. Children Write and Draw.—I can _____ and _____.
   (Simpler: I can _____. More complex: I can _____, _____, and _____.)

1. Experience—Photos of places in the community
2. Talk and List—Places in the community
3. Model—I went to the **library**.
4. Children Write and Draw—I went to the _____.
   (More complex: On Saturday, I went to the _____.)

1. Experience—Photos of family members brought from home
2. Talk and List—Brother, sister, mom, grandfather, etc.
3. Model—This is my **Uncle Tim**.
4. Children Write and Draw—This is my _____.
   (More complex: This is my _____ and my _____.)

Sentence Combining Frames

Once children have gained control of some basic English syntax, you may want to give them some instruction in sentence combining to help them learn to write more complex syntax. Again, you want to start with an experience, have the children talk about the experience, and create some kind of graphic organizer with the words. You can then model writing two simple sentences and combining them into one.

Here is an example for the topic animals:

Step 1

Experience—The class has been learning about mammals. They have watched many videos and researched mammals on the Web. They have read simple books about mammals, and the teacher has read aloud a variety of books.

Step 2

Talk and List—The teacher begins a chart to help them summarize what they have learned about mammals. Different children contribute ideas to the chart. Here is what the beginning of the chart looks like:

mammal	live	eat	look like	kinds
cat	all over the world	mice cat food	pointy ears tails	Siamese tiger alley
dog	all over the world	meat dog food bones	wagging tail	collie poodle terrier mutt
elephant	in Africa in Asia in zoos in circuses	grass	long trunks floppy ears huge wrinkly skin	Asian African

Step 3

Model—The teacher chooses a mammal and writes two short sentences about that mammal.

Elephants are mammals. They live in Asia and Africa.

Next, the teacher models how these two sentences can be combined into one longer one.

Elephants are mammals that live in Asia and Africa.

The teacher may want to write two more simple sentences and show how these can be combined.

Elephants are huge. They have floppy ears and long trunks.

Elephants are huge mammals with floppy ears and long trunks.

Step 4

Children Write—The children choose a mammal and write two short sentences about it. They share these sentences in small groups and decide how the sentences can be combined into one longer sentence.

Paragraph Frames

Paragraph frames can be used to help children learn the syntax of paragraphs. Paragraph frames follow the same four steps. Here is an example based on the same mammals topic.

Step 1

Experience—The class has been learning about mammals. They have watched many videos and researched mammals on the Web. They have read simple books about mammals, and the teacher has read aloud a variety of books.

Step 2

Talk and List—The teacher begins a chart to help them summarize what they have learned about mammals. Different children contribute ideas to the chart. Here is what the beginning of the chart looks like:

mammal	live	eat	look like	kinds
cat	all over the world	mice cat food	pointy ears long tails small	Siamese tabby alley
dog	all over the world	meat dog food bones	wagging tail different sizes	collie poodle terrier mutt
elephant	in Africa in Asia in zoos in circuses	grass leaves	long trunks floppy ears huge wrinkly skin	Asian African

Step 3

Model—The teacher chooses a mammal and writes a simple paragraph about that animal, using the information from the chart.

Elephants are *mammals* that live in Asia and Africa. They eat leaves and grass.

Elephants are huge animals with big floppy ears and long trunks. There are two kinds of elephants: African elephants and Asian elephants. Elephants are very big and interesting animals.

The teacher takes the paragraph modeled and asks one child to choose an animal and tell about it, using the same sentence structures used in her elephant piece. The child picks "cats" and the teacher asks, "Where do cats live?" The teacher erases elephants and writes cats there. She erases in Africa and Asia and writes all over the world. The teacher continues to ask the child questions and erase the parts of the paragraph that are particular to elephants and write in cat information. The finished paragraph looks like this:

Cats are mammals that live all over the world. They eat mice and cat food. Cats are small animals with pointed ears and long tails. There are several different kinds of cats, including Siamese, tabby, and alley cats. Cats are very clever and funny animals.

Next, the teacher erases all of the cat-specific information, leaving this paragraph frame. Children use this frame and the chart to write paragraphs about their chosen mammal.

_____ are mammals that live _____. They eat _____.

_____are _____ animals with _____. There are _____ different kinds of

_____, including _____. _____ are _____ animals.

Using Books as Models

Another way of providing writing frames for children that help develop their sense of English syntax and vocabulary is to use books as models. Many teachers use *The Important Book* by Margaret Wise Brown (HarperTrophy, 1990) as a model. In this poem, the first and last line are almost the same with the addition of the word **But**.

The important thing about _____ is_____.

But the important thing about _____ is _____.

After reading this poem to the children and talking with them about it, you can model the writing of your own important poem.

The important thing about me is that I am me!

I am a teacher.

My name is Mrs. Cunningham.

My favorite color is purple.

I like to read books.

I like to eat pizza.

But the important thing about me is that I am me!

Next, the children write important poems about themselves. They use the same first lines as the one the teacher modeled and fill in facts in between. After editing, a class book about "All of the Important People in Our Class" can be published and enjoyed by all. This "important thing" format can be used to review and write about various units or themes in the classroom. You could even create the "Important Book of Mammals" if that was how you chose to frame the writing children did about mammals. Many teachers help children make Mother's Day books using *The Important Thing* Model.

The important thing about my mother is that she loves me.

She goes to work at the hospital every day.

She takes me out for pizza.

She doesn't stay mad at me long.

She bakes me cookies on Sunday.

But the important thing about my mother is that she loves me.

Here are some other books which can serve as models and frames for children to write in ways that help them develop English syntax and vocabulary.

Alligator Pie by Dennis Lee (Macmillan of Canada, 1987)

Alison's Zinnia by Anita Lobel (Greenwillow, 1990)

Can You See Me? by Shirley Greenway (Ideals Publications, 1992)

Away from Home by Anita Lobel (Greenwillow, 1994)

Buzz Said the Bee by Wendy Cheyette Lewison (Cartwheel, 1992)

Brown Bear, Brown Bear, What Do You See? by Bill Martin, Jr. (Pearson Schools, 1999)

Caps, Hats, Socks, and Mittens: A Book about the Four Seasons by Louise Borden (Scholastic Paperbacks, 1992)

Fortunately by Remy Charlip (Aladdin, 1993)

A House Is a House for Me by Mary Ann Hoberman (Puffin Books, 1982)

My Cat Jack by Patricia Casey (Walker Books, 2004)

Q is for Duck: An Alphabet Guessing Game by Mary Elting and Michael Folsom (Clarion Books, 1985)

That's Good, That's Bad by Margery Cuyler (Henry Holt and Co., 1993)

Tomorrow's Alphabet by George Shannon (HarperTrophy, 1999)

Supporting Children Who Struggle with Writing

Writing may be the most difficult cognitive activity we do. You have to know a lot to write—a lot about the topic, a lot of vocabulary, a lot about how the language in which you are writing works, a lot of words and how to spell them, a lot of rules and mechanics, a lot of different forms and genres in which to write. You have to juggle all of these different "balls" at the same time as you write. Writing is hard, even for good writers who write a lot. It can be excruciating for children who, for a whole variety of reasons discussed in this chapter, don't write well. Yet, while writing is hard for all and very hard for some, all children need to learn to do it. The lack of writing skills of graduates is one of the most often cited complaints of employers about the young people they hire—college grads included.

Writing is hard for many teachers. Most teachers consider themselves good readers but are less confident of their writing skills. For all of these reasons, actually teaching children to write is often postponed, put off, or "just not gotten around to!" Yet, the ability to communicate clearly and persuasively in writing is one of the most valued skills in society. Your children may not ever be wonderful writers, but they can be better. Writing may not be their favorite thing to do, but they don't have to hate it. You may not feel as confident in teaching writing as you do in other areas, but you can dive in and "do your best." All children need and deserve to leave elementary school with the ability to communicate through writing. Hopefully, this chapter has empowered you to take on the challenge of making all of your children better writers. They will thank you for it someday!

Chapter 11
A Peek into Classrooms Later in the Year

In this chapter, you will return to Fourblox Elementary to take another imaginary trip with Tom Baldman and Margaret Wright. This visit takes place at the end of the school year, so you will see teachers whose classes have gone way beyond what they were doing at the beginning of the year. The Writing Block still begins with a mini-lesson taught by the teacher, thinking aloud and writing for the children, followed by the children writing and the teacher conferencing or editing with them about their writing. The block ends with a brief period of sharing. This chapter will give you an idea of what the Writing Block might look like "later in the year." Exactly what happens in Four-Blocks® classrooms during the Writing Block later in the year varies, depending upon the students, grade level, teaching style, and what has been introduced and taught daily during the school year.

During the school year Margaret Wright taught a 10-week workshop on writing for elementary teachers in this school district. Tom stopped by several times to lend his expertise and to share information with the teachers. The writing course included many of the new things you read about in the preceding chapters on getting started, editing, revision, conferencing, focused writing, genres, and teaching struggling writers. Tom and Margaret plan to visit many of the same classrooms today, during the last month of school, that they visited "early in the year." The focus of their visit is to watch the Writing Block and see the teachers putting into practice the information Tom and Margaret included in their writing course. They hope to see teachers putting into practice all of the "tips" they included and avoiding the CAUTION: DEAD ENDs they warned teachers about.

First, Tom and Margaret stop by the office to greet the principal, Claire Leider. Claire tells the visitors she has just finished writing a book with DeLinda DeLightful (one of the second-grade teachers) about using children's literature in reading instruction. "Writing a book was a lot more work than we thought," Claire says, "but we worked hard, and it is finished!" Tom, Margaret, and Claire agree that teachers will appreciate the help.

"Here's your schedule for today," says Claire, handing Tom a piece of paper with the times, teachers, grade levels, and classrooms. Tom and Margaret know they are sure to see some good teaching and gain some new ideas to help other teachers and students late in the year.

Here is what the schedule for their repeat visit looks like:

Time	Teacher	Grade Level	Room No.
8:30–9:15	Bea Ginning	Kindergarten	Room 4
9:15–9:55	Deb Webb	Grade 2	Room 25
9:55–10:35	Cece Southern	Grade 1	Room 11
10:35–11:15	DeLinda DeLightful	Grade 2	Room 22
11:15–11:55	Amanda Amazing	Grade 3	Room 33
12:00–12:30	Lunch	(with Claire Leider in her office)	
12:30–1:10	Randy Reid*	Grade 4	Room 44
1:10–2:15	Will Teachum	Grade 5	Room 50
2:15–3:00	Susie Science	Grade 3	Room 30

*Joe Webman is on a field trip today.

8:30–9:15 Bea Ginning Kindergarten 1 Room 4

As Tom Baldman and Margaret Wright walk down the hall and around the corner, they come to the kindergarten classrooms and stop at Bea Ginning's door. School has just started, but the kindergarten classes are having a Young Authors' Celebration and Muffins for Moms because it will be Mother's Day this coming weekend. The children will also be "reading" their individual student-authored books to this early morning audience and then serving their mothers, grandmothers, and guests muffins and milk. Tom cannot think of a better present for a mother than to hear her little five-year-old reading a book he has written and illustrated all by himself! As Tom and Margaret enter Bea's kindergarten class, they slip quietly into the back of the room and join the assembled guests. The children are gathered in a "big group" on a colorful carpet with Bea sitting in a rocking chair and the children sitting in four groups in front of her. They quickly go through the morning opening—calendar, weather, and the morning message. Bea writes the morning message on a piece of chart paper and reads it with the children.

> Today is Muffins for Moms Day.
>
> It is also our Young Author's Celebration.
>
> We will read the books we wrote.
>
> We will serve our mothers and other visitors muffins and milk.

Quickly, Bea reviews what the class will do this morning for the visitors. The children are in four groups, and each group of five or six students will read their student-authored books to their guests. Then, the young authors will serve their guests muffins and milk, and finally serve themselves. Bea introduces Margaret Wright and Tom Baldman to the class. Margaret is asked to join one group and Tom another group. Bea leads one group, and three parent volunteers are helping by leading the other groups.

Each child reads her book page by page, showing the illustrations on each page. When the book is finished, the child reads the page titled "All About the Author" at the end of the book. Each child has written a five-page book, and it seems like each child can read her book. (Well, perhaps one child in each group may need to get a little help from the "leader.") In Tom's group, Carolyn begins by reading her book titled *Sports*. She reads it loudly and proudly; she is proud of her writing and proud of her reading. Carolyn may enjoy sports and like to tell about the sports she plays, but it is also clear that she is a good kindergarten writer and reader! Jordan is next; he reads his book titled *T-Ball*. Jordan reads his book slowly, not missing a single word. He remembers the words because he wrote it. He stretches out some words and can write most of the words he already knows from memory. He has also practiced reading his book every day for the past week—practice that has paid off! When he is finished reading, it is Ashlyn's turn to read her book, *The Rabbit*. Tom smiles because Ashlyn is another confident reader and writer.

Finally, Jackie and Guiselle read their books (with help) and share their pictures. Bea glances around the room at each group and thinks to herself, "These children have come a long way since entering kindergarten." When school started, she knew that some children could read, but she also knew that no child in her kindergarten class could write. Today, they have all read books they wrote aloud to an audience. Some children have written two or three books and can read and write quite well now. Other children have written every day since January, and with her coaching, they can write five sentences on their chosen topic. These young children have really learned to write by writing.

When each group finishes reading, each child in that group goes to the table to get a muffin and a small carton of milk and takes it to his mother, using his best manners. Some children return for more refreshments as they have other guests to serve. Those with just one guest return for their own refreshments and using their best manners, eat with their guests. Tom and Margaret are each served a muffin and milk by students without parents present. They easily assume proud parental roles, bragging about the books the children wrote and read, and then thanking them for the delicious muffins. Looking at the clock on the classroom wall, Tom and Margaret realize that they are late. As some mothers leave quickly to get to home or to work, Tom and Margaret say their good-byes and are off to watch another writing lesson.

9:15–9:55 Deb Webb Grade 2 Room 25

Tom and Margaret are a few minutes behind schedule as they enter Deb Webb's second-grade classroom. The children are sitting on the carpet with their knees and noses pointed at Mrs. Webb, who is standing in front of a large piece of chart paper with lots of writing on it. Mrs. Webb reviews what the class is doing for the children and the visitors.

"On Monday, I started my story, writing a good beginning about my family's trip to Disney World® this spring. I wanted to hook my readers from the start. Then on Tuesday, I wrote the middle and let my readers know where we went and what my family did on our vacation. On Wednesday, I tried to write a good ending for this story. Since I have written many pieces this year and you seemed to enjoy this one, I thought I would publish this piece of writing just like you do. So, yesterday we read the story together, and you helped me with the revision or "making it better." We changed some words then added on to my story. We decided I needed more descriptive words, so I drew a colorful cartoon to describe the characters walking around the amusement park. We found a few places where I could have chosen a better word. I changed a noun (people to workers) and two verbs (ran to hurried and walking to wandering), and I worked on the ending, adding to it to make it more understandable and interesting.

"Today, I want you to be my 'partners' and help me edit this story using our Editor's Checklist. I have taught you to be aware of many things when writing this year, and these eight items I expect each one of you to be able to check, either with a partner or by yourself." (Deb started her checklist in September and has added to the list slowly but is now holding her second graders responsible for all of the items on this list. She has taught many editing mini-lessons, but she has taught much more than editing to the class this year.) She reads the first item on this list, "Do all the sentences make sense?" The children read each sentence and give her a thumbs-up for each sentence. All of the sentences make sense. So, Mrs. Webb puts one check at the top of her paper.

Next, she reads the items numbered two, three, and four, and they check each sentence for capitals and ending punctuation marks. A capital letter is at the beginning of each sentence, but Space Mountain is not capitalized and needs two capitals, one for Space and one for Mountain. Mrs. Webb then puts three more checks at the top of her paper. Next, she reads the fifth item on the list, "Are the words I need to check the spellings of circled?" The children find Word Wall words and comment that all of the Word Wall words are spelled correctly—as they should be. Next, they look at the spelling of words that are not on the wall but words that Mrs. Webb spelled by stretching them out and listening for the sounds. They think that the word "direcktions" needs a circle, and someone needs to check the spelling in the big dictionary on the teacher's desk. They find that the word is misspelled and cross out the "k." They read the story over again to see if every sentence stays on the topic—the trip to Disney World®. The children know this story has a beginning, middle, and end since the teacher has worked on each part on a separate day. Mrs. Webb then puts two more checks at the top of the paper.

The final read is for conversation and quotation marks. There are several sentences that need quotation marks and have none; the children are proud to find each one and tell Deb exactly where the quotation marks belong. Deb has talked about conversation and using quotation marks, even though she has not added it to her checklist. Not all of the students are ready for this item yet, but they will be next year. When the editing is completed, Deb tells the children that they will have 10 minutes to edit with partners one of the finished pieces in their notebooks, then 10 more minutes to edit their partners' pieces, and the final 10 minutes they can return to Self-Selected Writing or work on any writing they are in the process of publishing. Deb tells students, "Choose a piece of writing that is approximately a page in length; more than that might be too long and you won't get through it."

Here is a copy of the Editor's Checklist the children have stapled inside the front covers of their writing notebooks.

Editor's Checklist

1. Do all the sentences make sense?

2. Do all the sentences start with capital letters?

3. Do all the sentences have ending punctuation?

4. Do all people and place names have capitals?

5. Are words I need to check the spelling of circled?

6. Do all the sentences stay on the topic?

7. Does the piece have a beginning, middle, and end?

The children are sent back to their desks and chairs to work with a partner and edit each other's writing. Deb moves from the front of the classroom and roams around the classroom, making sure her second graders are on task editing with their partners and using the checklist. She reminds a student who has written a Word Wall word wrong that, "Word Wall words have to be spelled correctly even on first draft!" Deb then "oohs" and "aahs" over how well some students are editing and helps two or three partners who need a little help. When the students are finished editing, they return to writing for the last 10 minutes. Deb then puts on her editor's hat with the words "Editor-in-Chief" written across the front.

She calls Ashlyn to a side table and conferences with her. Ashlyn has written an interesting, imaginary story about one of the American Girl® characters. Since Ashlyn has been reading these books for two years, she understands how to write about a girl living in the past. Deb is quite proud of this second-grader's writing ability. Deb would never assign this kind of writing to her second graders, but she knows letting students write about what interests them leads to multilevel instruction—this girl is writing several years beyond the writing level of most of the class! Time is running out, so Mrs. Webb tells Ashlyn they will finish working together tomorrow, "Be sure you are ready to tell me who you want to dedicate this book to and what you want to write about the author (Ashlyn) on that page."

As Margaret and Tom begin to leave, sharing is beginning. They whisper to Deb that they are amazed at how far these students have come this year, both in the quantity of writing they can produce and the quality of their writing, revising, and editing. Tom tells Margaret, "You can tell Deb likes the Writing Block, but more importantly, she keeps up with the literature on writing and puts what she learns into practice in her classroom. I wish all teachers could talk with her and visit her!"

9:55–10:35 Cece Southern Grade 1 Room 11

Cece is gathering the children in front of the room around her overhead projector as Tom and Margaret enter and find two "big chairs" waiting for them in the back of the room. They sit and watch as Cece begins to talk to her students about what she will write about today in her mini-lesson. "Today, we are working on our animal reports. We have learned a lot about animals in science. Last week, we read four books about animals in 'book club groups.' (For more on book club groups, see *Book Club Groups: A Multilevel Four-Blocks® Reading Strategy* by Hall and Tillman, Carson-Dellosa, 2004.) Today, we will begin to write animal reports. I am going to start with a web to organize my information, then I will use the web to write. Next, we will see if we can 'make it better,' then edit or 'fix it.' Finally, we will write our reports in accordion books." Cece shows an accordion book to the children, and they look pleased that their reports will go into "special" books.

"We have made a web before. A web helps us organize our information. If I choose to write about elephants, the web will help me organize what I know about elephants. Then, I will use that web to write what I know about elephants." Cece starts a web, thinks aloud, talks, and writes." Since the animal I am going to write about is an elephant, I will put that in the middle. I want to tell where they live, what they eat, what they look like, and some interesting facts about different kinds of elephants. So, I will put those four things in ovals in the corners." (She makes the web as she talks.)

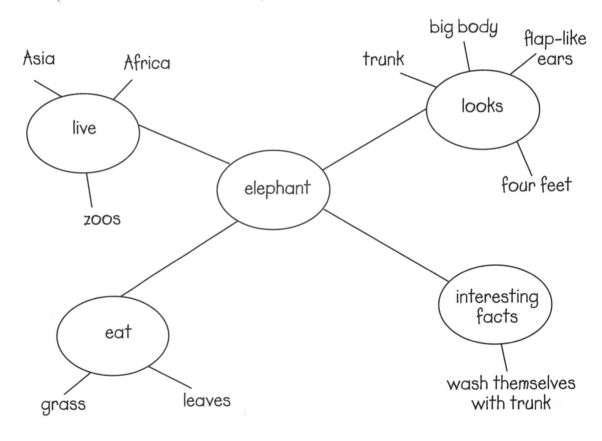

Cece then talks more about where elephants are found in the world as she fills in that "spoke" of the web. Next, she talks about what these large, heavy animals look like—their trunks, their ears, their feet, and that different elephants are either brown or gray as she fills in that "spoke." She talks about the third "spoke," which is what elephants eat, and tells the class she had to find that information in books. She decides that she might write about what people feed elephants that live in the zoo. When she gets to the final "spoke," she adds one interesting fact, then tells the class that she is reading an elephant book she borrowed from the library during her read-aloud today in Self-Selected Reading and will add more interesting facts before she begins to write tomorrow.

Cece tells the students that they will stop their Self-Selected Writing and start focused writing pieces. They will begin with webs and write about animals that interest them. She reminds the children of the many books in the Self-Selected Reading baskets; some her own, some borrowed from the school library, and others from the public library. The children have been reading animal books at Self-Selected Reading and studying animals at science time. They have watched movies and videos about wild animals and zoo animals. Mrs. Southern expects her first graders to select animals today and create webs, just like she did, during this Writing Block. Each child has a plain sheet of white newsprint on his desk when he returns to his seat. The children have a model of a web still on the overhead projector screen. They also have their teacher circulating, smiling, and helping those who are unsure of which animal to choose. Sometimes Mrs. Southern takes a book from a nearby book basket and asks a question like, "Would you like to write about bears or tigers?" as she shows the covers of two books, one book about bears and one about tigers.

Mrs. Southern wanders around the room, bragging about the wonderful web she sees and helping students who need help. She chats with a few students about their animals; she then sits at a table on the side of the room and calls a group of children to the table who seem to need and want more help than most of her other students. Tom and Margaret wander around the room, looking at the animals the students choose and the webs these young writers are creating. They are pleased that students who need extra help get it in Cece's classroom. Mrs. Southern ends the Writing Block by letting her students pair with nearby students and share their webs. In a few minutes, Cece has allowed all of her students to share their webs and get some feedback from a peer. As the adults listen, they hear some wonderful comments and some interesting, often helpful, questions.

10:35 –11:15 DeLinda DeLightful Grade 2 Room 22

As soon as Tom and Margaret enter DeLinda DeLightful's classroom, she greets them and says, "We are so glad you are here to visit us again; we just love to write!" The children are sitting in their special places on the colorful carpet. Mrs. DeLightful then goes over to her overhead projector and sits in front of it, facing the children. DeLinda seems delighted at what she will do today in her mini-lesson. "I am so excited about what we will do today. In second grade, we have learned all about nouns and verbs; we have even talked about adjectives. Today, I will write a short piece, and then I will ask you to find all of the verbs, the action words and words like is, are, and were. Watch as I write this for you."

DeLinda then writes on an overhead transparency while the children watch her and read as she writes:

> Yesterday I saw two small boys taking a shortcut down the alley in back of the drug store. Big boys were back there, throwing eggs and yelling. The owner came out. "I'm calling your grandmother." he said as he shook his finger at the two little boys.
>
> Their grandmother was waiting in the yard for them when they got home.
>
> "Grandmother, we didn't throw those eggs." they said. "Some big boys did."

Next, DeLinda asks her students to find the verbs in each sentence. The hands go up as she reads the first sentence, and one little boy tells her, "**Saw** and **taking** are the verbs in that sentence." DeLinda circles those two words with a blue felt-tipped pen and begins to read the second sentence. Another boy is happy to tell her that there are three verbs in that sentence: **were**, **throwing**, and **yelling**. She circles the three verbs in the second sentence. After reading the third sentence she calls on a girl who answers, "The verbs are: **came**, **calling**, **said**, and **shook**." The fourth sentence is easy for another student, who is pleased to announce, "**Was**, **waiting**, and **got**." For the final sentence, she lets all of the children tell her, "The verbs are: **throw**, **said**, and **did**."

"Our final task this morning is to see if we can replace any boring verbs with better verbs," Delinda says. The children decide that **saw** could be changed to **watched**, **said** to **yelled**, and **arrived** would be a better verb than **got** in that sentence. The transparency now looks like this:

>   watched
> Yesterday I ~~saw~~ two small boys (taking) a shortcut down the alley in back of the drug store. Big boys (were) back there, (throwing) eggs and (yelling). The owner (came) out. "I'm (calling) your grandmother." he (said) as he (shook) his finger at the two little
>   yelled
> boys.
>
>   arrived
> Their grandmother (was) (waiting) in the yard for them when they (got) home.
>
> "Grandmother, we didn't (throw) those eggs." they (said) "Some big boys (did.)"

After bragging about how smart the students are, Mrs. DeLightful sends them back to their seats and reminds them they can look at their writing today to see if they can find some verbs that could be replaced with stronger verbs to make their writing even better. When the children are all quietly in their seats and writing, DeLinda goes to the publishing table and begins her editing/publishing conferences.

There is a large, laundry-size basket full of student-authored books in the center; proof that this class has been busy writing and publishing this year. Once again, it is evident to the visitors that each child is delighted with his teacher's comments and questions during their conversations at conference time. The students are eager to please and seem to enjoy their task of simple revision, editing, and publishing. The block ends with Wednesday's children near the "Share Chair" ready to read. Each child is ready to read something she has written recently, either a just published piece or first draft. When children read published pieces Mrs. DeLightful reminds them of her rule, "Say something nice first, and then you can ask a thinking question." When a child reads a work in progress, she always leads the class to say, "We can't wait to hear the rest of your story!"

Tom and Margaret notice that it is time to leave this delightful teacher and her class for the last visit of the morning. Time goes by fast when you are watching good teaching! They also noted that writing usually is 30–40 minutes per day in Four-Block classrooms, and every teacher has taken 40 minutes today. Margaret comments how, during the first few weeks of school, writing was more like 15–20 minutes in some classrooms and 30 minutes in others. Once these children got into the routine of mini-lessons, writing, and sharing, many teachers stretched the time to the maximum—just like she did when she was a classroom teacher.

11:15–11:55 Amanda Amazing Grade 3 Room 33

As Tom and Margaret enter the next classroom on their schedule, they see Amanda Amazing sitting behind her overhead projector with her third-grade students gathered in a huddle in front of her. "Mother's Day is coming, and I brought some writing about mothers to share with you today. These are pieces of writing that were given as gifts. Have you ever thought about that? I thought that since Mother's Day was coming up, you might want to give some thought to giving a gift of writing to your mother or your grandmother this year. The three pieces I brought in to share mean a lot to me. My favorite piece is one my daughter wrote for me at Christmas. She wrote it when she was in third grade, like you, and she wrote about her Mimi—my mother. My mother died soon after, and Merrill Kaye and I both miss her very much. This piece of writing is one of the best presents I've ever received.

"The next piece I brought in is a poem written by one of my mom's students. This student wrote a poem about my mother as her teacher. I really do love the poem, it says a lot about who my mom was as a teacher.

"Finally, I even brought in some letters that mean a lot to me. They are special letters from my husband and children that they wrote to me over the years, and I have saved them. Sometimes the words we have trouble saying in person we can say on paper.

"Let's spend some time thinking together today about the types of writing you could use as gifts and make a list." Amanda then makes a list on a transparency as she shares her story, poem, and letters with her students. She reminds her students that these are three genres they learned about this year in third grade.

Gifts for Your Mother or Grandmother for Mother's Day

Write a story about your mother or a special time with her.

Write a poem about your mother or grandmother.

Write a letter to your mother.

The students seem anxious to return to their seats and begin this task. The samples their teacher brought in to share during her mini-lesson have sparked thoughts in their young minds—they CAN do this, and they will have wonderful gifts for their mothers! After the students write for 20 minutes, Mrs. Amazing asks them to stop writing, reminding them that they can continue tomorrow, but it is time to share right now. Today, they can share their writing if they want; if their writing is too personal, she suggests they share things they have written before and have not shared with the class. One girl shares a letter she has started to her French grandmother, whom she calls Memere. It is filled with wonderful memories of the things they did together over the years. The students' comments make it clear that she has done a good job, even if it is not finished. A boy tells about the letter he is writing to his mother, but he does not read it, and Amanda does not tell him he has to. She comments that letters are personal, and many personal letters should only be read by the people they were intended for. The next person to share reads a poem he has started about his mother; it is quite good. Another boy shares an acrostic poem he has written.

M is for the many things you do for me.

O is for one who cares for me.

T is for the time you took me to the beach.

H is for our home you keep so clean.

E is for everyone in our family, we love you.

R is for respect; I respect you and love you.

Tom glances at the clock and realizes another 40 minutes has flown by; he and Margaret need to be heading down the hall to the lunch Claire Leider has planned for them. As they leave the classroom, Tom says to Margaret, "That's Amanda, always amazing. Who would have thought about the children writing as Mother's Day gifts? They are doing a wonderful job writing to or about their mothers, though. It's a wonderful review of three genres she has taught her third graders."

12:00–12:30 Lunch with Claire Leider in Her Office

Claire has had the lunchroom staff prepare salads for their lunch. Summer is coming, and everyone is watching his weight, so Claire thinks she is safe ordering salads. As the trio eat and drink, they talk about how well things are going at Fourblox Elementary. Claire enjoys their compliments but knows she is also fortunate to have some wonderful teachers. She knows that using the Four-Blocks® framework is not easy; it requires a teacher to teach each of the four blocks and use whole class, small group, and one-on-one conferencing. She tells Tom and Margaret, "Good teachers don't mind working hard; especially if they see results, and they get results with the Four-Blocks® framework—good reading, good writing, and good test scores. What else could a teacher—or a principal—ask for? We're all looking forward to summer, though, just as much as the students. We work hard the whole school year, and now we need to rest and relax! Isn't that what summer is for? Maybe I'll have time to get caught up on my reading, too—all of those books I've bought and been given and just haven't had time to read. It seems that writing the book with DeLinda and now writing end-of-the-year reports has taken all of my time; never mind the plans I need to make for the next school year. School doesn't end any more without having to make plans for the next school year. There is still so much to do. Besides end-of-the-year tests, there are also end-of-the-year field trips and celebrations. It doesn't seem like a single day goes by without something going on in a classroom or some class going off campus on a field trip."

Margaret says, "I noticed all of the kindergarten classes had Muffins for Mom today and their Young Authors' Celebrations. It was just wonderful! All of the children in Bea's class did a good job writing and reading their books. We know we will miss seeing Joe today because his class is gone to Ramsey Creek Park for their end-of-the-year picnic. We also heard that the fourth-grade classes have invited a local author of children's books to talk to them at their Young Authors' Celebration next week."

Before Claire can respond, Tom glances at his watch and signals to Margaret. They both jump up to thank Claire for lunch, then rush off to Randy Reid's room.

12:30–1:10 Randy Reid Grade 4 Room 44

Today, as Tom and Margaret enter his room, Randy is just beginning his mini-lesson. Mr. Reid is talking to his students about writing to a prompt. "Today, you will have a focused writing assignment. I will ask you to write a letter to a friend. You will tell your friend where you want to go this summer and why. The place can be nearby or far away—that is your choice." Randy quickly passes a paper to all of his fourth graders, so they will have the prompt in front of them to refer to as they write. They also have a piece of lined paper to write on and a piece of unlined paper for planning.

Tom can tell Randy has analyzed this prompt before giving it to his students, just like they talked about in the writing course. The audience will be a friend. The students all know how to write about themselves—they have done that since kindergarten. The topic of this letter, and they all know how to write a friendly letter, is where they would like to go this summer and why.

Randy reminds his class that when they write to a prompt he does NOT conference with them. They are writing, and he cannot help. He tells them he will roam the room and make mental notes that he will share with them tomorrow, but his job for today is just to see that everyone is writing. As Randy passes by Tom and Margaret, he tells them that it is so hard not to be helping his students. He explains how much he enjoys both over-the-shoulder and shoulder-to-shoulder conferences, but he knows this is not the time for conferencing. Randy explains, "I would much rather be helping than just observing, but I need to see that all of my fourth graders can write to a prompt without my help." Tom and Margaret observe that all students understand what they are to do and begin to respond as soon as the teacher says they can begin. Randy also jotted the time the students started this assignment on the board. They have 45 minutes to write and no time to talk to anyone. Quickly his students begin the task, and most of these fourth graders are off to a wonderful start.

Tom and Margaret make a note that when students have had good instruction for four years, writing to a prompt is NOT a hard task, especially when some self-selection is still possible in a prompt.

When the 45 minutes is up, Randy collects the prompt and the students' papers. He will grade these papers tonight and return them tomorrow. "In fourth grade, parents want to know that I grade some writing, as well as teach writing daily. Besides, I am anxious to read all of your letters. Those letters I stopped and read while roaming the room were all quite good. Since you have written about so many interesting places, both near and far, you might want to pair and share, orally, what you wrote about today." Randy then gives the class five minutes to do just that—talk about their writing.

1:15–2:15 Will Teachum Grade 5 Room 50

As Tom and Margaret stroll into Will's fifth-grade classroom, the students are about to begin to analyze their folktales using a writing scale. Will's mini-lesson is focused on just how the students will do the task. "We have read several folktales and tall tales lately in the Guided Reading block. Then, I asked you to write folktales; some of you are almost finished. Today, I will talk about how you can analyze your writing with a writing scale that is used just with folktales." Then, Will begins to think aloud and talk about his folktale, analyzing it orally as he writes the scale on a transparency. This is the scale his uses to analyze his folktales as a final step.

Writing Scale for a Folktale

1. Does my paper have the same topic as the prompt?

2. Does my story have just a few characters?

3. Are the main characters either animals or common people?

4. Does my paper tell a simple story?

5. Does my story teach a lesson?

6. Does my paper begin like a folktale?

7. Does my paper end like a folktale?

Will has modeled each step for his fifth-grade students. First, he wrote a folktale over several days, then he spent a day revising the folktale and making it better. Next, he edited with his class for the items on their class checklist. Finally, they are going to analyze their folktale. Did they write a folktale with all of the features of a folktale? Each step has been modeled for the class, so they understand just what to do and how to do it. Will believes that "a picture is worth a thousand words," and that you can teach students to do most anything if you show them how, not just tell them to do it. For this final step, students are to use this scale to analyze their folktales. With the scale on the overhead and a copy for their writer's notebooks, the students are asked to return to their seats. When they have finished writing their folktales, they are to begin the task of analyzing it to the scale. Three or four students are finished writing, but all are anxious to see how well they have done to this point.

After the students are back in their seats and busy using the scale to analyze their folktales, Will begins roaming the room, conducting over-the-shoulder conferences to help. Tom and Margaret begin to roam the room as well, reading the folktales and watching the students analyze them. They see some good folktales and a few great ones. The scale helps one of the students realize he had failed to "teach a lesson" (#5) in his folktale, and he begins a revision. He seems happy to have noticed this before he passed his final paper in!

Seeing so many students engrossed in their assignment is exciting to both Tom and Margaret, but once again, it is time to move on, this time to their last class of the day.

2:15–3:00 Susie Science Grade 3 Room 30
(Susie Science's class has just returned from a field trip, and they are writing in their journals about what they saw.)

The last thing on the schedule is Susie Science's writing lesson. Susie writes at the end of the day with her third graders because, "Writing is a nice quiet, easy activity at the end of the day. My students like to write, and so do I. Some days, we can also review something we have learned or enjoyed doing." Today, the class visited the City Waterworks and have just enough time to write about their trip." Susie's class has just finished studying the water cycle, and she has integrated the science objectives on the third-grade state standard course of study into all four Blocks. During the Self-Selected Reading Block, the students have been reading books that will help them learn more about the water cycle and build their background knowledge. She believes they need to read more than just the science text. Ms. Science has borrowed many books on water and the water cycle (from the school and public libraries) to supplement her collection (which is quite remarkable.) During Guided Reading, the class reads *The Magic School Bus: At the Waterworks* by Joanna Cole (Scholastic, 1988), and during the Writing Block, they have written an informational piece about the water cycle as a focused writing lesson. For the Working with Words Block, Susie has had her third graders do a making words lesson using the word reservoir, and she also did a Guess the Covered Word lesson with some important vocabulary words.

Today, after a short mini-lesson where Ms. Science reviews their field trip and creates an outline with the class, the students are free to write about where they went, what they saw, and what they did. "Be sure to tell me what you learned, what happened, what you liked, etc. Anything you think I would want to know, let me know," she says. Susie's short mini-lesson outlines the trip, which she titles "Our Trip to the Waterworks."

Susie Science loves to teach science, and she wanders around the room to see what the children have written about the trip and the subject. She stops and helps children who are having trouble getting started or need help with what they are doing. To Margaret and Tom, it is evident that Susie likes writing almost as much as science.

Leaving Fourblox Elementary, Tom and Margaret comment on the fact that teachers were doing more. Margaret also saw them using the new information she talked about in her workshop. She says to Tom, "Lots of tips found their way into these classrooms, too. The best part of this job is the wonderful teachers we work with. We keep learning, and they keep learning—how fortunate for students! Spending a day with teachers and children is better than

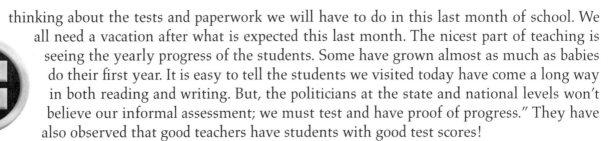

thinking about the tests and paperwork we will have to do in this last month of school. We all need a vacation after what is expected this last month. The nicest part of teaching is seeing the yearly progress of the students. Some have grown almost as much as babies do their first year. It is easy to tell the students we visited today have come a long way in both reading and writing. But, the politicians at the state and national levels won't believe our informal assessment; we must test and have proof of progress." They have also observed that good teachers have students with good test scores!

"But enough about school and writing. I'm off to my travel agent to look at cruises. Should I travel through the Panama Canal, go to Alaska, or maybe cruise the Mediterranean? What a wonderful way to learn and rest! What will you do this summer?"

Chapter 12
Why Do Writing the Four-Blocks® Way?

There are two dimensions of any instructional strand in school: the characteristics of the ongoing instruction and the ways that instruction changes through the year and across the grades. This chapter will review the research support for both dimensions of the writing instruction in Four-Blocks classrooms. Presented first are five research findings that support the day-to-day writing instruction in the Four-Blocks® framework. Then, five more research findings that support the ways writing instruction changes through the year and across the grades in the Four-Blocks® framework are discussed.

Research Support for the Day-to-Day Writing Instruction in Four-Blocks Classrooms

Teachers of writing, including Four-Blocks teachers, are fortunate to have a major published review of research on teaching writing to consult for guidance in determining the characteristics of effective, day-to-day writing instruction. Hillocks (1986; 1995) used meta-analysis to review the experimental research on teaching writing. Meta-analysis is a well-established procedure for mathematically combining the results of several related studies into a "meta-study." The procedure generates the statistic of average effect size that can then be used to compare the relative effectiveness of different instructional features, methods, or approaches. Hillocks' meta-analysis of writing instructional research gives us four findings that support the day-to-day writing instruction in Four-Blocks classrooms.

Research Finding #1: Focus on Teaching Students How to Write, Not about Writing

The first of the two major factors examined in Hillocks' meta-analysis was focus of writing instruction. For this factor, he collected the experimental studies that investigated the effectiveness of each of six instructional emphases in writing:

1. **Free writing**—Students write whatever they have on their minds in journals

2. **Grammar**—Students learn to identify parts of speech, parts of sentences, and kinds of sentences.

3. **Inquiry**—Students explore and discuss a set of items (leaves, rocks, seashells, pictures of people or objects, poems, maps, etc.) to prepare to write about them

4. **Models**—Students are presented with examples of good writing to show them what its characteristics are.

5. **Sentence combining**—Students learn how to merge two or more short sentences into one longer sentence.

6. **Writing scales**—Students learn to use specific criteria to evaluate and revise or edit a piece of writing or produce a better piece of writing of a similar kind.

Each study he found that compared one of these six focuses with a control condition was analyzed to generate an effect size for that comparison. To compute an effect size, the average score for the control group on the outcome measure is subtracted from the average score for the experimental group. This difference is then weighted by dividing it by the standard deviation for the control group on the outcome measure. The resulting statistic, Glass's statistic, is a measure of the size of the effect for that comparison in that one study. In other words, this procedure evaluates each experimental treatment in each study based on the proportion of a standard deviation that it moved the experimental group ahead of the control group on the outcome measure.

In a meta-analysis, the effect sizes of all of the studies that examined one type of treatment are then averaged together so that the general effectiveness of the treatment in all of the studies can be gauged. Hillocks applied this established procedure to each of the six focuses he looked at. The average effect sizes for the six focuses were as follows:

Grammar = -0.29

Free Writing = 0.16

Models = 0.22

Sentence Combining = 0.35

Writing Scales = 0.36

Inquiry = 0.56

The meta-analysis of experimental research on teaching writing shows that focusing on inquiry is the most effective emphasis of the six, while focusing on grammar is the least effective emphasis of the six. The ineffectiveness of grammar instruction in the meta-analysis is not news:

"Research over a period of 100 years has consistently shown that the teaching of traditional school grammar (TSG) has little or no effect on students, particularly on their writing." (Hillocks and Smith, 2003, p. 721)

Hillocks used the established distinction between procedural and declarative knowledge to interpret the results of the meta-analysis on focus of writing instruction:

"It is interesting to note that the [three] treatments with the largest gains all focus on teaching procedural knowledge, knowledge of how to do things . . . [Free writing] does not help students learn new . . . procedures. Both grammar and models focus on learning . . . declarative rather than procedural knowledge" (Hillocks, 1995, p. 223)

Declarative knowledge is simply knowledge you can "declare," that is, say or write down. For example, grammar instruction teaches students to declare such knowledge as the correct labels of the parts of speech in a sentence. For another example, models instruction teaches students to declare such knowledge as that good descriptive writing usually relies on figurative language. Hillocks' meta-analysis of writing instruction shows that focusing on teaching students knowledge about writing they can declare is not nearly as effective as teaching them to do the procedures that good writing includes. Of course, this makes perfect sense. No one can learn to play the piano by being taught the names of the parts of it or by listening to good pianists demonstrate specific techniques.

As you have seen throughout this book, Four-Blocks teachers focus on teaching students how to write, not about writing. This difference between writing the Four-Blocks way and other kinds of writing instruction that emphasize declarative knowledge, such as grammar, is strongly supported by the first research finding.

CAUTION: DEAD END!

When one becomes aware of how ineffective or even counterproductive a focus on grammar instruction is in a writing program, it is tempting to conclude that students' grammatical errors in writing can be ignored in elementary writing instruction. CAUTION, that is a DEAD END! All students must learn how to write with an acceptable level of grammatical correctness, or they and their writing will be discriminated against by their future teachers, employers, and anyone else unfortunate enough to need to read what they have written. This first research finding does not in any way decrease the necessity for students to learn how to write in an acceptable and conventional form. All it says is that students must be taught how to write correctly, not what correct writing is. Grammar instruction alone does not work. The goal of helping students learn to write grammatically correctly remains as important as ever. (Research finding #4 on page 224 will show how this goal and others like it can be achieved.)

Research Finding #2: Students Learn How to Write Better While Actively Engaged in Writing Activities, Rather Than Just Listening to the Teacher

The second of the two major factors examined in Hillocks' meta-analysis was mode of writing instruction. For this factor, he collected the experimental studies that investigated the effectiveness of each of four instructional approaches in writing:

1. Presentational/Traditional—The teacher explains how to write well, takes students through the composition parts of the language book, presents good models of writing as examples, gives specific writing assignments, and grades their papers.

2. Natural Process—Students participate in self-selected writing, mini-lessons, peer conferencing, revision, editing, and publishing.

3. Individualized Conferences—The teacher teaches the students how to write in individualized writing conferences.

4. Environmental—The teacher develops the writing activities, chooses the instructional objectives, models the procedures students are to follow, supervises and coaches the students as they engage in the activities. The students engage in inquiry (exploring and discussing the topic) before they write and use a writing scale (specific criteria) to read and evaluate their own papers after they write.

Again, each study he found that compared one of these four modes with a control condition was analyzed to generate an effect size for that comparison, and the effect sizes of all of the studies that examined a mode were averaged together. The average effect sizes for the four modes were as follows:

Presentational/Traditional = 0.02

Individualized Conferences = 0.17

Natural Process = 0.19

Environmental = 0.44

The meta-analysis of experimental research on teaching writing shows that natural process, individualized conferences, and environmental writing instruction are all superior to presentational/traditional instruction.

Traditional writing instruction, the kind you probably had as a freshman in college and possibly earlier, meets the first research finding discussed above: it attempts to teach students how to write, not just about writing, like grammar instruction does. However, Hillocks calls it "presentational" because in traditional writing instruction, "the teacher dominates the classroom, presenting information in lecture and from textbooks, setting assignments, explaining objectives . . ., outlining criteria . . . . Its essential feature is that teaching is telling" (Hillocks, 1995, p. 221). The meta-analysis shows that such instruction is much less effective than the other three modes where students learn how to write while writing, rather than from just listening to the teacher.

Actually, this second research finding should resonate with our common sense and experience. No one can learn to ride a bicycle or to swim by being told how to ride or swim. To learn how to ride a bicycle or swim, you have to get on a bike or in the water! It should be obvious that the same holds true for another complex behavior like writing.

As you have seen throughout this book, Four-Blocks teachers provide most of their writing instruction while students are engaged in some kind of writing activity, rather than expecting them to learn from just listening to the teacher. This difference between writing the Four-Blocks way and other kinds of writing instruction that emphasize teacher talk about what and how to write is strongly supported by the second research finding.

Research Finding #3: Students Learn How to Write Better When Their Writing Activities Are Designed and Supervised by the Teacher without Being Presentational

The third research finding also comes from the meta-analysis comparing modes of writing instruction. Why is environmental writing instruction the most effective of the four modes? "Environmental" writing instruction is Hillocks' term and not widely used, but the concept is certainly familiar to teachers in Four-Blocks classrooms. To Hillocks (1995), the term environmental means instruction that achieves a "balance" among the teacher, the student, and the writing to be done. Presentational instruction is out of balance and ineffective because it is teacher-centered, while the student and the writing matter less. Individualized conferences and natural process instruction are much more effective than presentational instruction because of research finding #2 (students learn how to write better while writing than just listening to the teacher), but individualized conferences instruction is still out of balance by being teacher-dominated, while natural process instruction is still out of balance by being student-centered.

As you have seen throughout this book, writing the Four-Blocks way resembles natural process and individualized conferences instruction much more than presentational instruction. This is in keeping with the first two research findings, discussed above. However, writing the Four-Blocks way is also balanced in the environmental sense. Writing process instruction is used, but the teacher designs and supervises all aspects of that instruction. Students are not expected to teach themselves how to write in peer groups or at learning centers. Individualized conferences are used, but the instruction provided therein is a "conversation" between teacher and student, and not a teacher presentation of what the student did or should now do. Writing the Four-Blocks way balances the teacher, the student, and the writing to be done. This difference between writing the Four-Blocks way and other kinds of writing instruction that are either teacher-centered or student-centered is strongly supported by the third research finding.

Research Finding #4: Students Must Learn How to Read and Evaluate Their Own Papers for Specific Criteria

One of the most common and persistent myths in writing instruction is that teachers help students learn how to write better by marking on their papers. However, the experimental research shows that this practice does not improve student writing:

"Teacher comment [written on students' compositions] has little impact on student writing. None of the studies of teacher comment . . . show statistically significant differences in the quality of writing between experimental and control groups. Indeed, several show no pre-to-post gains for any groups, regardless of the type of comment." (Hillocks, 1986, p. 165)

Instead, the results of both aspects of the meta-analysis demonstrate that the most effective writing instruction teaches students how to read and evaluate their papers for specific criteria they are taught to use. The results of the meta-analysis on six focuses of writing instruction indicated that writing scales (learning to use specific criteria to evaluate and revise or edit a piece of writing or produce a better piece of writing of a similar kind) is the second-most effective focus of the six. The results of the meta-analysis on four instructional approaches in writing indicated that "environmental" or truly balanced instruction (instruction where, among other things, students are actively involved in exploring and applying specific criteria to what they are going to write about or the papers they have written) is the most effective of the four.

CAUTION: DEAD END!

Grading and marking student writing teaches students little or nothing about how to write better. However, in almost all schools, teachers must grade their students in writing (or at least in language arts) and must be prepared to conference with parents about how their children are progressing in their writing. Here, there are two CAUTIONs. First, you need to have enough samples of each student's writing with your evaluation and marks on them to justify your grades in writing and to demonstrate to the parents how well she can write. To not do so is a DEAD END. That will undermine your writing instruction. Second, you must realize that your students are learning little or nothing about how to write better when you grade and mark their papers, regardless of how much you do it. To think that such grading and marking is teaching is also a DEAD END. The wise writing teacher grades and marks only as many papers as necessary and knows that instruction, rather than grading and marking, is what leads to improved student writing.

As you have seen throughout this book, Four-Blocks teachers do not depend on marks and grades to teach their students how to write better. Rather, they work hard to help all of their students learn how to read, evaluate, revise, and edit their own papers for specific criteria appropriate to their levels of writing development.

Research Finding #5: Build Students' Writing Fluency

In addition to the meta-analysis of experimental research on writing instruction that gave us research findings #1–4, more recent writing research has investigated the role of fluency in students' writing development. Writing fluency is the ease of writing. "Ease," itself, cannot be observed but is usually indicated by the quantity and speed of a student's writing. Writing fluency is correlated with writing quality (Berninger, Yates, Cartwright, Rutberg, Remy, and Abbott, 1992).

Research indicates that writing fluency is largely dependent on transcription skills—handwriting and spelling (Graham, Berninger, Abbott, Abbott, and Whitaker, 1997). While handwriting and spelling are not part of meaning construction or language expression, difficulties with transcription can cause students to write very little and to lack self-confidence in writing. Research finding #5 means that an effective writing instructional program will help students develop handwriting and spelling proficiency as they learn the other abilities that good writing requires.

CAUTION: DEAD END!

Traditionally, in the primary grades, handwriting and spelling were systematically taught, but writing was not. Unfortunately, whole language frequently reversed that. With a renewed emphasis on writing fluency today, some teachers may be tempted to return to a time when handwriting and spelling instruction replaced writing instruction. CAUTION, that's a DEAD END! The results of the meta-analysis of research on modes of writing instruction show that presentational writing instruction does not work. Handwriting and spelling are important skill areas that must be taught presentationally, but for that reason, they must support and never supplant writing instruction.

Four-Blocks teachers know the Working with Words Block provides essential skills instruction that they help their students transfer to their writing during the Writing Block. In Four-Blocks classrooms, students are taught phonics systematically during the Words Block and taught how to spell words phonetically when they write during the Writing Block. Students are also taught how to read and spell high-frequency words on the Word Wall during the Working with Words Block and are expected to spell those words correctly in their writing during the Writing Block. Students are also taught how to handwrite during Word Wall activities in the Words Block and expected to handwrite legibly in their writing during the Writing Block. These strong links between the Working with Words and Writing Blocks help Four-Blocks teachers build students' writing fluency. Children who can spell the high-frequency words correctly, many of the other words phonetically, write them all legibly, all while writing about things they want to write, are fluent writers.

Research Supports Teaching Writing Day-to-Day the Four-Blocks Way

These five research findings support the way Four-Blocks teachers teach writing from Building Blocks through Big Blocks:

1. Focus on Teaching Students How to Write, Not about Writing

2. Students Learn How to Write Better While Actively Engaged in Writing Activities, Rather Than Just Listening to the Teacher

3. Students Learn How to Write Better When Their Writing Activities Are Designed and Supervised by the Teacher without Being Presentational

4. Students Must Learn How to Read and Evaluate Their Own Papers for Specific Criteria

5. Build Students' Writing Fluency

Writing the Four-Blocks way changes dramatically as students move up through the grades and become more sophisticated writers, but the day-to-day instruction always remains consistent with these five research findings. As a result, writing the Four-Blocks way is both effective and a "balanced" writing program worthy of the label.

Why Writing Instruction Changes Through the Year and Across the Grades in Four-Blocks Classrooms

One of the most important aspects of the Four-Blocks® framework is how it changes and builds on what students have learned before. We distinguish among Building Blocks, Four Blocks as the specific program in grades 1–3, and Big Blocks. In addition, we are always concerned with maximizing how students develop in reading and writing through the school year, as evidenced, for example, in the *Month-by-Month Phonics* books (Cunningham and Hall, Carson-Dellosa) for the Working with Words Block.

As you have noticed throughout this book, writing the Four-Blocks way also changes through the year and across the grades so that new learning and growth can be built on previous learning and growth, rather than just assuming it. The specific dimensions of these changes occur because students' writing development is hindered by five major problems that almost all writers face as they are learning how to write.

The Motivation Problem

Young or struggling writers often attempt to avoid writing. Some claim they don't know what to write about. If you give them a topic, some claim they don't know anything to say about it, or that they can't write about it because they don't know how to spell the words. If you spell words for them, many will sit without writing, waiting their turn for you to tell them how to spell the next word. Regardless, when they do write, they usually only write a little and then say they're finished.

By observing and talking with these young or struggling writers, you soon become aware that most of them share a motivation problem. For example, consider Jamie. He failed the state writing test in the fourth grade. His writing is typically unelaborated and short. Occasionally in class, he refuses to write at all. Since kindergarten, he has pressured his teachers to give him at least a choice of topics to write about to help him get started, and he has almost never written more than the minimum amount set by his teachers. Jamie's motivation problem has made it very difficult for his teachers to teach him to write better.

The motivation problem in writing has at least three important aspects:

- Lack of self-efficacy in writing
- Lack of intrinsic motivation to write
- Lack of independence in writing

Self-efficacy in writing is the belief that one can write and that one can improve in writing. This kind of self-confidence is an essential part of motivation in writing and is related to writing performance and achievement (Pajares, 2003; Schunk, 2003). Intrinsic motivation in writing is the willingness to write without grades or other tangible rewards. The formation of students' academic intrinsic motivation begins early and is affected by the curriculum, specifically by "increasing the autonomy of students and reducing the use of extrinsic consequences" (Gottfried, Fleming, and Gottfried, 2001, p. 11). An important aspect of intrinsic motivation is that students with learning-oriented achievement goals have higher achievement than students with ego-oriented achievement goals (Meece and Miller, 1999). Learning-oriented students value learning for its own sake and feel a sense of accomplishment whenever they learn. Ego-oriented students want to perform better than other students and only feel successful if they do.

Independence in writing is the willingness to write without help. Of course, it is a manifestation of both self-efficacy and intrinsic motivation in writing, but it is also facilitated when students are writing in an environment that encourages, rather than discourages, risk-taking.

Throughout this book, you have seen that Four-Blocks teachers begin each year at every grade with writing activities (1) that require as little motivation as possible and (2) that are designed to gradually build students' motivation to write. These activities include:

- Self-selected writing
- Single-draft writing
- Phonic spelling
- Sharing first drafts in a positive atmosphere

Self-selected writing teaches students how to write about things they care about, rather than what you may suggest to them. Single-draft writing does not require nearly as much motivation as process writing does. Phonic spelling enables students to write independently without knowing how to spell very many words correctly. Sharing first drafts in a positive atmosphere teaches students that they enjoy having their peers listen to what they have written. These activities are not magic, but with a teacher's persistent and enthusiastic use over time, they help students overcome their lack of self-confidence, intrinsic motivation, learning-oriented achievement goals, and independence in writing.

In kindergarten and early in the year at every other grade, these four activities comprise the writing cycle (Writing Cycle 1). A writing cycle is the succession of steps that the students complete with a piece of writing and then repeat with the next piece of writing and the next. Writing Cycle 1 has the students repeatedly engage in self-selected, single-draft writing with phonic spelling, followed by sharing their first drafts in a positive atmosphere. Writing Cycle 1 continues to be the way each piece of writing is produced until the students have enough self-confidence, intrinsic motivation, learning-oriented achievement goals, and independence, as well as the writing skills, to be successful with Writing Cycle 2.

The Writing-Isn't-Speaking Problem

Almost all children are able to communicate in speech when they start to school, but as soon as they are expected to write something that others can read, they encounter the problem that writing isn't speaking. In other words, they confront the predicament that writing their speech down requires additional skills that speaking does not. This problem continues until students acquire some proficiency with the additional skills that writing requires. For example, consider Alicia. She is a third grader who is very expressive in her speech. The ideas and language in her writing are quite sophisticated and interesting, but it is hard to read because it is filled with mechanical errors. The other children criticize Alicia for making so many errors.

The writing-isn't-speaking problem has five important aspects:

- Handwriting
- Spelling
- Capitalization
- Punctuation
- Formatting

Handwriting and spelling are the transcription skills that comprise basic writing fluency (Graham, Berninger, Abbott, Abbott, and Whitaker, 1997). Capitalization, punctuation, and formatting (e.g., margins, centering, paragraph indentation) are the rule-governed mechanics of writing. Speaking requires none of these, but writing requires all five.

Four-Blocks teachers teach handwriting, phonics, and the correct spellings of commonly used words systematically during the Working with Words Block. Then, they provide two kinds of instruction during the Writing Block that help students gradually learn the basic rules that govern the mechanics of writing:

- Writing mini-lessons
- Editing instruction (how to use the Word Wall and Editor's Checklist to proofread and correct your own paper independently)

Writing mini-lessons are how Four-Blocks teachers teach students the rules that will then be placed on the Editor's Checklist. Editing instruction is how they teach students to proofread and correct their own first drafts for the correct spelling of the Word Wall words and the correct application of the rules on the Editor's Checklist. This approach is consistent with the long-established fact that grammar instruction doesn't help students learn how to write correctly (Hillocks and Smith, 2003) and with research finding #4 (students must learn how to read and evaluate their own papers for specific criteria) discussed in the first half of this chapter.

As soon as students' motivation in writing and writing fluency (handwriting, phonic spelling, and spelling of Word Wall words) are adequate to permit it, a simple writing process consisting of editing and publishing is added to the writing cycle (Writing Cycle 2). Writing Cycle 2 has the students repeatedly engage in self-selected, process writing with sharing of first drafts in a positive atmosphere, self-editing of first drafts, and publishing. Writing Cycle 2 continues to be the way each final draft is produced until the students have enough self-editing ability to be successful with Writing Cycle 3.

The Lack-of-Automaticity Problem

Why does the writing process exist at all? That is, why do many college-bound high school students, most published writers, and almost all professional writers work on drafts several times, usually focusing on different aspects of the message or form? They do this because they lack the automaticity with all of the parts of writing that would be necessary to write a piece once without rereading it and have it still earn a good grade or be publishable.

The lack-of-automaticity problem in writing is the natural inability to "juggle" all of the components of writing at the same time. Writing is complex and each part is difficult to learn and impossible to master. Unless a component of writing has been learned so well that it can be done well automatically, that component can always be improved if the writer rereads the paper, focusing only on that component to improve it. That is why the writing process evolved.

If a lack-of-automaticity is natural, even for adults who are professional writers, it is much more to be expected of children in the elementary grades. For example, consider Kevin. He is a second grader whose writing is about average. He can tell a much better story when the teacher lets him dictate to her rather than write it himself. His spelling on tests is much better than his spelling when he writes. He does well in "Daily Oral Language" and on grammar worksheets, but he makes frequent mechanical errors when he writes.

As you have seen throughout this book, Four-Blocks teachers teach students how to use the writing process (revision, editing, and publishing) so that they are able to independently produce final drafts that are longer, more sophisticated, and more mechanically correct than they are able to produce on first draft. At the same time, Four-Blocks teachers teach writing skills and the writing process in such a way that students gradually increase in their automaticity with the parts of writing so that their first drafts also gradually improve in length, sophistication, and mechanical correctness.

As soon as students' ability to self-edit their own first drafts is adequate to permit it, the full writing process consisting of revising, editing, and publishing becomes part of the writing cycle (Writing Cycle 3). Writing Cycle 3 has students repeatedly engage in Self-Selected, process writing with revision, self-editing, and publishing. Writing Cycle 3 continues to be the way each final draft is produced until the students have enough revision and self-editing ability to be successful with Writing Cycle 4.

The Multiple-Genres Problem

The first few years students are learning how to write are spent acquiring general writing abilities, abilities that almost all writing requires: handwriting, spelling, capitalization, punctuation, sentence formation, keeping to the topic, etc. However, once a student has developed general writing abilities at a basic level, a new problem arises: There are many different genres or types of writing, and each one must be learned separately. For example, consider Tish. She is a fifth grader who writes good stories (imaginative narratives). However, her reports are not well-organized and lack transitions. At times, Tish turns an assignment to describe or explain into a story.

Writing the Four-Blocks way builds on students' basic general writing abilities by teaching them how to produce the different major genres of writing. The three main tools that Four-Blocks teachers use to teach these genres are:

- Focused writing lessons
- Carefully crafted prompts
- Genre-based writing scales

Focused writing lessons are guided writing lessons built around prompts. These lessons are planned and taught to help students learn specific writing strategies, including how to successfully produce a certain genre of writing. The prompts that focused writing lessons are built around are carefully crafted to provide the right mix of challenge and support so that students are successful at learning new writing strategies.

Genre-based writing scales are developed for each of the genres students are being taught how to write in the focused writing lessons. The students are then taught how to read and evaluate their own first drafts for the criteria on the writing scale for the appropriate genre, and how to revise their own first drafts to bring them completely into line with the genre-based scale. By this process, students eventually internalize the genre so that they can usually produce a good example of it on first draft. This approach is consistent with research finding #4 (students must learn how to read and evaluate their own papers for specific criteria) discussed in the first half of this chapter.

As soon as students' general writing abilities are adequate to permit it, learning to write specific genres becomes the focal point of the writing cycle (Writing Cycle 4). Writing Cycle 4 has the students repeatedly engage in focused, process writing with self-evaluation using a genre-based writing scale, revision guided by the genre-based writing scale, self-editing, and publishing.

The Prior-Knowledge Problem

Through the year and across the grades, writing the Four-Blocks way gradually changes instructional emphases and the writing cycle to help students overcome the first four problems that almost all writers face. Each of the four problems is confronted in turn with instructional emphases and a writing cycle that minimize the problem and help students learn what they need to in order to rise above it.

There is another problem that almost all writers face, however, and it remains a problem across all of the grades regardless of the current writing instructional emphases or writing cycle. This is the prior-knowledge problem. This problem has three important ramifications for writing at every level:

- You cannot write well about what you don't know.
- You cannot write well about what you don't understand.
- You cannot write clearly and interestingly about something unless you know the vocabulary.

For example, consider Antuan. He is a first grader who is a good speller and who is learning to begin and end sentences with capitalization and punctuation. He likes to write, but his writing is short and simple. He just doesn't seem to know much about the world or have very many words to use to talk about it.

Because of the prior-knowledge problem, some of the changes across the grades in writing the Four-Blocks way extend beyond the Writing Block and even beyond the Four Blocks. The various changes occur as four kinds of instruction are brought into play:

- Self-selected writing
- Experience-based teaching of science, social studies, and current events
- Self-selected reading
- Inquiry-based writing lessons in the intermediate grades

Self-selected writing is an integral part of the first two writing cycles. In part, this is because it helps young or struggling writers overcome the motivation problem. Giving students a topic or a choice of topics to write about may stop them from saying they can't write because they can't think of a topic, but it doesn't motivate them to write, and their continuing lack of motivation is sure to manifest itself in other ways. Instead, teaching students that they can write about things they care about, and that writing is something related to life and not just school, is an essential strategy for motivating young or struggling writers.

Self-selected writing, however, is also important for all writers at every grade because it enables them to overcome the prior-knowledge problem. Every student has something that she knows and cares about; some experience to relate; some person, pet, or toy to describe; some point-of-view to express or argue. The prior-knowledge problem is largely solved in those cases because the student has much of the prior knowledge those pieces of writing require.

Experience-based teaching of science, social studies, and current events is beyond literacy, and therefore beyond the Four-Blocks framework. Yet, advocates for the Four-Blocks are also advocates of limiting the teaching of reading and writing to approximately two hours per day in grades 1–3, precisely because they understand how essential good content instruction is for building the prior knowledge both reading and writing require. They encourage and support experience-based teaching of science, social studies, and current events beginning in kindergarten because that is the only way schools can effectively build the prior knowledge, including the meaning vocabulary knowledge, that reading comprehension and sophisticated writing must have.

Likewise, the Self-Selected Reading Block has always been one of the Four Blocks because Self-Selected Reading is the primary way people build prior knowledge and meaning vocabulary for themselves as they grow older (Cunningham and Stanovich, 1998). Teacher read-aloud has also been shown to build prior knowledge and meaning vocabulary (Elley, 1989; Stahl, Richek, and Vandevier, 1991).

Four-Blocks teachers emphasize self-selected writing during the first three writing cycles, usually well into second grade. By the middle of second grade, students should have had enough experience-based science, social studies, and current events instruction, and should have done enough Self-Selected Reading and listened to enough teacher read-aloud that they have the prior knowledge and meaning vocabulary necessary to be successful when the emphasis switches to focused writing, as it does in Writing Cycle 4.

Inquiry-based writing lessons in Writing Cycle 4 are another way Four-Blocks teachers help their students overcome the prior-knowledge problem in writing. For these focused writing lessons, students explore a set of items in preparation for writing about them, often in cooperative learning groups. These items can be leaves, rocks, seashells, pictures of people or objects, poems, maps, or any other thing that will be the assigned topic in the prompt of a focused writing lesson. Under the supervision of the teacher, the students are encouraged to explore the particular set of items they have been given in creative and inquisitive ways that focus on understanding and appreciation, rather than "a right answer." They are often asked to compare and contrast the leaves, poems, or maps, etc., as they examine and discuss them, to decide how they are alike and different so that they can write about the characteristics of that kind of item as the topic. You may recall that in the meta-analysis of experimental research on six focuses in writing, inquiry had the largest average effect size of the six (Hillocks, 1986, 1995).

These four kinds of instruction play their respective roles at the proper time to help students overcome the prior-knowledge problem in writing. In writing the Four-Blocks way, students' lack of background knowledge is not allowed to hinder them from learning how to write well.

Why Do Writing the Four-Blocks Way?

Good writing instruction plays two important roles: it helps students learn how to write well and it is also one of the main methods of teaching reading. Moreover, because the Four-Blocks framework is a comprehensive program, the instructional activities across the blocks interact so that students are guided to apply in the Writing Block what they are learning in the Guided Reading, Self-Selected Reading, and Working with Words Blocks.

The day-to-day instruction through the year and across the grades in the Writing Block always remains consistent with the experimental research on teaching writing, discussed in the first half of this chapter. Yet, the instruction in the Writing Block gradually changes throughout the program in order to help students overcome the five main problems that almost all writers face as they are learning how to write, discussed in the second half of this chapter. Writing the Four-Blocks way is a practical and sound way of teaching students how to write from kindergarten through the end of the elementary grades. More importantly, students who receive instruction in "Writing the Four-Blocks Way" enjoy their writing time each day.

Professional Resources

Berninger, V. W., Yates, C., Cartwright, A., Rutberg, J., Remy, E., and Abbott, R. (1992). "Lower-level Developmental Skills in Beginning Writing." *Reading and Writing: An Interdisciplinary Journal, 4,* 257–280.

Caulkins, L. M. and Oxenhorn, A. (2003). *Small Moments: Personal Narrative Writing.* Portsmouth, NH: First Hand.

Clarke, L. K. (1988). "Invented versus Traditional Spelling in First Graders' Writing: Effects on Learning to Spell and Read." *Research in the Teaching of English, 22,* 281-30.

unningham, A. E. and Stanovich K. E. (1998). "What Reading Does for the Mind." *American Educator, 22 (1 and 2),* 8–15.

Cunningham, P. M, Hall, D. P., and Sigmon, C. M. (1999). *The Teacher's Guide to the Four Blocks®.* Greensboro, NC: Carson-Dellosa Publishing.

Cunningham, P. M., Hall, D. P., and Cunningham, J. W. (2000). *Guided Reading the Four-Blocks® Way.* Greensboro, NC: Carson-Dellosa Publishing.

Cunningham, P. M., Hall, D. P., and Gambrell, L. B. (2002). *Self-Selected Reading the Four-Blocks® Way.* Greensboro, NC: Carson-Dellosa Publishing.

Cunningham, P. M. and Hall, D. P. (1997). *Month-by-Month Phonics for First Grade.* Greensboro, NC: Carson-Dellosa Publishing.

Cunningham, P. M. and Hall, D. P. (1998). *Month-by-Month Phonics for Third Grade.* Greensboro, NC: Carson-Dellosa Publishing.

Cunningham, P. M. and Hall, D. P. (1998). *Month-by-Month Phonics for the Upper Grades.* Greensboro, NC: Carson-Dellosa Publishing.

Elley, W. B. (1989). "Vocabulary Acquisition from Listening to Stories." *Reading Research Quarterly, 24,* 174–187.

Gottfried, A. E., Fleming, J. S., and Gottfried, A. W. (2001). "Continuity of Academic Intrinsic Motivation from Childhood through Late Adolescence: A Longitudinal Study." *Journal of Educational Psychology, 93,* 3–13.

Graham, S., Berninger, V., Abbott, R., Abbott, S., and Whitaker, D. (1997). "Role of Mechanics in Composing of Elementary School Students: A New Methodological Approach. *Journal of Educational Psychology, 89,* 170–182.

Hall, D. P. and Cunningham, P. M. (1998). *Month-by-Month Phonics for Second Grade.* Greensboro, NC: Carson-Dellosa Publishing.

Hall, D. P. and Cunningham, P. M. (2003, 1997) *Month-by-Month Reading, Writing, and Phonics for Kindergarten.* Greensboro, NC: Carson-Dellosa Publishing.

Hall, D. P., Cunningham, P. M., and Arens, A. B. (2003). *Writing Mini-Lessons for Upper Grades.* Greensboro, NC: Carson-Dellosa Publishing.

Hall, D. P. and Williams, E. (2001). *The Teacher's Guide to Building Blocks™.* Greensboro, NC: Carson-Dellosa Publishing.

Hall, D. P. and Williams, E. (2002). *Predictable Charts.* Greensboro, NC: Carson-Dellosa Publishing.

Hall, D. P. and Williams, E. (2003). *Writing Mini-Lessons for Kindergarten.* Greensboro, NC: Carson-Dellosa Publishing.

Hillocks, G., Jr. (1986). *Research on Written Composition: New Directions for Teaching.* Urbana, IL: National Conference on Research in English/ERIC Clearinghouse on Reading and Communication Skills.

Hillocks, G., Jr. (1995). *Teaching Writing as Reflective Practice.* New York, NY: Teachers College Press.

Hillocks, G., Jr., and Smith, M. W. (2003). "Grammars and Literacy Learning." In J. Flood, D. Lapp, J. R. Squire, and J. M. Jensen (Eds.), *Handbook of Research on Teaching the English Language Arts, 2nd edition* (pp. 721–737). Mahwah, NJ: Erlbaum.

Leedy, L. (2004). *Look at My Book: How Kids Can Write and Illustrate Terrific Books.* New York, NY: Holiday House.

Levine, S. S. (1977). "The Effect of Transformational Sentence-Combining Exercises on the Reading Comprehension and Written Composition of Third-Grade Children." *Dissertation Abstracts International, 37,* 6431A.

Meece, J. L., and Miller, S. D. (1999). "Changes in Elementary School Children's Achievement Goals for Reading and Writing: Results of a Longitudinal and an Intervention Study." *Scientific Studies of Reading, 3,* 207–229.

Mooney, M. (1990). *Reading To, With, and By Students*. Katonah, NY: Richard C. Owen Publishers.

Pajares, F. (2003). "Self-Efficacy Beliefs, Motivation, and Achievement in Writing: A Review of the Literature." *Reading and Writing Quarterly, 19*, 139–158.

Schunk, D. H. (2003). "Self-Efficacy for Reading and Writing: Influence of Modeling, Goal Setting, and Self-Evaluation." *Reading and Writing Quarterly, 19*, 159–172.

Sigmon, C. M. and Ford, S. M. (2002). *Writing Mini-Lessons for Third Grade*. Greensboro, NC: Carson-Dellosa Publishing.

Stahl, S. A., Richek, M. A., and Vandevier, R. J. (1991). "Learning Meaning Vocabulary through Listening: A Sixth-Grade Replication." In *Learner Factors/Teacher Factors: Issues in Literacy Research and Instruction (40th Yearbook of the National Reading Conference)*, pp. 185–192. Chicago, IL: National Reading Conference.

Straw, S. B., and Schreiner, R. (1982). "The Effect of Sentence Manipulation on Subsequent Measures of Reading and Listening Comprehension." *Reading Research Quarterly, 17*, 339-352.

Tompkins, G. E. (2002). *Language Arts: Patterns of Practice, 5th edition.*, p. 179. Upper Saddle River, NJ: Pearson Prentice Hall.